中国思想文化术语多语种对外翻译
标准化建设项目成果

CHINESE THINKING AND CULTURE
MULTILINGUAL TERMINOLOGY DATABASE

中华源·河南故事
CHINESE CIVILIZATION
Stories from Henan

焦裕禄
A MODEL OFFICIAL — JIAO YULU

主编 张松文
EDITOR-IN-CHIEF: ZHANG SONGWEN

河南大学出版社
HENAN UNIVERSITY PRESS
·郑州·

图书在版编目（CIP）数据

中华源·河南故事.焦裕禄：汉英对照/张松文主编.－－郑州：河南大学出版社，2020.5（2020.7重印）
 ISBN 978-7-5649-4293-9

Ⅰ.①中… Ⅱ.①张… Ⅲ.①地方文化－河南－通俗读物－汉、英②焦裕禄（1922—1964）－生平事迹－汉、英 Ⅳ.①G127.61-49②D263

中国版本图书馆CIP数据核字(2020)第082276号

责任编辑	毛晓旭
责任校对	时　娇
封面设计	翟淼淼
出版发行	河南大学出版社
	地址：郑州市郑东新区商务外环中华大厦2401号　邮编：450046
	电话：0371-86059701（营销部）0371-86059753（大众读物分公司）
	网址：hupress.henu.edu.cn
排　版	河南博雅彩印有限公司
印　刷	河南博雅彩印有限公司
版　次	2020年5月第1版
印　次	2020年7月第2次印刷
开　本	710 mm×1010 mm　1/16
印　张	16.5
字　数	228千
定　价	86.00元

版权所有　侵权必究
本书如有印装质量问题，请与河南大学出版社营销部联系调换。

"中华源·河南故事"系列丛书编委会

顾　　问	黄友义　杨　平　范大祺
名誉主任	穆为民　何金平
主　　任	付　静
副 主 任	陈志伟　刁玉华　李向前　李　镇　梁留科
	刘金锋　孔留安　史永庆　许二平　万正峰
	杨建伟　杨玮斌　王建修　王自文　张改平
	张松文　赵卫东

主　　编	付　静
执行主编	杨玮斌
编　　委	陈玮　丁锐　高阳　徐恒振

中华源·河南故事·焦裕禄

主　　编	张松文
副 主 编	席建设　赵淑芬　钱建成（英文）
中文撰稿	王文凯　明洋　张静　赵兴国
	张冲　王蕾
英文译者	黄为葳

The Editorial Committee
Chinese Civilization
Stories from Henan

Consultants	Huang Youyi Yang Ping Fan Daqi
Honorary Directors	Mu Weimin He Jinping
Director	Fu Jing
Deputy Directors	Chen Zhiwei Diao Yuhua Li Xiangqian Li Zhen
	Liang Liuke Liu Jinfeng Kong Liu'an Shi Yongqing
	Xu Erping Wan Zhengfeng Yang Jianwei
	Yang Weibin Wang Jianxiu Wang Ziwen
	Zhang Gaiping Zhang Songwen Zhao Weidong

Chief Editor	Fu Jing
Executive Chief Editor	Yang Weibin
Editors	Chen Wei Ding Rui Gao Yang Xu Hengzhen

Chinese Civilization
Stories from Henan
A Model Official — Jiao Yulu

Editor-in-Chief	Zhang Songwen
Associate Editors-in-Chief	Xi Jianshe Zhao Shufen
	Qian Jiancheng (English Text)
Writers	Wang Wenkai Ming Yang Zhang Jing
	Zhao Xingguo Zhang Chong Wang Lei
Translator	Huang Weiwei

1963年9月，焦裕禄在他亲手栽种的泡桐苗旁留影

A snapshot taken in September 1963, in which Jiao Yulu is seen standing close to a tall paulownia sapling which was planted by him.

念奴娇·追思焦裕禄

习近平

中夜，读《人民呼唤焦裕禄》一文，是时霁月如银，文思萦系……

魂飞万里，盼归来，此水此山此地。
百姓谁不爱好官？把泪焦桐成雨。
生也沙丘，死也沙丘，父老生死系。
暮雪朝霜，毋改英雄意气！

依然月明如昔，思君夜夜，肝胆长如洗。
路漫漫其修远矣，两袖清风来去。
为官一任，造福一方，遂了平生意。
绿我涓滴，会它千顷澄碧。

注：

①该词最早发表在1990年7月16日的《福州晚报》上，作者习近平时任中国福建省福州市委书记。

②焦裕禄于1962年12月—1964年5月在中国河南省兰考县任县委书记，当年为了防风固沙，领导农民摆脱贫困，焦裕禄提倡广泛种植泡桐树。如今，兰考县泡桐如海，焦裕禄当年亲手栽下的幼桐已长成参天大树，人们亲切地叫它"焦桐"。

③焦裕禄临终前说："我死后只有一个要求，要求党组织把我运回兰考，埋在沙丘上。活着我没有治好沙丘，死了也要看着你们把沙丘治好！"

Jiao Yulu in My Nostalgic Memories

— *to the tune of Nian Nu Jiao*

Xi Jinping

I did not finish reading the article "Jiao Yulu—A True Public Servant Revered by the People" until the wee hours, when the silvery moonlight was so generous with its fluid gleam. And then my mind waxed nostalgically lyric …

Away into the unfathomable void of the cosmos
Although his soul chooses to traverse,
Yet it never gives up pining for the particular whereabouts.
Has there ever been the case
Where a nice Jack would bear malice
Towards unselfish public servants?
That's why at the very spot where still now stands
The paulownia sapling, which, been so unanimously claimed it has,
Was planted with Jiao Yulu's own hands.
Sees so frequently lamentation nippingly lachrymose!
In the face of hardship and self-sacrifice,
Never deserted him his supreme heroic urges —
Not even for once.

Tonight the moonlight here is as brilliant as it ever was.
To my nocturnal routine has been added the process
Of summoning every night to my mind your reminiscence.
This can hugely purify my mind and redouble my militance.
Though the official career he brought himself to traverse
Was rather long, yet he never for once
Let himself succumb to glamorous lure or tinseled vice.
Throughout his official career, each of his tenures of office
Invariably turned out to be a spell of deluging bliss
To benefit the local population; and that precisely was
The goal he ordered himself to unfailingly chase.
All droplets of beatitude he had offered to the populace

Are bound to ultimately conglomerate with plenty of pace
To form an ocean of supreme blessedness and grace.

Notes

1. This poetic piece by Xi Jinping was first carried by *Fuzhou Evening Paper* on July 16, 1990. At that time, he was in office, working as secretary of the Fuzhou Municipal Committee of the Communist Party of China (CPC). (Fuzhou is provincial capital of Fujian Province.)

2. From December 1962 to May 1964, Jiao Yulu worked in Henan Province as secretary of the CPC Lankao County Committee. In the course of his tenure of office there, he led the local population to subdue the monster in the form of gale-force winds which, being devilishly powerful in stripping the arable land of both its moisture and its fertile topsoil and in turning it barren, had been irrevocably and mercilessly impoverishing the local people for eons. He tried his utmost to persuade and organize the local people to grow paulownia tree — also called Chinese parasol tree — in every part of Lankao County. Now the county is safely canopied with numerous close-knit paulownia trees. The paulownia tree, which was planted by Jiao Yulu, has now shot skyward to look like a gorgeous and imposing giant. And the local people now fondly call it "Dear Jiao's Paulownia".

3. The only deathbed wish voiced by Jiao Yulu is this: "The last and only craving I cherish prior to my demise is this: The Party organization to which I have been duly affiliated will see to it that my remains, after having been conveyed back to Lankao County, be interred somewhere in a dune there. As I did not succeed in protecting all the dunes there from the encroachment of the gale-force winds in my life, I yearn to see in my afterlife how the local people continue to battle the winds until they are irrevocably subdued."

2018年11月12日,国际媒体代表团参观兰考县展览馆
On November 12, 2018, members of a delegation from international media visited the Lankao County Exhibition Hall.

2019年6月28日,国际嘉宾出席在焦裕禄干部学院举办的"中国共产党的故事——习近平新时代中国特色社会主义思想在河南的实践"专题宣介会
The thematic event on "Stories of the Communist Party of China — Henan's Achievements in Practicing Xi Jinping Thought on Socialism with Chinese Characteristics for a New Era" was held in Jiao Yulu Executive Leadership Academy on June 28, 2019. Participants in the event hail from all over the world.

1969年12月焦裕禄的母亲李星英（中）与阿尔巴尼亚留学生合影

The group photo was taken in December 1969. In the photo are Li Xingying, Jiao Yulu's mother (middle) and four students from Albania.

阿尔及利亚友人拜谒焦裕禄烈士墓

Visitors from Algeria are seen in the photo paying homage to Martyr Jiao Yulu's Grave.

总 序

中国是世界四大文明古国之一,也是世界上唯一的古代文明传统未曾中断的国家。河南省地处中国中东部,是中华文明和中华民族的重要发祥地,在中国五千年的文明史上,河南作为国家政治、经济、文化的中心就长达三千多年。从某种意义上讲,一部河南史就是半部中国史。这里是中华人文始祖黄帝的故乡,是古丝绸之路的东方起点,是少林功夫和陈氏太极的发源地,这里创建了中国历史上最早的都城,镌刻了中国最古老的文字,诞生了中国最初的商业文明。

伴随着新时代的荣光,河南经济社会发展迅速,人民生活水平显著提升,这是自力更生、艰苦奋斗的历史结果,也是对外开放带来的益处。河南经济社会的发展、人民生活方式的改变都植根于深层次的文化积淀。为了让世界更多地了解河南,让河南更好地走向世界,2018年以来,河南省外事办认真研析了这片古老土地上的历史文化资源和时代风貌,组织各领域权威专家学者,编译了"中华源·河南故事"中外文系列丛书,选取少林功夫、太极拳、中医、汉字、文物、焦裕禄、红旗渠、丝绸之路、古都、农业、手工艺等多个主题,力图以故事的方式向世界展现一个立体、全面、真实的河南。

当今世界,人类文明无论在物质还是精神方面都取得了巨大进步,特别是物质的极大丰富是古代世界完全不能想象的。同时,当代人类也面临着许多突出的难题,比如,贫富差距持续扩大,物欲追求奢华无度,个人主义恶性膨胀,社会诚信不断消减,伦理道德每况愈下,人与自然关系日趋紧张,等等。要解决这些难题,不仅需要运用人类今天发现和发展的智慧和力量，而且需要运用人类历史上积累和储存的智慧和力量。河南历史文化底蕴深厚、包容性强，在今天仍极具现实意义。中原文化蕴含的思想智慧有助于修身养性，推动人类社会进步发展，焦裕禄精神、红旗渠精神所体现的为民爱民、艰苦奋斗的价值取向是构建人类命运共同体的力量源泉。我们期待与读者们一起从河南故事中汲取更多的智慧和力量，共同创造更加美好的未来。

Series Foreword

China is one of the four ancient civilizations in the world, and is also the only country in the world where the ancient civilization has not been interrupted. Located in east-central China, Henan province is an important cradle for the Chinese nation and the Chinese civilization. In the course of the five thousand years of Chinese history, for more than three thousand years it served as the political, economic and cultural center of the country and therefore, as generally accepted, represents half of the history of China. Henan is the native place of Yellow Emperor, the cradle of Chinese culture, the starting point of the ancient Silk Road in the east, and the birthplace of Shaolin Kungfu and Chen-style Taijiquan—typical examples of the world-renowned Chinese martial arts. It was here that the earliest capital city in China was founded, the oldest Chinese characters engraved, and the earliest commerce took shape.

In the new era, Henan has witnessed rapid growth in its economy and remarkable improvement of people's living conditions, owing to the national reform and opening-up policy and unremitting endeavoring of the people. Modern economic achievements and social development as well as the changes of way of life could be traced back to its traditional values and cultural heritages. To enable people from other countries to understand Henan, and let the province integrate more efficiently into the world development, the Foreign Affairs Office of the People's Government of Henan province, has organized teams of authoritative experts and scholars in relevant fields to compile this *Chinese Civilization: Stories from Henan* in Chinese and other foreign languages since 2018, by crystallizing the excellence of traditions and outstanding features of modern development. The book series include *Shaolin Kungfu, Taijiquan, Traditional Chinese Medicine, Chinese Characters, Cultural Heritage, A Model Official — Jiao Yulu, Man-made River — Hongqiqu Canal, the Silk*

Road, *Ancient Chinese Capitals*, *Handicraft* and *Feeding the People — Agriculture*, etc, attempting to present a panoramic picture of the province.

In today's world, human civilization has made great progress in both material accumulation and cultural and ethical advancement, and the great abundance of materials today, especially, is beyond the imagination of the ancient people. At the same time, however, modern people are also confronted with a lot of problems, such as the widening gap between the rich and the poor, the indulgence in pursuit of luxury and extravagance, the undesirable extension of individualism, the decline of social integrity, and the increasing tension between man and nature. To solve these problems, we need to draw on the wisdom and powers developed today as well as those accumulated in the past. Henan is endowed with a rich historical and cultural heritage characterized by its inclusiveness, and such a heritage remains significant today. The intelligence and wisdom in Henan culture are conducive to self-cultivation and to the promotion of social development. The spirit of serving the people and relentless struggle, as embodied in *Jiao Yulu* and *Hongqiqu Canal*, provides source of strength for building a community with a shared future for mankind. It is our hope that, wisdom and strength from Henan stories, could lead us to a shared brilliant future.

前　言

在历史的天空中，总有一些人物，如恒星般熠熠发光，催人自省，给人力量。这其中，中国优秀县委书记的榜样——焦裕禄，以其对国家的无限忠诚、对人民的深沉热爱燃尽了生命之火，树立了一座亿万人民心中永不磨灭的精神丰碑。中国国家主席习近平曾说，焦裕禄虽然离开我们50年了，但他的事迹永远为人们传颂，他的精神过去是、现在是、将来仍然是我们党的宝贵精神财富，我们要永远向他学习。

焦裕禄出生于1922年，那时的中国正处于半殖民地半封建社会，政局动荡、民不聊生，无数中国的仁人志士都在寻求救国之路。年轻的焦裕禄也投身于时代的洪流之中，他经历了儿时的辗转奔波和悲惨的逃荒生活，后来在抗日战争中当过哨兵，在解放战争中打过仗，为支援前线送过粮，为剿匪反霸流过血，为工业生产立过功，一步步由热血青年成长为成熟的管理干部，为民族解放和工业建设贡献了自己的力量和智慧。他的身上闪耀着一个中国青年忠于国家、任劳任怨、不屈不挠、敢于斗争的精神光芒。

1962年，40岁的焦裕禄临危受命，担任兰考县委书记，为治理风沙、内涝、盐碱三大自然灾害，解决群众的吃饭和生存问题，他立誓"拼上老命大干一场，决心改变兰考面貌"。他忍着病痛，涉洪水、查风口、探流沙，凭着一双铁脚板和一辆自行车，在群众中找到了治理"三害"的办法。在风雪夜，他带领干部冒沙尘、顶风雪，走村串户，访贫问苦，给困难户送去了救济粮，而他自己却要去最穷的群众家里吃百家饭（群众外出逃荒讨饭，要来的诸如窝窝头、红薯片等吃的东西）。他对群众说："我是您的儿子。"道出了他与群众的深情厚谊，也赢得了群众的永远铭记。没有一种根基，比扎根群众更坚实；没有一种力量，比从群众中汲取更强大。人民怀念焦裕禄，是因为焦裕禄这座丰碑上永远铭刻着人民的利益。"百姓谁不爱好官？把泪焦桐成雨。"习近平主席的深沉感念，道出的是一种历史真理，写就的是一曲为民之歌，更是对传承弘扬焦裕禄精神的殷殷厚望。

焦裕禄被誉为"毛泽东的好学生"。他去世后，河南省人民政府追认他为革命烈士。2000年，在新华社《时事资料手册》的百年中国回顾中，焦裕禄同孙中山、毛泽东、邓小平等一起被评为"百年中国十大人物"。在庆祝中华人民共和国成立60周年时，焦裕禄入选"100位新中国成立以来感动中国人物"。在庆祝中华人民共和国成立70周年时，焦裕禄又荣获中央宣传部、中央组织部等九部委授予的"最美奋斗者"称号。半个世纪以来，焦裕禄亲民爱民、艰苦奋斗、科学求实、迎难而上、无私奉献的事迹和精神激励了无数中国公职人员不忘初心、牢记使命、前赴后继、开拓进取。同样，焦裕禄精神也会感染世界各国的公职人员，激励他们为摆脱贫困、促进经济发展而努力，为增进民生福祉、保持社会和谐稳定、构建人类命运共同体而勤勉工作。

本书还原了焦裕禄的人生经历，叙述了他作为革命战士、企业领导、地方领导时发生的感人故事，展示了在他的精神鼓舞下兰考县实现脱贫、经济社会发展取得巨大成就的生动实践。相信本书对于中外读者了解焦裕禄以及中国公职人员的工作作风、理解习近平治国理政思想有着重要的参考价值。

Preface

There are no eras in the history of the Chinese nation but have their respective dazzling luminaries shining in diverse fields of the nation's civilization, just as there are no quarters of the welkin but have their respective glaring constellations. Memories of dazzling luminaries in our history constitute a momentum capable of both motivating us to execute severe self-scrutiny and redoubling our self-confidence. Of all the dazzling luminaries in the history of the Communist Party of China (CPC), Jiao Yulu sparkled, who was an impeccable and exemplary secretary of the CPC Lankao County Committee before his demise. His allegiance to our nation and unfathomable love of our people triggered him to do everything in his power and exhaust all his vitality, physical strength, and wisdom without even the least trace of egoism, simply for duly fulfilling his duty as an official. Thus, his image and memory have now been so dignified as to have attained monumental stature and would be forever cherished by our nation. "Although Jiao Yulu is no longer with us for half a century," said President Xi Jinping, "yet his splendid memory would stay with us for eons. His personality now remains and will persist to remain to be a portion of our Party's most valuable moral heritage, wherefrom we will incessantly imbibe spiritual nutriment."

Jiao Yulu was born in 1922. That year witnessed China managed to survive as a semi-colonial and semi-feudalistic regime, which, while being politically unstable, was hopelessly irresponsible and inane in the act of salvaging the populace from starvation. At that time, myriads of patriots were striving to formulate or implement a strategy that could be proved truly effectual to secure salvation for the Chinese nation. Jiao Yulu was then one of such patriots. He had a wretched childhood, which saw his family, being then victimized by famine, undergo a long spell of miserable vagrant life. Later he joined the army led by the Communist Party of China. In military confrontation with the Japanese aggressive forces, he used to be detailed by his infantry unit to stand sentinel. In the period of the liberation warfare launched by the Communist Party against the Kuomintang regime, his infantry unit was long involved in combat activities on battlefield. Sometimes he was assigned to work for the department of military logistics. Once he was seriously wounded while carrying out the campaigns against some bandits, bullies, and outlaws. After the establishment of the People's Republic of China, he was assigned to work in the realm of industrial production, where his excellent performance and fulfillment of his duty won for him successive citations from his superiors. Thus, he matured from a warm-hearted and pure-minded youth into a professionally competent administrator who had exerted himself to the utmost in the interest not only of liberation but of industrialization of our country. He was the quintessence of loyalty, fortitude, resilience, and just militance. And these qualities of his will blaze forever in our nation's memory of him.

In 1962, hunger and famine overtook the population of Lankao County. Extremity and exigency of the situation there urgently called for a most moral and capable leadership to exercise sagacious administration over the county. Jiao Yulu who was then forty was under the circumstances appointed to the post of secretary of the CPC Lankao County Committee. He knew the shocking enormity of the adversity he had to face in order to subdue the macabre magic wielded by gale-force winds, wantonly shifting sand dunes, waterlogging, and invidious alkaline soil, so as to wring back from nature the local people's survival and social development. "Striving to thoroughly reshape Lankao's physiognomy," he vowed, "I'd stick at nothing and fight to accomplish it even at the cost of my life!" Being faithful to his oath, he set out to conduct a markedly expansive spectrum of geographical, ecological, and meteorological surveys in the county. In the courses of those arduous and painful investigations, illness and fatigue tortured him. In some cases, he had to wade across treacherous torrents or climb up sheer icy cliffs to locate a wind gap or trace movements of wind-blown sand. All the transportational facilities available to him, while he was carrying out those exploratory errands, were nothing but his own feet and, sometimes, a bicycle. In due course, he succeeded in formulating, together with the local multitude of the county, a resourceful strategy for contending with the "three demons"— namely, straying sand dunes, waterlogging, and pernicious alkaline soil. It is usually on blizzardy nights that he would sally forth from his shabby office, together with a number of administrative personnel to rush to hosts of penurious households in the county for offering to them gratuitous provisions or shelter from the storm. Often in the course of discharging his official duty, he had to eat his meals — though such meals were never provided gratis — at homes of ordinary inhabitants in the county. As the county's economy was anything but commendable at that time, such meals he was provided with were literally an assortment of foods — such as steamed corn bread, desiccated slice of cooked sweet potato — most worthy of a beggar. "I'm just one of your children, you know," most candidly he would pronounce when chatting with senior inhabitants in the county. Sincerity and profundity of his ingrained affection for the county population was irrefutably self-evident and would be indelibly engraved in the memory of generation after generation of the local population. Popularity that is grounded in morality and propriety can be everlasting. Moral support can carry an amazing clout only when it owes its origination to the public's general consensus. Memory of Jiao Yulu inevitably triggers the general public to appreciate his love of and total devotion to our nation. An infectious wave of formless public yearning for renewing his memory actually sweeps our nation from time to time. That's why President Xi Jinping was motivated to compose the following lines:

"Has there ever been the case
Where a nice Jack would bear malice
Towards unselfish public servants?
That's why at the very spot where still now stands
The paulownia sapling, which, been so unanimously claimed it has,
Was planted with Jiao Yulu's own hands.
Sees so frequently lamentation nippingly lachrymose!"

In these lines of President Xi's is revealed his candid adoration for Jiao. President Xi truly admires heroes who devote their lives to our nation unselfishly, and earnestly hopes that Jiao's unstinted fervor and verve that kindled him to serve our nation selflessly would be faithfully inherited by our future generations.

People appreciate and praise Jiao Yulu, and honor him as "Chairman Mao Zedong's distinguished disciple". Official acclaim has been proclaimed by Henan

Provincial Administration for Jiao's strikingly eminent service, and the posthumous title of "a revolutionary martyr" has been awarded him. Collected in a publication published in 2000 and entitled *Anthology of Archived News Reports* and compiled by Xinhua News Agency is an article bearing the title "A Survey of China in the Last One Hundred Years". In the article is nominated China's ten top luminaries in the last one hundred years, and the name of Jiao Yulu is among those of the other nine luminaries including Sun Yat-sen, Mao Zedong, Deng Xiaoping. On the 60th anniversary of the People's Republic of China, Jiao's name was officially proclaimed to be included in "a galaxy of names of one hundred most brilliantly didactic luminaries in People's Republic of China". On the 70th anniversary of the founding of People's Republic of China, nine CPC's top authorities — including the Central Publicity Department, the Central Organization Department, etc. — jointly announced the conferment upon Jiao Yulu of the title, "the unrivalled endeavorer". His distinguished career, which was devoted to the Chinese people, epitomizes such superb qualities as allegiance, aplomb in the face of danger or difficulty, political sagacity, unselfishness. Over the past five decades, journalistic presentation of his official career has inspired numerous public servants to strive to be perennially and steadily mindful of the noble lifetime goal which each of them set for himself (or herself) at the inception of his (or her) official career and to urge himself (or herself) to unfailingly attain his (or her) lifetime goal. It is apparently conceivable that the moral heritage bequeathed us by Jiao Yulu can certainly be availed of as a universal didactic momentum, as it is believed to be capable of actuating public servants all over the world to strive to flay poverty from any part of the surface of the earth, promote global economic growth, improve life quality everywhere, and redouble security and social harmony in every part of our planet, so as to expedite the genesis of such an international communal settlement as ensures that the entire human race can without fail share one and the same future.

In this memoir is realistically presented Jiao Yulu's life story. Vivid narration amply supplied in this biographical work serves to highlight not just his keen sense of responsibility but his fiery and unfading passion which impelled him to dutifully and selflessly fulfil his duty initially as a revolutionary soldier, later as an administrator of a state enterprise, and still later as a top leader of a county government. Graphically delineated in this memoir is a panoramic background to the crisis occurring in the county concerned in the form of desperation experienced by the masses pending their being deprived of the last hope of survival. This memoir tells how the population of Lankao County rose to stave off impoverishment and desperation and remarkably achieved its local economic and social development by imbibing moral vitalization from Jiao's exemplary life career. It is only commonsensical to conclude that this memoir is able to provide its readership, domestic and abroad, with essential information concerning the commendable style of fulfillment of duty adopted by the majority of public servants in China in general and by Jiao Yulu in particular. Moreover, this memoir can help its readership with comprehending the theory, evolved by President Xi Jinping, of the art of executing governance over a nation.

目 录　　Contents

第一章　短暂而光辉的一生　　001
　　一、出生孔孟之乡　　002
　　二、艰难成长岁月　　006
　　三、积极参加革命　　010
　　四、投身工业建设　　020
　　五、献身兰考热土　　024

Chapter I　He had a brilliant, though brief, life!　　001
　　I. He was well acquainted with the fundamentals of Confucianism.　　005
　　II. His harrowing juvenile years　　009
　　III. He zealously volunteered to have himself affiliated with the revolution led by the Communist Party of China.　　015
　　IV. So he glowed on the industrial front too.　　021
　　V. After Weishi it was to Lankao that Jiao riveted his devotion.　　027

第二章　时代的呼唤　　039
　　一、"跑题"发言　　042
　　二、首次报道　　044
　　三、深度发掘　　046
　　四、三次热潮　　052

Chapter II　Our era calls on us to learn about and follow Jiao Yulu.　　039
　　I. A speech delivered at a conference was irrelevant to the main thrust of its agenda.　　043
　　II. The debut official news release in China on Jiao Yulu's life and career　　045
　　III. The follow-up unearthing of the treasure trove of Jiao Yulu's morality　　047

IV. The three upsurges in the duration of the nationwide movement of "learning about and following Jiao Yulu" 053

第三章　一本永远读不完的书 061
　　一、亲民爱民 064
　　二、艰苦奋斗 080
　　三、科学求实 090
　　四、迎难而上 112
　　五、无私奉献 134

Chapter III　An undrainable fountainhead of wisdom 061
　　I. Jiao's philanthropic rules of behavior 065
　　II. Jiao's unswerving adherence to frugality in performing his official duty 081
　　III. One of Jiao's rules of behavior is: "Always strive to think logically and fulfill my duty faithfully, practically, and sensibly." 091
　　IV. Jiao's deeply ingrained sense of duty endowed him with courage, ingenuity, and insight. 111
　　V. Jiao's selfless dedication 135

第四章　历久弥新的精神 151
　　一、教育了公职人员，争做为民、务实、清廉的表率 152
　　二、鼓舞了广大群众，自力更生实现了农业丰收 170
　　三、带动了文化旅游，引领了文化观光基地集群 176
　　四、做强了特色产业，助推兰考民族乐器走向世界 192
　　五、推进了减贫事业，为构建人类命运共同体做出了有益示范 200

Chapter IV　Jiao Yulu's tremendous bequest to us 151
　　I. From Jiao, all government staff can learn how to serve the people in an unselfish and pragmatic way. 153
　　II. The moral bequest left behind by Jiao is blossoming in Lankao. 171
　　III. Development of cultural undertakings and tourism and creation of a series of cultural-touristic interests in Lankao 177
　　IV. The emergence in Lankao of a brand-new and unique industry — the musical instrument industry 185

V. Lankao's success in poverty reduction encourages the rest of China to follow suit, and inspires the international community to strive to build a community with a shared future for mankind. ... 191

附 录 焦裕禄经典语录 ... 217
 一、公仆情怀 ... 218
 二、求实作风 ... 218
 三、奋斗精神 ... 219
 四、道德情操 ... 219
 五、十条工作经验 ... 220
 六、干部十不准 ... 220

Appendix Quotations from Jiao Yulu ... 217
 I. Quotations describing his reflection on the role played by a government official ... 222
 II. Quotations that mirror Jiao Yulu's down-to-earthness ... 223
 III. Quotations that mirror Jiao's indomitability of will and valor ... 223
 IV. Quotations serving to outline Jiao's morality ... 224
 V. Quotations that summarize the experience Jiao had learned from his official career ... 225
 VI. Quotations from Jiao that illustrate the ten taboos for government officials in Lankao ... 225

后 记 ... 228
Postscript ... 230

第一章

短暂而光辉的一生

Chapter I

He had a brilliant, though brief, life!

焦裕禄1922年出生在中国山东省淄博市博山县（现为博山区）一个农民家庭，只接受了小学教育。成年后的焦裕禄，身高1.78米，英俊潇洒。在生活上，焦裕禄懂浪漫、有情调、爱生活。他爱好广泛，学过吹号、唱戏，还会拉二胡。他喜欢打篮球，被称为球场上的"灵魂"。在工厂中，他还学会了俄文，会跳交际舞。在家庭里，他尊重长辈，孝敬父母，爱自己的妻子，关心孩子。

当时的中国面临着内忧外患，与其他生活在中国社会底层的民众一样，焦裕禄经历了无数艰辛，他接受先进思想洗礼，走上了革命道路。苦难磨砺了他的心智，决不向命运屈服。参加革命后，焦裕禄是个有勇有谋的人，敢于冒着战火向前冲。在工作中，焦裕禄是个具有优秀领导才能的人，他口才好，善于总结，会说顺口溜，有灵活的工作方法和丰富的管理经验，经常开"诸葛亮会"。在人际关系方面，焦裕禄是个能够团结他人、与同事和睦相处的人，他是个热心肠，经常帮助同事下属解决难题。

一、出生孔孟之乡

齐鲁大地，历史悠久，山河毓秀，人才荟萃，是著名的孔孟之乡、礼仪之邦。博山县位于山东省中部，矿产资源丰富。这里是孝文化的发源地，还流传着一个美丽的故事。

几千年前，博山县有一户农家，儿媳俭朴持家、孝顺公婆。不幸的是，她的丈夫病死了。失去儿子的公婆心生怨恨，每天都让儿媳往返几十里山路挑水做饭。怕儿媳歇脚偷懒，婆婆特地把水桶做成尖底的。然而不管严寒酷暑，儿媳任劳任怨。天上的神仙被她的坚韧所感动，送她一根神奇的马鞭，让她藏在家里的水缸中，只需摇一下马鞭，缸内就有泉水汩汩流出。谁知婆婆发现后，趁她不在时将马鞭拿了出来，哪知泉水突然喷涌而出，从山顶流到山洼，形成了一条河流。儿媳为了救婆

Jiao Yulu was born in 1922 to a peasant family in Boshan County (the present-day Boshan District in Zibo City), Shandong Province. In days prior to his teenage, his family finances could only afford to give him elementary education. Advent of his adulthood saw him gain 1.78 meters in stature. At that time, he was a young man handsome and optimistically equable. Being temperately passionate in nature, he was cultured, unusually perceptive, and eclectic in taste. Once he became infatuated with bugling and trumpeting and then took a fancy to singing operatic arias before letting himself be obsessed with the art of playing a typical Chinese string instrument called "erhu". As a veteran basketball player, he answered to the sobriquet "basketball addict". During his tenure as an administrator of a state enterprise, he addressed himself in his leisure hours to learning Russian and the skill of social dance. He revered all his seniors and superiors, fondly cherished China's traditional family values and sentiments, and was most sincere in offering filial respect to his parents, marital fidelity to his wife, and paternal love to his children.

Before the foundation of the People's Republic of China, his family belonging to the lowest social stratum, led a miserable life under the Kuomintang regime, whose incompetent, corrupt and unscrupulous governance left the country lethally crippled with irrelievable social upheavals at home and unshunnable and aggressive invasions from foreign powers. The early part of Jiao Yulu's life was the epitome of stark deprivation that often landed him on extremity in seeking his survival. Anyway, racking adversities just served to fortify his resilient character and turn him virtually refractory to his outrageous fate. Thus, in due course in his early adulthood he began to embrace revolutionary ideology and aspire to live as an active revolutionist. This is how he came to devote his life to the revolutionary cause carried on by the Communist Party of China in the 1940s. Since he became a revolutionist in deed directly under the command of a specific organization of the CPC, his practical performance in the course of fulfilling his duty witnessed that he was not only brave but also versed in doing strategic planning and skillful deploying. Never could a perilous mission daunt him. He was a remarkably talented administrator or leader. His eloquence was simply overwhelming. Moreover, his sagacity and integrity enabled him to be very quick in detecting or ascertaining the lesson to be aptly drawn from a failure or accident. He had the aptitude of composing impromptu comic jingles to amuse his audience or enliven the atmosphere of a routine assemblage. It is always with superb

焦裕禄在博山的老家
Jiao Yulu's former residence in Boshan County

婆，舍身坐在水缸上，水势得到了控制。后来，为了纪念她，博山的群众就把这条河叫作孝妇河。

孝妇河旁有一座山叫作崮山。崮山北面有一个村庄叫北崮山村。这里石层厚，土质薄，乱石成滩。遇上大雨，土层冲走；遇到大旱，颗粒不收。

19世纪末20世纪初，中国处于农耕时代，生产力水平低下。在外来势力的侵略下，清政府的统治日薄西山，国家处于风雨飘摇之中。1911年，辛亥革命爆发，清政府随后倒台，中国结束了两千多年的封建帝制，进入半殖民地半封建社会。

1922年8月16日，焦裕禄出生了，按照家谱排序，爷爷给他起名"裕禄"，寓意全家过上富裕、厚禄的生活。关于他的家庭情况，焦裕禄在一份写给组织的资料中记载：八岁至十五岁，家庭十五口人，十三亩地，牛二头，骡子一头，房子廿余间，全家种地，冬闲时开一个小油坊，打蓖麻油，资金大部分是借外债。资料中所说的十五口人，包括焦裕禄的太奶奶、爷爷、奶奶、父亲、母亲、哥哥、叔叔、婶婶和他们的儿女。

tact and consideration that he went to carefully exercise the administrative leadership he was charged with. Never for once had he failed to have timely recourse to due flexibility in properly handling a devilish dilemma. He had a preference for holding diverse, yet irregular, "caucuses" attended by colleagues under his direct command for finalizing an important decision or arrangement. He was astoundingly popular with his juniors as well as seniors, because of his integrity and sincere amiability. He wanted himself to be constantly obliging to all those in his surroundings.

I. He was well acquainted with the fundamentals of Confucianism.

Jiao Yulu's hometown, Boshan County, is in close vicinity of both Confucius' and Mencius' places of birth — places where the influence of Confucian ideology remains indelibly sturdy in spite of historic vicissitudes. Honesty, propriety and decency are virtues constituting the moral forte of the majority of natives of this region. Boshan County, in the central part of Shandong Province, is famous for its unusually ample mineral resources and was the place of origination of ancient China's filial piety culture and tradition. A touchingly didactic legend was told, so it has been alleged, by remotely ancient population of the county. And the legend goes like this:

Millennia ago in Boshan lived, on the top of a hill, a peasant family. Originally, there were four members in the family: the old master, his wife, their son, and their daughter-in-law. Then the son met a gratuitous death. Thus his wife, namely, the daughter-in-law, as she did not choose to embark on a second matrimonial union, remained to live in the family and continued to be in charge of its housekeeping. The young woman was a consistently virtuous and pure-minded soul. She had been impeccably devoted to her parents-in-law and commendably frugal and resourceful in discharging her household duty in all the years before her husband's demise and did not in the least diminish her filial devoutness ever since. Unfortunately, the heart-rending sorrow inflicted upon the old bereaved parents by their son's unexpected death appreciably warped their mentality, so much so that they harbored gratuitously the suspicion that it was their daughter-in-law who had engineered their son's mysterious death. Motivated by such a crackbrained idea and viciously intent on avenging their son' death, they peremptorily ordered their daughter-in-law to

青年时期的焦裕禄
photo of the juvenile Jiao Yulu

二、艰难成长岁月

1931年，9岁的焦裕禄在本村上小学。读了四年小学后，焦裕禄转到南崮山村博山县第六高级小学继续读书。家里贫困，为节省笔墨钱，他就用树枝在地上学写字。他学习认真，写的一篇作文《阚家泉的风景》受到老师的表扬。作文中写道："仁者爱山，智者乐水。我钦佩那些为国建立过功勋的仁人智者，更爱哺育过无数仁人智者的好山好水。而最令我喜爱的，就是岳阳山南山脚与崮山西山脚交会处的阚家泉……"

后来，因家中变故，16岁时焦裕禄被迫辍学，在家务农，挣钱贴补家用。他经常和父亲推着独轮车，到县城运煤卖煤，甚至还到本地的煤

trudge for a rugged and very long distance of downhill trail to fetch from a fountain there fresh water for the family's culinary use. They gave the young woman a pair of pails and a shoulder pole for carrying the water uphill. The bottom of either pail they gave her was not flat but shaped in the form of a cone protruding from the lower end of the pail, so that neither pail could be left to stand erect on the ground, or else the water it contained had to be spilt. This was meant for depriving the young woman, while carrying the water uphill, of the possibility of putting the pails full of water down on the trail for taking a short rest even if she felt intolerably fatigued, because the conically-bottomed pails could not be left to stand erect to keep the water unspilt. The old couple plotted against her. But, year in year out, the daughter-in-law willingly subjected herself to the ordeal imposed on her by the old couple without even the least resentment. Later, growing sympathetic towards the tolerant and gentle victim, a divinity descended from heaven to offer her a magic lash as a gift, telling her to affix the magic lash to the bottom of the vat, which was kept in the family's kitchen for storing the water she brought back from the fountain. The divine being told her that simply by gently swaying the lash already affixed to the bottom of the vat, a tamed spurt of fresh water would spontaneously issue from the lash. Before long, however, her mother-in-law discovered the lash and stealthily managed to detach it from the vat bottom. The instant the lash was dislodged, a torrent of fresh water gushed forth unexpectedly from the bottom of the vat and soon the torrent swelled to the dimension of a deluge which, having rushed into a ravine, surged forward to fashion itself into a river. The moment the torrent began to burst forth from the bottom of the vat, the young woman, on seeing that the torrent might drown her mother-in-law, strove to stop the torrent by stretching herself prone across the mouth of the vat. In this way, she gradually succeeded in blocking the torrent. To pay homage to her heroic act that was successful in finally containing the deluge, the local people reverently called the river fashioned by the initial deluge "the Devoted Daughter's River". Close to the bank of the river stood Gu Hill. To the north of the hill was a hilly village going by the name of Beigushan. Arable land here was very scanty because there was only a very thin layer of surface soil, which just barely covered up a very thick rocky stratum. Expanses of the arable land peripheral to the village were densely dotted with clusters of masses of rock cropping up here, there, and everywhere. Every downpour in a year tended to flush a portion of thin layer

1943年初,焦裕禄被押到东北抚顺大山坑煤矿,被迫给日寇做苦工
Early in 1943, he was escorted to Dashankeng Colliery in Fushun in China's Northeast. There he was forced to do most tormenting labor.

窑里挖过煤。

　　1941年秋天,山东地区大旱,农业绝收,焦裕禄一家断粮少食,欠下了不少外债。当时,博山被日伪军占领,苛捐杂税严重。保长(保甲制的一种职位。民国时期10户人家设立一甲长,管理甲长的则是保长,一个保长管理10个甲长)上门收租时,焦裕禄一家交不起钱,就被强迫收走了二亩地抵偿地租,这让焦家的生活难以为继。焦裕禄的父亲整日愁闷,在深秋的一天夜里,上吊自杀了。焦裕禄的父亲死后,焦家失去了顶梁柱。焦裕禄的爷爷面对突如其来的打击,病倒在床。焦裕禄的哥哥流落在外,联系不上。嫂子带着孩子,看不到生活的希望。

　　然而,祸不单行,1942年8月的一天,村里来了日军和汉奸,堵门抓

of surface soil off its rocky bottom. When the drought came, the arable land was rendered stark barren.

At the turn of the last century, agrarian economy monopolized China, thus pinning her national productivity down to a pitiably low level. At that time, having been turned hopelessly imbecile in the face of aggressive warfare successively launched by various imperialist powers, the Manchu government of the feudal Qing Dynasty was on the verge of an abrupt downfall, and social disturbances were literally unbridled. Then the 1911 Revolution led by Dr. Sun Yat-sen swept the feudal dynasty into the historical bin and leveraged all the political resources the revolution had mustered to bring the then China to accept a semi-colonial and semi-feudal social system in the wake of the cessation of the two-millennia-long era of autocratic monarchy.

On August 16, 1922, Jiao Yulu was born. His given name is "Yulu" — a name which his grandpa came up with in compliance with the rules stipulated by his tribe exclusively for creating a given name for each of its offspring. The two Chinese characters "裕禄" — pronounced yulu — carry the connotation that the household concerned would be endowed with wealth and prosperity. According to an autobiographical report submitted by Jiao to the CPC set-up to which he was once affiliated, his household consisted of fifteen members, when he was between eight and fifteen, and was in possession of thirteen *mu* (1 *mu* ≈ 0.067ha) of arable land, two oxen, and one mule. At that time, there were altogether twenty odd residential chambers within the precincts of his family compound. His household was actively engaged in farming and would manage to leverage some loan for operating a small-scale castor oil extraction mill in wintertime when farming had to suspend. As for the fifteen household members, they included Jiao's great grandma, grandparents, parents, uncles, aunts and some cousins.

II. His harrowing juvenile years

He began his primary education in 1931 when he was nine and attended a local village school and later went to Nangushan Senior Elementary School No. 6 to finish his primary education after he had done his first four years at the previous village school. As penury rid him of money for buying stationery, he impelled himself

壮丁。焦裕禄在家被日军抓住,送到县城宪兵队监狱,在狱中受尽毒打和折磨。

1943年初,日军用火车将焦裕禄等20多人押到济南,后又将他们送到抚顺大山坑煤矿做劳工。抚顺是当时重要的煤炭基地,19世纪初先后被俄国和日本占领。他们用"人肉开采"的办法,掠夺中国的煤矿资源。大山坑煤矿位置偏僻,几十里不见人烟。在煤矿里,日本监工们不管劳工的死活,让劳工们每天在暗无天日的矿井做十几个小时苦工。劳工们住的是阴暗潮湿的工棚,吃的是玉米面窝窝头,很多劳工因劳累得病而死。6月的一天,焦裕禄在当地一个老乡的帮助下,历经艰险逃出了煤矿。

一段时间后,焦裕禄辗转回到博山家中。因没有了"良民证"(抗战期间,日本伪政权为了确定人员身份,维持占领区的安全,对中国老百姓实行身份管理制度,为每一位占领区百姓发放"良民证"),在家乡恐再生变故,焦裕禄决定离开家乡,和家人外出逃荒。9月,他们逃荒到了江苏省宿迁县城东15里的双茶棚村,之后焦裕禄到一个地主家里做了两年雇工。

三、积极参加革命

1945年8月,中国抗日战争取得了胜利,新四军收复了宿迁,建立起了人民政权。焦裕禄听到博山县城也被收复的消息后,怀着喜悦的心情,用扛长工的钱买了一头骡子,带着家人回到博山。

此时的家乡是一片崭新的天地。过去被日军、汉奸欺压得直不起腰的人们,现在挺直了腰杆,开始了生产自救。北崮山村也开始有了中国共产党的党组织,民兵队长焦方开就是共产党员。他介绍焦裕禄加入了区武装部。焦裕禄积极参加了斗地主、押俘虏、送情报、打土匪等行动,得到了党组织的认可。经过多次申请,1946年1月,焦裕禄在焦方开

to wield a short twig for a pen to trace in the dirt the stroke structure of a Chinese character he had just learned or tried to learn. He was a particularly diligent pupil. "The Scenic Landscape at Kanjia Spring", one of his compositions he wrote as a little pupil, was warmly acclaimed by his teachers. In it run many beautiful passages, one of which reads, "People with a gracious turn of mind tend to get fascinated with mountainous landscape, whereas people with a sagacious turn of mind tend to be obsessed with riverine scenery. As for me, I admit I am 'incorrigibly' addicted to paying my profoundest homage to those benevolent or sagacious historic figures who have accomplished invaluable exploits to benefit the Chinese nation. Above all, I am more than head over heels in reckless love with our superb territory, which succeeds in bringing up myriads of benevolent or sagacious historic figures just referred to above. But it is Kanjia Spring rippling and gurgling at a tiny locale where the southern base of Yueyang Hill and the western base of Gu Hill meet …"

Then disaster overtook his family, and he had, at sixteen, to drop out of school because he had to do farm work and odd jobs for supporting his family. Together with his father, he had from time to time to transport coal in a large wheelbarrow to markets for sale in the county. Now and then he had even to go to work in a nearby coal pit as a hired laborer. In the fall of 1941, a catastrophic drought hit his hometown and neighboring regions and, moreover, had in tow a famine, which apart from threatening to curtail his family's survival, left it badly in debt. At that time, Boshan County was occupied by a detachment of poorly-armed quisling-like Chinese soldiers dispatched by the headquarters of Manchukuo Armed Forces. The detachment mercilessly extorted and ravaged the county. The lackeys, whom the detachment sent out to collect from the local population land rent, an assortment of fees, and material resources, were all ruthless hoodlums. It so happened that one day a small band of lackeys intruded into Jiao Yulu's house to exact land rent. As his parents were verily unable to pay it, the band of lackeys peremptorily confiscated two *mu* of the Jiao family's arable land as a penalty for the family's failure to pay the land rent. The confiscation landed the family in an unabatable and prolonged starvation and rendered his father irretrievably dejected. Before long, he was completely overwhelmed with hopelessness and committed suicide on a night late in the fall of that year. In years before his death, he had been mainstay of his family. His tragic and unexpected death was too much for Jiao Yulu's grandfather who fell seriously ill

1948年焦裕禄随渤海地区南下工作队离开家乡来到尉氏县
Bohai Regional Southbound Task Force reached Weishi County, Henan in 1948. Jiao was transferred to the task force at that time.

的介绍下在本村加入了中国共产党。此后，焦裕禄由一个普通青年成长为革命战士。在这期间，他与民兵们试制了高效的大青石炸药，还策划了"空城计"。

1946年前后，中国国民党军队大举进攻中原解放区，内战全面爆发。中国共产党领导人民解放军粉碎了国民党军队的正面进攻和重点进攻，解放战争由战略防御转入战略进攻阶段。在这期间，焦裕禄随民兵连调到鲁中武装部，配合部队主力参加了莱芜战役。

1947年秋，华东分局按照中共中央指示，决定从解放区抽调一批政治思想作风好、有一定指挥能力和工作经验的干部随军南下支援前线。于是，焦裕禄被上级组织抽调参加渤海地区南下工作队——淮河大队，焦裕禄被分到一中队一分队当班长，开始南下。在行军途中，焦裕禄经常帮助队友背被包、扛行李，还组织队员排演了大型歌剧《血泪仇》。

shortly afterwards. At that time, as Jiao Yulu's eldest brother had long since strayed distantly away from Boshan, and as it was inconceivable that the Jiao family — particularly his wife — could reach him soon enough, she had no alternative but to struggle, though full of despair and disappointment, to bring up her child all by herself.

Sometimes, it is the way with luck to let disasters that are to befall a victim pile on one another. What happened to Jiao in 1942 seems to corroborate this. One day in August that year, a small contingent of Japanese infantry, together with some Chinese collaborators (Chinese quislings) serving as its guides, marched into Jiao's village to round up all the able-bodied young men from all the households there in order to conscript them. Jiao was then among those who were thus arrested and before long escorted to a prison affiliated to the Japanese gendarmerie in the county. There he was brutally tortured with flogging.

Early in 1943, together with twenty odd young male conscripts, he was transported in a Japanese army train to Jinan before these conscripts were finally sent to Dashankeng Colliery in Fushun in China's Northeast. There, he was forced to do inhuman labor. At that time, Fushun was an important center of coal industry in the then China and had been conceded successively to tsarist Russia and Japan in the early part of the 19th century. The guideline, which was aimed at savagely plundering China's natural resources and persistently followed by governments of the two imperialist powers, was "extraction of underground coal resource be effected solely by dint of manual labor". The said colliery was located in an area remote and desolate. The area was enclosed by a circular, bleak and unpeopled expanse of barren land. The distance between the two margins of the expanse measured scores of miles. In the colliery, Japanese foremen compelled the Chinese coolies to do painfully exhausting physical labor in completely sunless and suffocating pits for more than ten hours per day. The humid shanties which housed these Chinese coolies were very badly lit and ventilated. The only staple diet for them was loaf of steamed corn dough. Thus, a shockingly great number of these Chinese coolies died of overfatigue or excessive exhaustion. In June that year Jiao succeeded in fleeing the colliery with the help of a native peasant.

He had to stray from place to place for a spell after his hazardous flight from the colliery before he thought it safe for him to return to Boshan simply because

1949年春，焦裕禄在尉氏县宣传党的土改政策，发动群众进行土地改革
In the picture, Jiao is seen talking to peasants in a village on the suburbs of Weishi County, expatiating on the land reform program formulated by the Communist Party of China and mobilizing the local population to take part in the land reform move.

焦裕禄在河南省尉氏县工作时的照片
A snapshot of Jiao Yulu taken at the time when he worked as a government functionary in Weishi County, Henan

his "safe conduct" which had been issued to him by the Japanese occupation forces headquarters was confiscated by a Japanese foreman at the colliery. Without his "safe conduct", it would be dangerous for him to take up residence in Boshan. Therefore, he decided that thenceforth he had to make his life elsewhere than his hometown. Thus, in due course he managed to sneak back to Boshan once just for having a secret rendezvous with his family members and persuading all of them to quit, together with him, Boshan eternally for making their life elsewhere in China. In September that year, he and all his family members succeeded in taking flight from Boshan and migrating to a village in the South of China. The village bore the name of Shuangchapeng was located eight kilometers to the east of Suqian County, Jiangsu Province. There Jiao was hired as a farm hand working for a landlord living in the village. For two years he lived in that way in the village.

III. He zealously volunteered to have himself affiliated with the revolution led by the Communist Party of China.

China won the victory in the war she waged against the aggressive Japan in August 1945. Before long, the New 4th Army led by the Communist Party of China grabbed hold of Suqian County from the Kuomintang regime. Promptly a new civil administration was set up in the county. Accidentally from a news report released at that time by the local communist administration, Jiao learned that Boshan, his hometown, had already been captured by the People's Liberation Army. The news enraptured him. Promptly he went to the market, taking with him all the money he had earned from doing farm work for the landlord. There he bought a mule with all the money he had. Now, since Boshan was a liberated county, it would be most appropriate and auspicious for him and his family members to quit Suqian and return to their native place. The mule he bought would be used as a beast of burden for carrying all the belongings owned by him and his family members to facilitate their migration back to their hometown. In due course, they started on their home journey.

With the liberation, social life in Boshan experienced a restructuring. Those local people who had been, in the years of Japanese occupation, cruelly oppressed and downtrodden by the Japanese armed forces and the Chinese quislings now stood up

1950年10月21日,焦裕禄(前排右一)在省团校第四期三支七组的毕业留影

The political course run by the Youth League and attended by Jiao in June 1950 concluded on October 21, 1950. The course had already run three terms before Jiao was admitted to it. It was to the fourth term of the course that Jiao was admitted. The group photo shows all those who attended the fourth term of the course. In the photo Jiao is seen taking the first seat from the right in the front row.

　　1948年1月,淮河大队到达河南省尉氏县,焦裕禄所在的分队留在了尉氏,参与当地党组织建立政权、土地改革等工作,还组织发动群众镇压土匪恶霸。当年11月,淮海战役打响,焦裕禄任担架队大队长,带领队员执行支前任务。

　　1949年1月,焦裕禄由淮海战役前线返回尉氏县,调到大营区任副区长、区长,领导工作队百余人开展剿匪反霸斗争。其间,铲除了以黄老三为首的恶霸团伙。

　　1950年6月,焦裕禄在河南省团校学习半年,在这期间与新民主主义青年团尉氏县委女青年徐俊雅的感情得到进一步发展。10月,结束学习回到尉氏继续工作,后与徐俊雅结婚。

exultant and proud since they were rid of all manner of indignities imposed on them by Japanese aggressors and their lackeys. Moreover, all the local population actively took the initiative in setting in motion a program aimed at stepping up the local agricultural productivity as a primary measure to counteract natural disasters. A CPC branch had already gone into operation in Beigushan village. Jiao Fangkai, captain of the village's detachment of militia, was a member of the Communist Party. He took the initiative to ask for permission from the district militia command to recruit Jiao Yulu as a member. Thus, Jiao Yulu was provided with opportunities that allowed him to enthusiastically participate in such activities as debunking the unlawful landlords, escorting prisoners of war, making or providing safe delivery of secret information, nabbing robbers or outlaws. Jiao Yulu's excellent and dutiful performance at that time was highly appreciated by the CPC local branch. He had sincerely and repeatedly presented to the local CPC branch his application for acquisition of CPC membership. On the strength of cogent recommendation given by Jiao Fangkai, party membership was formally conferred on Jiao Yulu in January 1946 by the local CPC branch. Thus, Jiao Yulu succeeded in turning himself from an ordinary young man into a genuine revolutionist. In the meantime, in collaboration with the village's militia detachment, a deadly high explosive was invented by Jiao Yulu. And he dubbed it "the green stone explosive". Moreover, he helped the militia detachment with mastering a series of maneuvers needed for executing "the empty fort stratagem" which served to cunningly mislead the enemy which was Kuomintang troops.

The advent of 1946 saw an astoundingly massive offensive launched by the Kuomintang armed forces to make inroads into the Central-China-Plains liberation area. This was Kuomintang's initiative to ignite an all-round civil war. The CPC led the People's Liberation Army to thoroughly defeat both frontal onslaughts and attacks against key strategic positions, which were mounted by the Kuomintang armies. Thus, the warfare conducted by the CPC against the Kuomintang had to end its stage of strategic defense and switch to the new stage of strategic offense. At this juncture, Jiao Yulu was transferred to Central-Shandong Militia Command, because the militia company, to which he belonged organizationally at that time, was ordered to be incorporated into Central-Shandong Militia Command. Such a redeployment of the militia company was meant for redoubling the support that the said militia command could summon for the People's Liberation army corps, which were

焦裕禄（右）在辽宁省大连市工作时的照片（左为焦裕禄爱人徐俊雅）
This photo of Jiao Yulu (right) and Xu Junya (left), his wife, was taken at the time when he worked in Dalian City, Liaoning Province.

20世纪50年代初期的焦裕禄
A picture of Jiao Yulu, which was taken in the early 1950s

prepared to launch the "Lai-Wu Campaign" against the Kuomintang troops.

In fall 1947, in compliance with a decree from the CPC Central Committee, the CPC East-China Bureau proclaimed the order that a considerable batch of politically and morally commendable, experienced, efficient, and popular leaders be chosen from administrative positions now governing all the liberated areas and that such outstanding leaders, after their having been gleaned, be organized into various task forces which will be incorporated into different People's Liberation army corps. These army corps were to march southwards to liberate China's southern provinces. Under such circumstances, Jiao Yulu, having been chosen as a leader qualified for being enlisted in the aforementioned task force, was assigned to Huaihe Echelon which was at that time affiliated to another task force bearing the name of "Bohai Regional Southbound Task Force". While working with Huaihe Echelon, he was appointed a squadron chief. Thenceforth his echelon started to go southwards in fall 1947. Although the expedition was a very trying one, he was sincerely obliging and genial as usual to all his companions, helping them out with moving bulky and heavy luggage or accoutrements. Once he even took upon himself the responsibility of organizing a magnificent theatrical performance of "The Unabatable Enmity", a high operatic drama. The cast consisted mostly of members of his echelon.

Huaihe Echelon, for which Jiao worked in the capacity of squadron chief, pressed forward into Weishi County, Henan in January 1948. By and by the echelon was ordered to station there temporarily and charged with the responsibilities of establishing the local administrative setup in cooperation with the local CPC branch, setting the land reform program in motion, and mobilizing the local population to arrest and punishing the local tyrants, hooligans, and outlaws. Pending initiation of the famous "Huaihai Campaign" started in November that year, Jiao was appointed captain of a stretcher-bearer team which was charged with the duty of executing battlefield first aid.

At the end of "Huaihai Campaign" in January 1949, Jiao was discharged from his post as captain of a stretcher-bearer team and transferred back to Weishi County, where he was promoted to assume the post of deputy governor of Daying district in the county. Before long, he was further promoted to full governorship of the said district. Moreover, he was assigned to head a large work team consisting of one hundred people. The team was a militant group in charge of carrying out ferocious

在尉氏，焦裕禄带领工作组到大营区搞土改试点。因工作出色，他先后任团陈留地委宣传部长，团郑州地委宣传部长、第二副书记，这为其以后的地方领导工作奠定了坚实的基础。

四、投身工业建设

1953年秋，根据国家大规模工业化建设的需要，党组织选调焦裕禄到洛阳矿山机器厂工作，任筹建处基建科副科长。焦裕禄正式从地方革命斗争转岗到工业建设上。

1954年3月，为畅通物资输送通道，焦裕禄带领工人修建了一条由金谷园车站到矿山机器厂的公路。任务完成后，厂里派焦裕禄等几个管理人员到哈尔滨工业大学学习。12月，焦裕禄经过努力学习完成了初、高中课程，考试合格，准备转入本科学习。突然，厂里来通知，要他们提前结束学习返厂工作。焦裕禄等人服从安排，回到厂里工作。

1955年3月，厂里安排焦裕禄到大连起重机厂实习，他被分配到机械车间，担任车间实习副主任。实习期间，他经常向苏联专家请教，努力学习俄文，努力钻研工艺技术，熟悉工作计划，积累管理方法。在起重机厂期间，焦裕禄连续在厂报发表了题为《对工段长工作方法的几点体会》《谈谈前方竞赛中的问题和意见》《机械车间三季度竞赛总结》等几篇文章。在文章中，焦裕禄为车间基层干部总结了十条工作经验。厂党委采纳了这些经验建议，改进了管理方法，调整了生产，增加了效益。

1956年12月，近两年的实习结束，焦裕禄等人即将返回洛阳。大连起重机厂的工人们依依不舍，多次向厂里提议把焦裕禄留下来。工人们都说："焦主任是全厂最棒的车间主任。"

回洛阳矿山机器厂后，厂里任命焦裕禄为一金工车间主任。他把学到的先进经验和技术与车间实际相结合，攻克重重技术难关，最终试制成功了中国第一台2.5米大型卷扬机。他的车间多次被评为"红旗车

campaigns against bandits, local tyrants, and thugs and could justifiably boast of the exploit of extirpating a local-tyrant clique headed by a notorious cutthroat, Huang Laosan by name.

He was enrolled on a political course for six months in June 1950. The course, which was financed by the New-Democratic-Youth-League Henan Provincial Committee, was run by the Youth League Institute and terminated in October that year. In the same month, he went back to Weishi to resume his official position. In the six months in 1950, he first became acquainted with Xu Junya, a female functionary, who was then working for the New-Democratic-Youth-League Weishi County Committee, and then fell in love with her. And she responded to his infatuation with an equivalent emotional intensity. Later the two were joyously united in matrimony.

During the period of time he held his administrative post in Weishi County, he led a work team to Daying district to set in motion a tentative program for land reform. In this, his accomplishment was amazingly impressive. Consequently he was promoted first to directorship of the department of publicity of the CPC Chenliu Prefectural Committee and then to directorship of the department of publicity of the CPC Zhengzhou Prefectural Committee and concurrently secondary deputy secretary of the CPC Zhengzhou Prefectural Committee. Experience and knowledge he acquired through fulfilling official duties at his previous posts served very well to lay a solid foundation on which he could build later a very promising official career.

IV. So he glowed on the industrial front too.

Early in the 1950s, New China needed to develop her industry on an unusually massive scale. This called for a stunningly large supply to her industrial front of com-petent and dutiful leaders. Thus, in fall 1953, Jiao was under the circumstance transferred to Luoyang Mining Machinery Plant, which was at that time merely an embryonic enterprise. There Jiao was at first installed as deputy chief of the infrastructure construction section, which was an integral part of the plant's "plans and programs formulation panel". In this way, Jiao was irrevocably relieved of his official post as a militant functionary having worked for diverse local administrations and went to fill a position on the industrial front.

In March 1954, he was appointed to head a team of workers. They were

焦裕禄(右二)和干部们认真学习工业管理知识
In the photo Jiao (second from the right) is seen attending a seminar of industrial management.

1956年7月22日,焦裕禄(中排左四)与大连起重机厂机械车间工人文艺组合影
Apart from Jiao (the fourth from the left in the second row), all the rest in the group photo were at that time members of a workshop's amateur theatrical group. The photo was taken on July 22, 1956.

assigned the task of constructing a highway stretching between Jinguyuan Railway Station and his plant. The highway, once constructed, would immensely facilitate the transportation between the railway station and his plant. Construction of the highway was satisfactorily completed on schedule. Then his plant dispatched him and some members of its administrative staff to attend an educational set-up run by Harbin Institute of Technology. The set-up offered a spectrum of junior-middle-school as well as senior-middle-school courses to its enrollees. In December that year, Jiao completed all the courses he had been instructed to take and successfully passed all the examinations required of him. Now, he was on the verge of going to take some college courses to be offered by the set-up. But his plant abruptly ordered him and those members of the plant's administrative staff, who attended the set-up together with him, to immediately quit the set-up and return to his plant for resuming their services. None of them was disobedient.

Jiao was appointed in March 1955 as deputy director of a team of apprentices whom were dispatched by his plant to Dalian Crane Factory. There they would be assigned to work as apprentices in different workshops so that they could learn or be trained in the techniques and knowledge of using various machines imported from the then Soviet Union. As deputy director of the team, the task, which Jiao was charged with at that time in relation to the team, was to supervise and look after each member of the team. There was a team of experts from the Soviet Union working with the factory at that time. Fulfilling his duty as deputy director of his team of apprentices, he needed not only to learn the techniques and knowledge these apprentices needed to master, but also to frequently consult the experts from the Soviet Union who worked there. Therefore, he strove to the utmost to learn the Russian language, study relevant technological knowledge from various publications, acquaint himself with work plans drawn up by different workshops in the factory, and take pains to sort out some puzzling issues in the realm of business administration or industrial management. In the spell when he assumed deputy directorship at the factory, he even went academic and wrote a number of essays which were later carried in the factory's technological journal and bore respectively the following titles: "My Comment on the Managerial Methods Prevalently Adopted by Section Chiefs", "My Reflections on the Competition Going on on the Workshop Front", "A Summary of the Competition Taking Place in the Last Fall". In one of these essays, he sets

间"。他还善于发明创造，用土办法制造了车间使用的充电机。

1959年春天，厂里选派焦裕禄到调度科任科长。在这期间，他科学调度，合理安排生产任务，让厂里的生产效率得到了很大提升。他提出：调度科要了解上级的文件精神，熟悉全厂的中心工作，把握轻重缓急；要注重调研，经常下车间检查生产环节。除此之外，他还关心职工生活，帮助职工解决生活难题。

因经常加班，劳累过度，焦裕禄的身体出现了不适。洛阳矿山机器厂的领导安排他进了医院。经检查后，确诊为肝炎。厂领导出于对其健康的考虑，说服焦裕禄回尉氏县专心养病。1962年6月，组织上安排焦裕禄到尉氏任县委书记处书记。在尉氏，焦裕禄并没有安心治病，而是为贾鲁河的水患问题、农业生产问题到处奔波。

五、献身兰考热土

在尉氏工作半年之后，同年12月，焦裕禄来到风沙、盐碱、内涝三大自然灾害严重的兰考县工作。上任前，开封地委主要领导对焦裕禄说："兰考有三个最，最苦、最穷、最难。"俗话说，"灾区栽干部"，很多干部都不愿意去兰考。焦裕禄却对上级组织说："感谢组织把我派到最困难的地方，越是困难的地方越能锻炼人。请组织上放心，不改变兰考面貌，我决不离开那里。"

到兰考后，焦裕禄得知灾民外流问题严重，就带领县委干部到火车站，查看群众外出逃荒要饭的情况，让县委干部认识到问题的严重性和迫切性。为进一步了解灾情，焦裕禄随后到各公社大队调查第一手资料，倾听群众意见。他主动与群众同住、同吃、同劳动，积极向群众请教。经过了解，焦裕禄认为，对兰考群众生产生活影响最严重的问题，就是风沙、内涝、盐碱三大自然灾害。

随后，他把兰考县治"三害"办公室改为除"三害"办公室，并把

forth ten suggestions which are conducive to improving the quality of management exercised by a workshop headman. As a result, the factory's CPC committee adopted the ten suggestions raised by Jiao. From then on, the managerial efficiency of the factory began to turn for the better, and the factory's productivity was on the increase. The team of apprentices stayed with the factory for nearly two years and concluded its apprenticeship in December 1956. However, workers of the factory got so endeared to the apprentices in general and to Jiao Yulu in particular, as could not bring themselves to see Jiao Yulu and the apprentices depart and go back to Luoyang Mining Machinery Plant. Therefore, the factory workers repeatedly appealed to their factory manager, asking him to persuade both Jiao and the team of apprentices not to go away from the factory. The factory workers believed that if Jiao consented to work for their factory from then on, he was bound to become the best officer in their factory in the foreseeable future.

  Now, Jiao was back at Luoyang Mining Machinery Plant and immediately appointed director of its metal-processing workshop. He was remarkably smart in turning all the knowledge he had mastered in the spell he worked with Dalian Crane Factory to appropriate and good use in solving various problems confronting him as director of the metal-processing workshop. Thus, his workshop was able to surmount all manner of technological and technical impediments and snags and succeeded in building on its own a 2.5-meter double-drum winch. This winch is the first of its kind ever built in China. On the strength of the feat of successful construction of the gigantic winch, the workshop he headed was repeatedly awarded the title "A Red Flag Workshop" with prize that went with it. Jiao's keen intellect gave him creativity. As his workshop was badly in need of a powerful charger, he volunteered to manage to build for his workshop a makeshift charger all on his own.

  Then he was appointed in spring 1959 by the leadership of his plant to assume the post of chief of the plant's scheduling department. Now, his official duty included formulating correct and precise scheduling programs and drawing up appropriate and feasible production routines for all the workshops of the plant. He succeeded in very efficiently fulfilling his duty and thus significantly boosting his plant's productivity. Efficient scheduling, so he pointed out to his colleagues, presupposes that all those who are in charge of doing scheduling need to fulfill the following points:

  (1) They should attain a full knowledge of all the relevant instructions given

除"三害"作为全县的中心工作。焦裕禄带队下去搞调查,许多同志劝他不要下去,待在家里听汇报,可是焦裕禄却说:"吃别人嚼过的馍没味道。"他抽调120名干部、群众、技术员组成"三害"调查队,全方位摸清了风沙、内涝、盐碱等自然灾害的分布情况。

1963年8月,双杨树村村民用兑粮食、鸡蛋等方式筹钱购买牲口、种子,坚持走自力更生的道路,被焦裕禄称为"双杨树的道路"。

Shuangyangshu, was once a severely-afflicted village in one of the disaster areas in Lankao. But villagers there were totally undaunted by the scourge, on which they fought to turn the tables by organizing themselves into a collective-farming team. They never looked to the outside world for succor or relief. As the collective-farming team was devoid of financial resources for buying seeds, farming tools, draft animals, all villagers volunteered to give gratis their sideline products such as eggs, grain, to the team so that it could sell them in the rural market for cash. With the cash thus acquired, the team was adequately equipped for starting farming anew after the natural disaster was over. The villagers' heroic spirit of self-reliance and abstinence was highly praised by Jiao Yulu who warmly acclaimed the expedient adopted by villagers of Shuangyangshu of organizing a "collective-farming team" as "Shuangyangshu's creative way of combatting the natural disaster".

and documents released by the leadership of the plant, so that they can succeed in achieving a balance and adequate scheduling by dint of their having mastered a comprehensive knowledge of the plant's currently pivotal role and mission.

(2) They should have regular access to various workshops for surveying how each of them is actually carrying on its operational procedure in the course of fulfilling both its productivity quota and an extra order.

As chief of his department, he was very kind and generous in providing his colleagues with feasible solutions to their specific problems stemming from some domestic complications. His sense of duty impelled him to voluntarily and frequently work overtime. This entailed that overfatigue eroded his health. By and by, he sank and fell ill. The plant leadership was worried and made arrangement for his hospitalization. The preliminary checkup gave the diagnosis of hepatitis. Therefore, being most anxious about his recuperation, the plant leadership earnestly persuaded him to quit his post in Luoyang and immediately go back to his family in Weishi County for taking up a new, less burdensome or even just nominal official post there, assuming that hearth and home could be most helpful to his recovery. Consequently, in June 1962, he was transferred to Weishi County. There he was installed as member of the secretarial panel of the CPC Weishi County Committee. He never was a man to stay idle at his post or to wallow in self-pity. On the contrary, at his new post he took to busying himself with exploring solutions to the natural disaster originating with inundation of the Jialu River and to a lot of knotty problems that hindered enhancement of agricultural productivity in Weishi.

V. After Weishi it was to Lankao that Jiao riveted his devotion.

His tenure in office in Weishi lasted for six months. Then to Lankao County he was transferred in December 1962. The county was notorious for its three outrageous visitations in the forms of gale-force wind randomly dislodging dunes, arable land turning saline and alkaline, and waterlogging. Pending his departure from Weishi to take up his new post in Lankao, one of his superiors took pains to prewarn him of all the monstrosities lying in store for him once he was in Lankao to perform his official duty, saying: "There are, you know, three funny epithets with which Lankao has been

焦裕禄带领群众植树造林

Local people were led and encouraged by Jiao to quicken afforestation in the county.

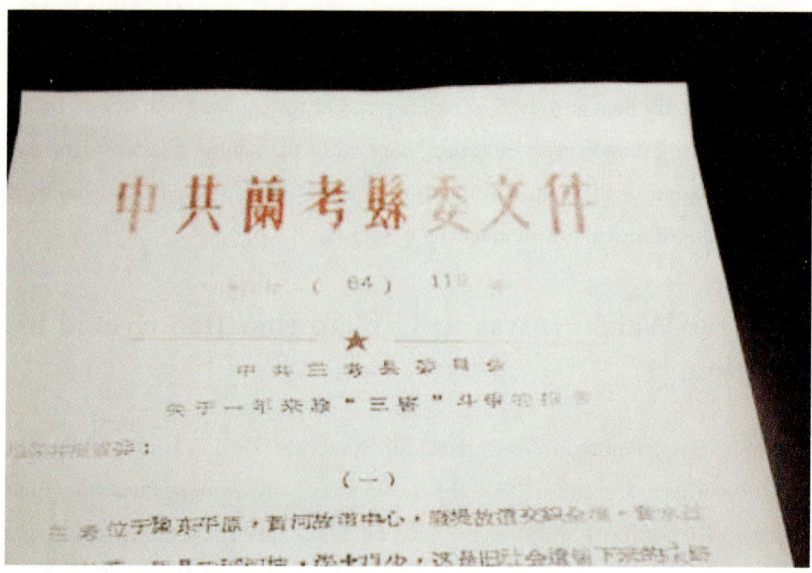

兰考县委向上级报送的除"三害"报告

The photo shows a copy of an official report sent by the CPC Lankao Committee to higher authorities. In the report is summarized the then development of the "campaign to eliminate the three banes".

dubbed. They are 'the land of the direst deprivation', 'the land of the most persistent impoverishment', and 'the land with the toughest resistance to any attempt to turn it for the better'." The forbidding ambience reportedly enclosing Lankao at that time induced the popular inventive verbal humor to come up with the following witty and sardonic remark, "A region where natural disasters tend to strike is hopefully the pitfall, into which a government official loves to dive." To tell the truth, a considerable number of government officials in Henan Province decided to keep as far away from Lankao County as best they could. But what was unique about Jiao Yulu was his response he gave to his superiors concerning his appointment to an official post in Lankao. And his response was: "I am sincerely grateful to my superiors who are so trustful of me as to send me to fill a position in a locality so ruthlessly beset with disasters and handicaps. But I believe that the harshest the disadvantage one is subjected to is, at the same time, the best circumstance one can take advantage of for multiplying one's moral caliber. So, please do rest assured that I will never quit Lankao unless its plight will have been completely done away with."

Soon after he had formally taken up his post in Lankao, he was keenly aware of and rather shocked by a mass exodus of the locals mortally inflicted by the then ongoing natural disaster. Thus, he led a small party of officials working for the CPC Lankao County Committee to dash to Lankao Railway Station to carry out a field investigation there for getting a whole picture of the woeful exodus. His intention in rushing part of his colleagues to the railway station was impelling them to see for themselves what a chaotic plight the pathetic exodus tumbled into and what a desperate situation the local people were in at that time. Jiao wanted his colleagues to be awakened right away to the stunning severity of the situation and the nagging exigency calling for unconventional and instantaneous actions on the part of the county administration not just for bringing relief to the local population but also for effectively stemming the onslaught of the natural disaster. Afterwards he toured all the villages on the suburbs of the county for obtaining an in-depth knowledge of devastation and ruin left behind by the natural disaster and of how the victimized villagers were struggling to survive. He was there also for getting himself fully informed of all the prevalent cravings of the local rural population. On arriving at a village, he chose to sojourn in a villager's home and would eat at his host's table and then go together with the host's family members to do physical labor in the field, so

焦裕禄组织的"三害"调查队勘察风沙灾害
The photo shows members of the task force were at work.

焦裕禄带领干部下乡访贫问苦
Together with some of his colleagues, Jiao went down to the rustic suburbs of Lankao to visit and comfort families in poverty and suffering.

that he could know the rural life there better. As a result of the arduous investigation he carried out in the rustic suburbs of Lankao County, he came to realize that the deadliest detriments threatening the survival of the local population were gale-force wind randomly dislodging dunes, arable land turning saline and alkaline, and waterlogging. They were the three banes of the county.

There had been once established by Lankao County Administration an agency going by the name, "office dealing with three-banes-related affairs". The office was still in operation at the time when Jiao came to Lankao. Then he decided to alter its name to "office for eliminating the three banes" and solemnly declared that elimination of the three banes ought to figure highest on the list of the county administration's priorities. On the eve before the departure of a work team headed by him to carry out extensive investigations and surveys that were requisite to formulating strategy for fighting the three banes, a lot of his colleagues tried hard to dissuade him from going on the expedition, being very anxious about his fragile health. They told him that it would be most advisable and appropriate for him to refrain from setting out on the expedition together with the work team. "Just stay put in your office," so they said to him, "there you can either read the reports they send you from the sites of their field investigations or listen to the oral reports which they come back to your office to give you. In that way you can play the part of a county administrator not a whit undutifully." To such a piece of advice, Jiao's rejoinder was: "To gnaw on a chew which has already been munched and enjoyed by somebody else is simply disgusting!" He organized a task force and assigned it to carry on the mission of investigating the widespread destruction and damage the three banes had inflicted on the county. The task force, one hundred and twenty strong, was an assemblage consisting of government employees, local inhabitants, and technicians and later succeeded in collecting full and detailed information concerning geographical distribution of each of the three banes within the periphery of the county.

Findings from the investigation and analyses the task force had carried out indicated that the size of arable land in the county was 900,000 *mu*. Of them, 240,000 *mu* were sandy and on shifting dunes and crisscrossed with blasts issuing from altogether 84 wind gaps. There were around 1,600 shifting dunes. The total size of land with saline or alkaline soil was 260,000 *mu*. The portion of land with the worst saline or alkaline soil was literally barren. There were roughly 280,000 *mu*

1963年秋，赵垛楼大队七季受灾一季翻身
Peasants of Zhaoduolou village in Lankao are seen in the picture extremely busy on the threshing ground while bringing in a bumper harvest in fall 1963, after the village had experienced seven consecutive seasons of natural disaster.

　　经过调查分析，焦裕禄了解到：全县总耕地面积90万亩，其中沙荒地24万亩，风口84个，沙丘沙岗近1600个；盐碱地26万亩，重碱地寸草不生；低洼易涝地近28万亩，阻水工程160多处。焦裕禄把全县所有的洼地、淤塞的河道全部绘图编号，在此基础上拿出一幅改造兰考的蓝图，制订了《中共兰考县委员会关于治沙、治碱、治水三、五年的初步设想（草案）》。焦裕禄在上面加注一句话——"拼上老命大干一场，决心改变兰考面貌，不达目的，我们誓不罢休。"

　　1963年初，为防止干部铺张浪费，搞特殊化，焦裕禄专门组织起草了一个《干部十不准》的文件，规定任何干部都"不准用国家和集体的粮食大吃大喝，请客送礼；不准参加封建活动；不准赌博"等。

　　在实践中，焦裕禄探索出了治沙、治水、治碱的方法。治沙，要坚持造林防沙、育草封沙、翻淤压沙三管齐下。治涝，要坚持以排为主，排、灌、滞、涝、台、改兼施的方针，实施上下游兼顾、不使水害"搬

of low-lying land most liable to get waterlogged. Besides, there were already more than 160 water-blocking projects in operation in the county. Jiao took pains to make comprehensive arrangements for drawing a detailed map not only for each expanse of arable land which was liable to get waterlogged but also for each watercourse which tended to be silted up. Then he assigned respectively to each of such expanses and each of such watercourses a number as its identification figure. On the basis of all these preparatory and preliminary efforts, he was able to produce the blueprint epitomizing the forthcoming transformation Lankao County was striving to undergo. Later he addressed himself to drawing up the draft document, "A Tentative 3-to-5-Year Plan Laid down by the CPC Lankao County Committee for Effectively Harnessing Gale-Force Storm and Drifting Dunes, Eliminating Saline and Alkaline Soil, and Removing Waterlogging". As a postscript to the draft document, he wrote down the following words: "I vow that I would strive to thoroughly reshape Lankao's physiognomy, stick at nothing, and fight to put the PLAN into effect even at the cost of my life!"

Later, with assistance from his staff he set about, in the beginning of 1963, writing a draft of the document "Ten Bans for All Government Cadres" which was aimed at rigidly curbing proclivities among government officials towards extravagance, wastefulness, and sinisterly grabbing prerogatives. It was laid down in the draft document that a government cadre is allowed neither to feast or send gifts to anybody at the cost of state fund or public fund, nor to take part in any feudal and superstitious activity or gambling.

It is in the course of arduous and persistent practice and doing experiments that Jiao discovered the most effective way and strategy to conquer the three banes. So far as harnessing gale-force wind and drifting dunes was concerned, a triple-initiative scheme was finally resorted to, which consisted of the three measures of afforestation, grass-planting, and stabilization of a dune with an envelope of silt. As for removal of waterlogging, the cardinal strategy adopted was finalization of construction of draining channels. And such a cardinal strategy was complemented with a spectrum of secondary strategies including rechanneling, appropriate irrigation, terrace planting, and elevation of surface soil. As a result, all the troubles that had adversely affected both the upstream regions and the downstream regions of rivers in the county were actually removed step by step, rather than being just displaced to some new locales.

1963年6月麦收前夕，秦寨大队用不同方法改良的盐碱地种植的麦子长势情况对比
Shown in the picture are diverse groups of bundles of mowed wheat with its blades intact. Each group is wheat cultivated according to a specific farming method. Though the farming method differs from one group to another, yet all the methods were intended for improving productivity of the wheat grown in saline-alkaline soil. These varieties of wheat were all grown by the Qinzhai Production Brigade. All these bundles were brought in pending the wheat harvest scheduled to take place in June 1963.

家"的政策。关于治碱，提出了翻淤压碱、开沟淋碱、打埂躲碱、台田试种、引进耐碱作物等措施。

1963年10月，兰考县召开四级干部大会，号召干部群众奋发图强，自力更生，大战"三害"。会上，焦裕禄树立了四个先进典型，将它们誉为"四面红旗"——韩村的精神、秦寨的决心、赵垛楼的干劲、双杨树的道路，激发全县群众治理"三害"、彻底改变兰考面貌的干劲，兰考的封沙、治水、改地斗争正取得节节胜利。

然而，繁重的工作压垮了焦裕禄的身体，严重侵蚀着焦裕禄的健康，他的肝病越来越严重了，但他仍坚持工作。有一次，焦裕禄在下乡

As for elimination of saline and alkaline soil, measures such as replacement of saline and alkaline surface soil with a layer of silt, encirclement of a plot of arable land with ditches for draining the saline or alkaline water contained in the plot, construction of encircling low ridges around a plot to keep saline or alkaline water away, elevation of surface soil of a plot of arable land, terrace cultivation, expansion of cultivation of alkali-resistant crops were adopted.

A meeting, which was convened in Lankao in October 1963 and attended by all the cadres working on the four local hierarchical levels and at which Jiao took the chair, issued a clarion call to all the inhabitants of the county, asking them to tone up to the utmost their morale and energize their spirit with a passion characterized by self-reliance, so that the county could turn out triumphant in its confrontation with the three banes. At the meeting, Jiao announced that in the campaign carried on so far against the three banes, four paragons of outstanding exertion had made themselves prominent and admired. Jiao declared that the four paragons were respectively in the forms of the high morale of the inhabitants of Hancun village, the irreversible determination of the inhabitants of Qinzhai village, the ambitious and passionate drive of the inhabitants of Zhaoduolou village, and the advisable strategic orientation followed by the inhabitants of Shuangyangshu village. "The four ought to be warmly acclaimed," emphasized Jiao, "as 'four red flags' that constitute the crucial dynamic impelling the Lankao people to finally subdue the three banes and confer a most decent facelift on the county. It is undeniable that the meeting signified that progress was being made in Lankao's endeavor to overcome the three banes."

But what is equally undeniable is the fact that overwhelmingly heavy official duty was wreaking life-threatening havoc on Jiao. Accordingly, his hepatitis got increasingly mortal. But he would not at all consent to recede a bit from the lethal enfeeblement his official duty imposed upon him. Once on a tour to a village for carrying out an investigation he suddenly fainted and was immediately sent by Lankao County administration to a hospital in Kaifeng City. There he pleaded with the doctors not to provide him with a special and comfortable guest-house accommodation. He said to them, "All I want from you now is nothing more than a diagnosis of my condition. I need no treatments here, because I want to go back to my county as soon as possible. In my county, I shall and can get my treatment while regularly fulfilling my duty and daily routine." As a matter of fact, he had later

调研时晕倒了，组织决定送他到开封治病。在医院就诊时，焦裕禄不住单人房间，他对医生说："在这里把病检查清楚，就回县里去，一面治病，一面工作。"1964年4月上旬，在北京的一家医院里，焦裕禄被确诊为"肝癌后期，皮下扩散"。

1964年5月14日9点45分，焦裕禄在郑州去世。去世时，焦裕禄留下了遗愿：活着我没有治好沙丘，死了我也要看着兰考人民把沙丘治好。

那一年，他年仅42岁。

to be rushed to a hospital in Beijing for his treatment. Early in April 1964, he was eventually diagnosed with "liver cancer in an advanced stage with liver metastasis".

In Zhengzhou, he passed away at 9:45 on May 14, 1964, when he was only forty-two! The deathbed wish he left us is this: "Now that it's impossible for me to see with my own eyes the ultimate conquest of the three banes, I pine only for the opportunities in my afterlife to observe Lankao triumph over them!"

第二章

时代的呼唤

Chapter II

Our era calls on us to learn about and follow

Jiao Yulu.

美国总统肯尼迪曾说:"不要问国家能为你们做些什么,要问你们能为国家做些什么。"不管在美国还是在其他国家,不管是过去还是现在,公职人员恪尽职守、讲付出、讲奉献都是各个国家所倡导的。正如英国哲学家洛克所说,政府的目的是为人民谋福利。焦裕禄是亲民爱民的典型代表,作为一个县的主政领导,他始终怀着一颗真诚为民的赤子之心,为了让群众不挨饿不受冻,他在群众最困难的时候送去救济粮和棉衣棉被,想方设法发展生产。进入21世纪,为什么还要学习焦裕禄?因为每个国家都需要千千万万个焦裕禄这样的公职人员履职尽责,推动社会发展。学习焦裕禄是时代的呼唤和人民的要求,社会管理需要焦裕禄这样认真负责、有方法、有经验的干部,发展经济需要焦裕禄这样敢于创新、敢闯敢干的干部,推动工作需要焦裕禄这样做事高效、执行力强、能干事、干成事的干部,群众工作需要焦裕禄这样接地气、能与群众打成一片的干部,维持社会和谐稳定需要焦裕禄这样善于作为、敢于担当的干部。

"Ask not what your country can do for you, ask what you can do for your country," so advised John F. Kennedy, the 35th president of the US. As a matter of fact, it is obligatory for a government functionary — whether he, or she, is an American or a national of any other country than America, and whether he, or she, is our contemporary or lived in a past century — to behave dutifully, dedicatedly, and selflessly. Not a country, whether it existed in a past century or is contemporary, would ever countenance one of its government officials to behave otherwise. John Locke (1632 — 1704), an English philosopher, was most sagacious in asserting, "The aim in establishing a government is to dedicate its best efforts to benefiting the public." Jiao Yulu was an epitome of dedication to the public. As a top leader of a county administration, his unfailing devotion to his official duty was impeccable. Striving to his utmost to opportunely provide poverty-stricken people with relief stuff such as provisions, bedding, clothing in the dead of winter, so as to save them from the ordeals of starvation and freezing cold, he willingly subjected himself to most excruciating trials and tribulations in the form of virtually unbearable physical and mental exertions and exhaustion arising from working overtime for excessively long hours in very trying circumstances, even though this evidently devastated his health. In a word, he did all things in his power to make the economy of his county flourish. But, why do we exert in the early decades of the 21st century to activate anew our move aimed at motivating our country to learn more about Jiao Yulu and earnestly follow him in our everyday life? Because we are firmly aware that all countries across the world are without exception in dire need of a great multitude of such loyal government officials as are analogues to Jiao Yulu, otherwise their social fabrics would sink in stagnation. In other words, our era calls on us to learn more about and follow Jiao Yulu. Peoples all over the world are calling for the initiation of a global move focusing on propagating information in relation to Jiao Yulu's life and exploits. The world will come to realize that to bring about an improvement in social life in a country calls for the emergence of a group of government officials who are morally on a par with Jiao Yulu who was dutiful, commendably experienced, and aptly flexible in fulfilling his duty. To steadily promote economic growth of a region needs a sizeable batch of government officials, in whom can be adequately mirrored Jiao Yulu's ingenuity and unbeatable initiative in making pioneering exertions. To enhance administrative efficiency necessitates a large number of government officials

一、"跑题"发言

焦裕禄去世后，兰考县广大干部群众沉浸在无限悲痛中。有的群众自发组织前往郑州烈士陵园拜谒，有的收集焦裕禄的遗物、看望焦裕禄的亲属。1964年5月下旬，河南省在民权县召开全省沙区造林会议，4位沙区造林先进县的县长在大会上发言，发言时间均为一个小时。第二位发言的是兰考县县长，他介绍了兰考县的造林情况、成绩和经验，还讲述了他的革命战友、兰考县委书记焦裕禄在除"三害"（风沙、盐碱、内涝）工作中的感人事迹。但参会人员发现，沙区造林越讲越少，而带领人们进行沙区造林的焦裕禄的事迹越讲越多。当讲到焦裕禄说"我死后只有一个要求，要求党组织把我运回兰考，埋在沙丘上。活着我没有治好沙丘，死了也要看着你们把沙丘治好"时，他已经泣不成声。会场许多人流下了眼泪。一个小时过去了，主持会议的省领导也被感动，他站起来说："讲，不受时间限制。"就这样，兰考县县长讲了两个半小时，全场泣不成声。会议结束时，省领导宣布："转变会议主题，下午集体讨论焦裕禄事迹。"

who are equal to Jiao Yulu in being very capable and efficient in fulfilling duty. To mobilize the populace to rally support for the government requires the emergence of batch after batch of government staff who are, like Jiao Yulu, free of arrogance, presumptuousness, or cynicism. To fortify social harmony and stability is plainly in need of the emergence of a multitude of government staff who have, like Jiao Yulu, high ambition, enormous integrity, and a clear moral code.

I. A speech delivered at a conference was irrelevant to the main thrust of its agenda.

Heartrending sorrow overtook the entire population of Lankao after Jiao passed away. Some Lankao natives hurried to the Revolutionary Martyrs' Cemetery in Zhengzhou on their own initiative in order to pay homage to him. Others strove to collect as best they could mementos and keepsakes by which to honor his memory; still others went of their own accord to visit Jiao's family members or relatives to offer condolences to them. Late in May 1964, a conference whose agenda focused on the issue of "afforestation in level desert plains in Henan Province" was held in Minquan County which is a county in the eastern part of the province. At that time, four counties, among which Lankao County was one, topped any other county in the province in developing afforestation in level desert plains. Thus, one representative from each of the four counties was invited to give a speech, delivery of which was scheduled to last inside of one hour, at the aforementioned conference held in Minquan County. When the deputy secretary of the CPC Lankao Committee, as representative of Lankao County, to attend the conference, took the floor, his speech touched at first upon the progress having been made in Lankao in developing afforestation on a massive scale and then upon the experience and lessons drawn by Lankao County from its afforestation efforts, before he waded passionately into recount in great detail the stunningly brilliant and touching deeds — deeds that were for subduing the three devilish banes — accomplished by Jiao Yulu who was his dearest comrade-in-arms. However, participants in the conference became aware before long that the bulk of his speech was not so much about the progress of afforestation in Lankao as about noble and heroic exertions of Jiao Yulu in carrying out the program of level-desert-plains afforestation. On coming to tell the conference

二、首次报道

全省沙区造林会议结束后不久,河南省委就做出向优秀共产党员焦裕禄学习的决定。1964年10月,新华社河南分社安排记者到兰考采访,焦裕禄的事迹被报道后,引起了新华社领导的重视。随后,《人民日报》发表了主题为"焦裕禄同志为党为人民忠心耿耿",副题为"中共河南省委号召全省干部学习已故前兰考县委书记为人民服务的革命精神"的通讯报道。紧接着,《河南日报》转载了该报道,还开辟了《学习焦裕禄同志为人民服务的革命精神》专栏。这些报道发出后,焦裕禄的名字开始走出兰考,在河南乃至全国范围内传播。

about the deathbed wish enunciated by Jiao Yulu pending the minute he breathed his last, the deputy secretary of the CPC Lankao Committee was almost stifled in tears. And the faces of his audience were all glistening with tears. Now sadness reigned over everybody present at the conference, as the deputy secretary reiterated Jiao's deathbed wish, "Now I have only one unrequited desire: my remains will be sent back to Lankao and buried in a dune there. Now that it's impossible for me to see with my own eyes the ultimate conquest of the three banes, I pine only for opportunities in my afterlife to observe, with my own eyes, Lankao triumph against them!" At this moment, even the high-ranking official who was sent by Henan Provincial Administration to preside over the conference was overwhelmed with the touching pathos of the audience. The speech given at the conference by the Lankao deputy secretary had by now already much exceeded the one-hour-stint and ought to have been interrupted under ordinary circumstance, but at this juncture, the high-ranking official who presided over the conference stood up abruptly and roared, "Go on. Don't cut down on your account of Jiao's story. There is no time limit to your talk!" Thus, the Lankao deputy secretary went on for two and half an hour to give rise to a heartrending ambience around the audience. When the conference had to be adjourned pending noon, the high-ranking official who presided over the conference rose to declare, "The original agenda for the afternoon session is abolished and to be replaced by the new agenda: all representatives to this conference are asked to take part in reviewing and discussing Jiao Yulu's life and career."

II. The debut official news release in China on Jiao Yulu's life and career

Soon after the conclusion of the promoting-afforestation-in-level-desert-plains conference, which was held in Minquan County, the CPC Henan Provincial Committee publicized its decision that a mass movement be set afoot for learning about and following Comrade Jiao Yulu. In October 1964, the Henan branch of Xinhua News Agency dispatched a reporter to Lankao for collecting relevant information. This was the initial media's effort to unveil Jiao Yulu's story, which galvanized the leading stratum of Xinhua News Agency. Thus, *People's Daily* carried a news report with the title, "Comrade Jiao Yulu's Allegiance and Devotion to Our

三、深度发掘

1965年底，时任新华社副社长的穆青和记者冯健去外地开会路过郑州时，在河南分社记者会上听当地记者讲了几个月来在灾区采访的见闻，很受触动。穆青决定，派记者到豫东灾区采访干部群众的抗灾情况。

河南分社记者周原第一站到了兰考邻县杞县，在这里周原没有找到新闻挖掘点。第二天周原乘汽车返回时，没有问路线，走了一段才知道上错车了。就这样，周原到了兰考。到了兰考，周原发现，县委大院就在汽车站旁边。说来也巧，周原走进县委大院，迎面碰上了平常跟着焦裕禄下乡的兰考县宣传干事刘俊生。刘俊生看了周原的记者证，把他领进办公室。

穆青、周原在兰考采访
The photo shows Mu Qing and Zhou Yuan were at an interview in Lankao.

Party and People". It was highlighted by a subtitle, "The CPC Henan Provincial Committee Calls upon All the Communist Party Members in Henan to Learn about and Follow the Revolutionary Initiative of Late Secretary of the CPC Lankao County Committee to Serve the People". *Henan Daily* not only hastened to reprint from *People's Daily* the news report but also started a special column which was entitled "Let Us Rise to Learn About Comrade Jiao Yulu's Revolutionary Initiative in Serving the People". All these were just media overtures debuting the name of "Jiao Yulu" on the ethical horizon of the Chinese nation and at the same time swept it to enliven not only the entire expanse of Henan Province but the entire territory of China.

III. The follow-up unearthing of the treasure trove of Jiao Yulu's morality

Mu Qing, the then deputy director of Xinhua News Agency and Feng Jian, a Xinhua-News-Agency reporter, chanced to come to Zhengzhou on their way to attend a meeting, which was to be held in another city. In Zhengzhou, both of them were invited to an assemblage of reporters who worked with the Henan branch of Xinhua News Agency. There Mu Qing and Feng Jian were deeply touched by a striking assortment of thrilling reports and stories recounted at the assemblage by reporters of the branch, who had just returned from their missions of press coverage carried on for months in disaster areas. Therefore, Mu Qing decided that a new batch of reporters should be sent to various disaster areas in the eastern part of Henan Province. There they were to carry out the mission of achieving the press coverage of how cadres and local populations there rose to fight the natural disasters and struggle to survive.

Thus, Zhou Yuan, a reporter affiliated at that time with the Henan branch of Xinhua News Agency, was assigned to go to an area in the eastern part of Henan. And promptly he embarked on his journey. His first stop was Qi County, which is a neighbor to Lankao County. In Qi County, he failed to ferret out any information anyway newsworthy. So, he left Qi County by taking a bus in the morning of the day after, intending to return to Zhengzhou. But he was rather absent-minded the moment he was about to get on board a bus and actually took a wrong bus which it

周原对刘俊生说："新华社副社长穆青同志，想写一篇豫东、鲁西南、皖西北改变灾区面貌的报道，让我先探探路，打个前站，摸摸线索……"

刘俊生脸上掠过一丝惊喜，打断周原的话："你们快来吧！俺兰考开展除'三害'斗争，把县委书记都累死了！"刘俊生激动地向周原介绍了焦裕禄的事迹，周原听后深受感动，决定留在兰考采访。12天后，带着第一手素材的周原回到郑州向穆青汇报，穆青听后对这个新闻线索非常认同，决定亲自到兰考采访。

穆青一行在兰考采访了和焦裕禄有过接触的当地干部和群众。哪知，讲的人哭着讲，听的人哭着听，一屋子记者也哭成泪人。穆青悲恸得不能自持，眼泪抹了一把又一把。中午大家也没吃饭，都在哭。下午继续讲，可一谈到焦裕禄的事，接受采访的人就哭，记者也伤心得握不住笔。到了晚上，穆青说："现在就要立刻着手写焦裕禄的长篇通讯。"穆青一行又去了焦裕禄生前下乡蹲点的韩村、张庄等地进行现场调研。根据调研材料，穆青、冯健、周原形成了初稿。初稿清样打出后，新华社要求兰考方面进行核实，"必须保证全部事实绝对无误"。最终，1966年2月7日，《人民日报》在头版头条发表了长篇通讯《县委书记的榜样——焦裕禄》，并配发社论《向毛泽东同志的好学生——焦裕禄同志学习》。之后，焦裕禄的事迹被传到了中国的大江南北。

was already too late for him to become aware of. The bus finally took him to Lankao. Walking out of the Lankao bus stop, he was pleased to find that the building housing the CPC Lankao County Committee stood just next to the bus stop. Thus, he sauntered leisurely into the building and soon ran fortuitously into Liu Junsheng, a government functionary working at that time for the department of publicity under the CPC Lankao County Committee. Liu had been regularly assigned to accompany Jiao Yulu as an assistant when the former needed to do investigation, inspection, or survey in a rural area. Now Zhou Yuan presented his journalist's ID card to Liu as was required by the formalities and was led into an office.

"Comrade Mu Qing, deputy director of Xinhua News Agency," so Zhou Yuan explained to Liu Junsheng, "desires that adequate press coverage can be brought about in regions such as the eastern part of Henan, the southwestern part of Shandong, the northwestern part of Anhui, so as to keep the Chinese people well informed of how local populations of these parts have fought so heroically to remold their native lands. Mu Qing sent me here as herald of the forthcoming media endeavor. I hope I can be allowed to go about some preparatory exertions …." A barely visible trace of pleasant surprise flitted across Liu's face, and he hastened to cut in saying, "I just fervently hope you, journalists, can be spirited out here in no time. Natives of Lankao here have been fiercely fighting to subdue the three banes. And the bestial enormity of the struggle has already cost the life of our beloved secretary of the CPC Lankao County Committee. He died of outrageously inhuman exhaustion!" Then he went on to passionately and briefly recount Jiao's life and career to Zhou Yuan. Zhou was so deeply moved as to instantly decide that he ought to stay put in Lankao to immediately start his investigation and interview with the local people. Twelve days later, Zhou left Lankao for Zhengzhou where he was to report to Mu Qing, taking with him a wealth of firsthand information concerning how people in Lankao strove undauntedly to get the better of the natural disasters. Having listened carefully to what Zhou Yuan had told him about how things stood in Lankao, Mu Qing fully advocated Zhou's conclusion that Lankao was a press-coverage bonanza and decided that he himself should immediately leave for Lankao in order to plunge into the bonanza to fully utilize it.

In Lankao, the party of journalists led by Mu Qing tried their utmost to interview all of those people who had come in direct personal contact with Jiao

穆青（右一）、冯健（中）、周原（左一）拜谒焦裕禄烈士墓
Mu Qing (on the right), Feng Jian (at center), and Zhou Yuan (on the left) are seen in the photo paying homage to the grave of Jiao Yulu, a revolutionary martyr.

纵观焦裕禄事迹的发现过程，看似偶然，实为必然。焦裕禄事迹被发现是偶然，但焦裕禄在兰考做出的感天动地、实实在在的功绩，是事迹被发现的必然因素。焦裕禄在灾害面前无所畏惧，在病魔面前视死如归，以"革命者要在困难面前逞英雄"的奋斗精神，以"心中装着全体人民"的爱民之心，带领兰考人民与风沙、内涝、盐碱做斗争。在人生最后的一段日子里，为了省钱，他拒绝吃药打针，用硬物顶着肝部缓解疼痛。在兰考，他与时间赛跑，与自然灾害抗争，大干了475天，用自己的生命换取兰考人民的幸福。

Yulu. Then an interview was held by Mu Qing. On that occasion, apart from the interviewees involved, some of the journalists were also present. Much to Mu Qing's stunning and disconcerting surprise, none of his interviewees could refrain from shedding a profusion of tears as they recalled Jiao Yulu's life and career. The journalists who attended the interview were no less pink-eyed and lachrymose than the interviewees. Even Mu Qing's mind went so unanchored as to leave his tears gushing out quite uncheckedly. The interview was still going on at full throttle when noon was just minutes impending. Nobody had appetite for a lunch now, what with the suffocating lachrymosity which none of them who were present at the interview was in a position to elude. However, the interview was interrupted anyway but was resumed in the afternoon. In the afternoon session of the interview, lachrymosity rose to reign for a spell whenever someone attending the interview chanced to refer to Jiao Yulu's life or career. All the journalists, who were present at the interview, were not just as sorrowful but grief-stricken as the interviewees and found themselves too enervated to even wield the pen for jotting down notes. In the evening Mu Qing insisted imperatively that each of the journalists who were present at the interview held in the daytime that day should right away set about writing a news report focusing on Jiao Yulu. The next day saw Mu Qing and his journalists set out for localities such as Hancun, Zhangzhuang, all being villages, each of which Jiao Yulu had frequented for doing field study or field investigation among villagers for an appreciably long stint. Now in each of these villages Mu Qing and his journalists were to carry on preliminary investigations that would facilitate their media coverage.

Basing themselves on the findings from all the firsthand media coverage in relation to Jiao Yulu's life and career, Mu Qing, Feng Jian, and Zhou Yuan succeeded in jointly working out a draft news report on Jiao's life and career. Then a typewritten copy of the draft news report was without any delay submitted to Xinhua News Agency which immediately directed it to Lankao County Administration and asked the latter to check whether the content of the draft news report was faithful to the reality. "You need to guarantee that every detail of the draft news report," Xinhua News Agency advised the county administration, "is totally authentic." Consequently, on February 7, 1966, *People's Daily* gave its front-page headlines to a long news report bearing the title, "Jiao Yulu, a Model for Secretaries of All CPC County Committees to Follow". Together with the news report went an

四、三次热潮

1. 第一次学习热潮

长篇通讯《县委书记的榜样——焦裕禄》刊发后,中央各部委、各中央局、各省市县先后发出《向焦裕禄学习》的通知。之后《人民日报》又连续发表了《要有更多这样的好干部》《在用字上狠下功夫》《调查就是解决问题》《最有力的领导》等7篇社论,在中国掀起了第一次焦裕禄精神学习热潮。

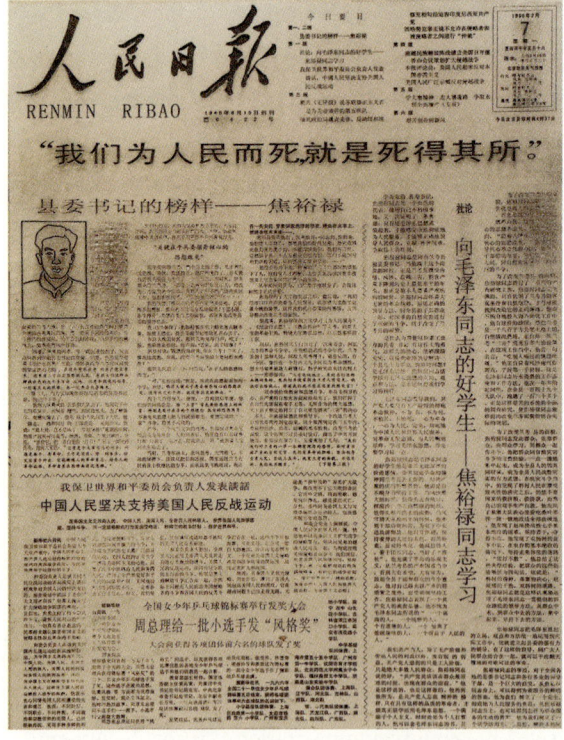

1966年2月7日,《人民日报》在头版头条刊发了长篇通讯《县委书记的榜样——焦裕禄》
On February 7, 1966, *People's Daily* gave its front-page headlines to a long news report bearing the title, "Jiao Yulu, a Model for Secretaries of All CPC County Committees to Follow".

accompanying editorial, "Let Us Learn about and Follow Jiao Yulu, a Distinguished Disciple of Mao Zedong". The news report and the accompanying editorial served to propagate nationwide Jiao Yulu's life and career.

A careful review of the process in which Jiao Yulu's legendary life and career have eventually come to light would reveal that the process could not be otherwise than a necessity, though a casual glance at the process might incline you to think that accidentalness alone governed it. It is true that the discovery of Jiao's life and career was just triggered by an accident. But what Jiao Yulu had achieved in Lankao were exploits stunningly thrilling, thrillingly significant, and significantly instructive. Being great exploits undeniably and immensely beneficial to the people, what Jiao had achieved is actually a formless monument that is naturally immune to anonymity. He was a hero from whom a natural disaster used to eventually pull back in awe. When coming to meet Death face-to-face, he did not even bat an eye. He adhered unfailingly to his mottos that "a revolutionist should behave like a hero when confronting adversity", that "my heart goes out to all of my people" when he strove to lead the population of Lankao to march on and subjugate the three banes. On being aware that his illness was totally beyond cure, he declined to receive any more treatments, simply because he could not bring him to further waste medical resources. When the sharp pain in his liver was too excruciating for him to endure, he would use a slender, rigid pole, or something like that, to prop forcefully against his chest. This could somewhat divert his attention away from the intolerable pain in his liver and made him feel a bit relieved. His tenure of office in Lankao can be metaphorically described as "a race against time" or "a relentless and prolonged tussle with natural disaster" — a tussle that lasted for 475 days. In the spell of the less than five hundred days, he relinquished his life in exchange for the beatitude that was Lankao people's due.

IV. The three upsurges in the duration of the nationwide movement of "learning about and following Jiao Yulu"

1. The first upsurge

Soon after the release of the long news report, "Jiao Yulu, a Model for Secretaries of All CPC County Committees to Follow", all the ministries and Commissions

1966年9月15日,毛泽东主席接见了焦裕禄的二女儿焦守云。同年10月1日,毛主席又接见了焦裕禄的大儿子焦国庆。周恩来总理也接见了焦裕禄的大女儿焦守凤。

2. 第二次学习热潮

1990年1月1日,电影《焦裕禄》在中国上映。1990年7月8日,新华社播发长篇通讯《人民呼唤焦裕禄》。这在中国广大干部群众中再次掀起学习焦裕禄精神的热潮。

1990年6月15日,邓小平为纪实文学《焦裕禄》一书题写书名
In the photo is shown the front cover of *Jiao Yulu*, a documentary novel in Chinese. The three Chinese characters are in Deng Xiaoping's handwriting. Deng did the inscription on June 15, 1990.

under the Chinese Central Government, all the regional bureaus under the CPC Central Committee, and all the provincial, municipal, or county administrations respectively issued to all the units or organizations under their jurisdiction a notification urging everybody to take the initiative in learning about and following Jiao Yulu. Later, seven editorials were published in a row by *People's Daily* to invigorate the initiative in ushering in an upsurge to the nationwide movement motivating people to learn about and follow Jiao Yulu. And the upsurge was the first of its kind in China. Titles of four of the seven editorials are respectively: "We Need More and More Exemplary Cadres like Jiao Yulu", "Do Strive to Put Truth into Practice", "Dealing with Difficulty Presupposes Carrying out Effective Investigation", and "On the Most Resourceful Leadership".

Jiao Shouyun, second daughter of Jiao Yulu, was received by Chairman Mao Zedong on September 15, 1966. Jiao Guoqing, eldest son of Jiao Yulu, was received by Chairman Mao on October 1, 1966. Later Premier Zhou Enlai received Jiao Shoufeng, eldest daughter of Jiao Yulu.

2. The second upsurge

Nationwide premiere of the film *Jiao Yulu* was scheduled on January 1, 1990. On July 8, 1990, a long news report, "Jiao Yulu—A True Public Servant Revered by the People", was released by Xinhua News Agency. Both the film and the news report triggered off the second upsurge in the nationwide movement of "learning about and following Jiao Yulu".

Jiao Yulu, a documentary novel written in Chinese, was published by Huaxia Publishing House. The title printed in the front cover of the novel is an inscription in Deng Xiaoping's hand. He did the inscription on June 15, 1990. Xi Jinping was at that time secretary of the CPC Fuzhou Municipal Committee. On July 15, 1990, he composed a poetic work "*Jiao Yulu in My Nostalgic Memories — to the tune of Nian Nu Jiao*". Added to it he had some preludial words which read, "I did not finish reading the article 'Jiao Yulu—A True Public Servant Revered by the People' until the wee hours, when the silvery moonlight was so generous with its fluid gleam. And then my mind waxed nostalgically lyric …"

President Jiang Zemin, came to Lankao on February 9, 1991 and visited and laid a wreath on Jiao Yulu's grave. Then he wrote down an inscription, "Let us learn about and follow Comrade Jiao Yulu and serve our people wholeheartedly".

1990年6月15日，邓小平为华夏出版社出版的纪实文学《焦裕禄》题写了书名。同年7月15日，时任中共福州市委书记的习近平，夜读《人民呼唤焦裕禄》一文，有感而发，写下词作《念奴娇·追思焦裕禄》。

1991年2月9日，时任中共中央总书记的江泽民来到兰考，向焦裕禄陵墓献了花圈，并题词"向焦裕禄同志学习，全心全意为人民服务"。

1994年5月，胡锦涛到郑州参加焦裕禄同志逝世30周年大会，并为焦裕禄同志纪念馆落成剪彩。2003年12月，时任国家主席的胡锦涛视察兰考。

3. 第三次学习热潮

从2009年到2014年，习近平三次到兰考，多次提炼焦裕禄精神，把焦裕禄精神概括为"五种精神""四种内涵""四有""四个人""三股劲"。至此，在全国掀起了第三次焦裕禄精神学习热潮。

2009年4月1日，习近平来到兰考，在兰考县干部群众座谈会上总结了焦裕禄的"五种精神"：亲民爱民、艰苦奋斗、科学求实、迎难而上、无私奉献。

In May 1994, Hu Jintao came to Zhengzhou for attending a memorial meeting for observing the 30th anniversary of Jiao Yulu's death and for cutting ribbon at the opening ceremony of a memorial to Comrade Jiao Yulu. In December 2003, he went to Lankao to conduct an official inspection there.

3. The third upsurge

Between 2009 and 2014, Xi Jinping came to Lankao three times. (It is in this period that he was promoted from the post of vice president of our republic to that of president of our republic.) He has, repeatedly and from different perspectives, summed up the morality that governed Jiao Yulu's rules of behavior. Listed here are titles of Xi's relevant and very pithy comments, "Jiao's Five Guidelines", "The Four Prominent Features of Jiao's Personality", "The Four Items of Jiao's Moral Asset", "The Four Features of Jiao's Personages", and "The Three Types of Jiao's Initiative". Thus, the third upsurge in the nationwide movement for motivating people to learn about and follow Jiao Yulu rose in full swing.

On April 1, 2009, Xi Jinping was in Lankao. At a forum on that day, which was attended by government functionaries and local inhabitants, he expatiated on the five guidelines Jiao adhered to in performing his official duty, and they are:

(1) Be affectionate to and intimate with the people.

(2) Be willing to endure hardship and work hard for the people.

(3) Be methodically-minded and practical.

(4) Never sidestep a difficulty.

(5) Serve the people selflessly.

On March 18, 2014, Xi Jinping came to Lankao again for conducting an official inspection. This time he expatiated on the four prominent features of the personality of Jiao Yulu as a government functionary. And the four features are:

(1) He was solicitous only about interests of the people but completely negligent of his personal interests.

(2) He never evaded truth, invariably went to get the firsthand information by going to investigate on his own, and was always pragmatic.

(3) He was always an undaunted pioneer and irreversibly heroic in confronting adversity.

(4) He was unfailingly dutiful, and frugal and never stooped to grabbing any privilege.

2014年3月18日，习近平到兰考视察，又将焦裕禄精神提炼为"四种内涵"："心中装着全体人民、唯独没有他自己"的公仆情怀，凡事探求就里、"吃别人嚼过的馍没味道"的求实作风，"敢教日月换新天""革命者要在困难面前逞英雄"的奋斗精神，艰苦朴素、廉洁奉公、"任何时候都不搞特殊化"的道德情操。在同中共中央党校第一期县委书记研修班座谈时，习近平要求，县委书记要做到"心中有党、心中有民、心中有责、心中有戒"，努力做"政治的明白人、班子的带头人、群众的贴心人、发展的开路人"，还要求干部认真学习焦裕禄的"三股劲"：对群众的那股亲劲、抓工作的那股韧劲、干事业的那股拼劲。

2014年5月9日，习近平到兰考视察，在焦裕禄干部学院参加并指导兰考县委常委班子专题民主生活会。

At a forum which was organized by Party School of the Central Committee of CPC and attended by the first batch of the trainees enrolled by a seminar that was run exclusively for secretaries of CPC county committees, Xi Jinping delivered a speech in which he urged each of his audience to strive for the following attainments: (1) political wisdom, (2) capability to execute an exemplary style of leadership, (3) sincere intimacy with the public, and (4) acumen in pioneering social and economic development of the region to be placed under his (or her) jurisdiction. To acquire these attainments, so Xi stressed, calls for each of his audience to behave in full devotion to Communist Party of China, to the Chinese people, to adhering to sense of duty, and to maintaining constant vigilance against even the slightest moral lapse. A government functionary, so Xi Jinping further expounded, needs to learn about and follow the three patterns of dynamics in which Jiao was indisputably unique. And the three patterns are: (1) perennial passion for endearing himself to the populace, (2) unsurpassable toughness in the face of adversity, and (3) one hundred percent dedication to his duties.

On May 9, 2014, again Xi Jinping came to Lankao for conducting an official inspection. There at Jiao Yulu Executive Leadership Academy, was held at that time a regular "awayday" focusing on achieving smooth coordination between programs or types of personnel — the "awayday" was attended exclusively by members of the standing panel of the CPC Lankao County Committee. Xi Jinping was invited to attend the "awayday" and delivered a speech there.

第三章

一本永远读不完的书

Chapter III

An undrainable fountainhead of wisdom

焦裕禄在兰考时的照片

A picture of Jiao Yulu, which was taken in Lankao

当今世界格局正处在一个快速变化的历史进程之中,和平、发展、进步的阳光已经穿透战争、贫穷、落后的阴霾。然而六十年前,中华人民共和国成立不久,举国上下积贫积弱、百废待兴,解决吃饭问题首当其冲。焦裕禄深知民以食为天,民生问题是社会稳定的基础。他一生都在带领群众与贫穷、落后做斗争,最后累死在兰考的沙土地上。为什么从国家领导人到民众都称赞他、怀念他?因为他有一颗高尚纯洁的心,他努力保障人民的权利,努力满足人民对美好生活的向往。放眼世界,他的事迹能够凝聚人心,他的精神具有强大的感召力和借鉴价值。

Now the world is in a historical stage marked by an accelerated universal development. As a result, military confrontation, impoverishment, or underdevelopment can no longer act as a critical impediment to peace, development, or progress in any part of the world. However, a glance in retrospect over the past sixty years of Chinese history would certainly lead us to recall how, in the few years immediately after the establishment of the People's Republic of China, our nation was trapped in a virtually impossible mess and compelled to solve myriads of issues or complications without delay. Of those issues or complications, how to spare the nation from hunger should be prioritized over anything else. Of this Jiao was fully and keenly aware, knowing intuitively the truth that being adequately fed is the primary element to sustain a human soul. To ensure that people be totally free of hunger or starvation is to ensure that social fabric has been founded on an invulnerable basis. Throughout the stage of his life when he worked in Lankao, Jiao exerted to the utmost to lead the Lankao people to fight back the encroachment of impoverishment and social stagnation until his overfatigue and serious illness that were induced by his overexertion in the interest of the local people stripped him of his life. Why is there, surging towards Jiao, such a durable flood of acclaims issuing not only from the supreme leaders of the country but from the entirety of the people? Because his soul was pure and saturated with dignity. And because he spared no efforts in securing protections for people's civil and political rights and in gratifying the craving and needs of the public for a better life. From his life and career have engendered and will continue to engender an inspiration and also dynamics that can help form global consensus and global initiative. Moreover, his life and career can stand out as a book for universal reference.

一、亲民爱民

1. 夜访火车站

焦裕禄初到兰考时,发现很多干部对抗灾有畏难情绪,开展工作时积极性不高,执行力不强。为此,在一个北风怒吼、风雪交加的夜晚,焦裕禄通知在家的县委委员开会。大家到齐后,焦裕禄说:"同志们,请大家跟我出去一趟,到火车站去看看。"

到火车站后,他们看到候车室里挤满了逃荒的灾民,有的横躺着,有的竖卧着。焦裕禄走到灾民面前,询问他们是从哪儿来的,准备到哪儿去。灾民都说家乡连年遇灾,家里面实在没有吃的东西,活不下去,为了生存,只有离开家乡外出要饭。焦裕禄心情沉重地对身边的县委委员们说:"同志们,这些人绝大多数是我们的阶级兄弟,是灾荒逼迫他

焦裕禄去火车站查看灾民逃荒情况(舞台剧剧照)
The photo shows a scene in a drama performed on the stage. Shown in the photo is a scene whose setting is the Lankao Railway Station where the actor enacting Jiao is seen talking to some victims of natural calamity.

I. Jiao's philanthropic rules of behavior

1. A nocturnal inspection conducted in the railway station

Shortly after his arrival for the first time in Lankao following his being appointed to the official post there, he became aware that as timidity was evident with a large number of local government officials in taking measures to fight the natural disasters, they had little enthusiasm for or initiative in putting counteractive endeavors against natural disasters into effect. In order to rid these colleagues of their inertia, Jiao deliberately took advantage of a freezing and late evening with howling north wind and blinding blizzard to order all members of the CPC Lankao County Committee — as these committee members had already retired home after finishing normal activity for a day — to rush to a meeting to be held in his office in the county-committee building. As soon as they were all present in his office, Jiao said, "Comrades, now I ask all of you in the first place to immediately go with me to the railway station and observe for yourselves what is going on there."

It is on arriving at the railway station that Jiao, together with his retinue, was stunned to find every waiting room there was littered with recumbent human bodies on the floor as well as in chairs. Jiao went to talk with them, desiring to know why and whence they came and whither they would leave. Their answers to Jiao's questions were similar and let him understand that natural calamities and famine for years in a row in their native counties left them no alternative but to desert their homeland and resort to vagrant beggary in order to grab a chance for survival. Brimming over with abject dejection, Jiao said to all the county-committee members in his company, "Comrades, you see most of them come from the same social origin as you and me. It is the natural disaster that turns them out of their homeland. It isn't their fault at all that they are plunged into such a miserable plight. It is public servants like you and me who ought to be held responsible for their wretchedness. Our Party has entrusted us with the duty of improving the lot of the 360,000 people. But we funked it. It is us who ought to feel ashamed and deeply remorseful!" Jiao's enunciation impelled himself and his companions to shrink with shame into an unseemly slouch. It is just at this moment that these county-committee members began to awake to Jiao's motivation in rallying all of them in the dead of a freezing and stormy night to the railway station.

们背井离乡的，这不能怪他们，责任在我们身上，党把三十六万群众交给了我们，我们没能领导他们战胜灾荒，过安居乐业的生活，应该感到羞耻和痛心。"讲到这里大家都低下了头。此时，这些县委委员们才理解焦书记为什么深更半夜领着他们来到风雪严寒中的火车站。

回到县委，已是午夜时分，这时会议才正式开始。同志们发言时都很激动。焦裕禄静静地听着，听完后他说："我们经常口口声声说要为人民服务，实际上我们在这方面做得不够，我希望大家牢记今晚的情景，这样我们就有决心去领导群众改变兰考的面貌。"会议整整开了一夜，天亮才结束。县委委员们怀着激动的心情，分别回到各自的战斗岗位上。

2. "我是您的儿子"

1963年冬的一个晚上，北风呼啸，大雪纷飞，雪下了一夜。第二天，天刚亮，他就把县委院里的同志叫到会议室开会。焦裕禄说："同志们，在这大雪封门的日子里，我们不能坐在办公室里烤火，应该到群众中间去。共产党员应该在群众最困难的时候，出现在群众面前，在群众最需要帮助的时候，去关心群众，帮助群众。"

焦裕禄的话引起了县委同志们的共鸣。会后，同志们立即分头出发了。这一天，焦裕禄带领同志们顶着风雪跋涉几十里，走过九个村庄，慰问了几十个生活困难或身患重病的老贫农。

在梁孙庄，焦裕禄来到老贫农梁俊才家。梁俊才身患疾病，梁大娘双目失明，生活极其困难。

焦裕禄一进屋，就坐到梁大爷的床头问候他说："梁大爷，您的病怎么样？生活有困难吗？"

梁大爷在床上颤悠悠地坐起来，睁开眼睛问："你是谁啊？"

焦裕禄亲切地回答："我是您的儿子。"

Chapter III An undrainable fountainhead of wisdom

It was not until midnight that Jiao and his company got back to his office in the county-committee building. Then he formally announced it was time for them to properly start their meeting. Jiao sat mute and intently listening while others vied with each other to talk and got very much agitated. At last, Jiao said, "All of us have been persistently letting the catchword 'we devote ourselves to serving the people' race through our lips. But as a matter of fact, we have been till now lagging well behind in our exertion. I hope none of us is to let slip from our memory what we had just seen happened at the railway station tonight. The memory will certainly back us up on our determination to lead the local people to completely refashion Lankao." The peep of dawn saw the meeting at an end. A roaring fire now sparked in all members of the CPC Lankao County Committee when they strode back to their respective official posts.

2. "Now, I'm your son!"

Throughout the night — a night in the year 1963 — it snowed, with the gale-force wind from the north furiously roaring. A new day began in Lankao as dawn cracked and saw Jiao Yulu go about summoning all the government staff who lived in the county-committee compound to attend a meeting to be held in the conference room in the county committee building. As soon as the meeting was afoot, Jiao said to his audience, "Comrades, snow has blocked access to almost all houses and buildings in the county. We can't so fondly indulge ourselves by staying snug by the stove in our offices and call it a day, can we? No. It is obligatory for us to be together with our people. A communist ought to be in the midst of his multitude whenever adversity looms, and would exert to the utmost to do things beneficial to his people whenever they are in need of his exertion. He ought to be deeply concerned about them and give them comfort." His audience chimed in with him without reserve. The meeting terminated. Now all those who had attended the meeting split into groups and sallied forth energetically from the county-committee compound. Braving the elements, they went on their respective tours to visit elderly people and the needy in the county. Trudging through blinding snow and nipping wind, the group which was led by Jiao traveled on that day scores of kilometers, dropping in on scores of elderly people, the sick, and the needy living respectively in nine villages.

In Liangsun village, Jiao went to visit Liang Juncai, an aged and impoverished peasant. Liang fell seriously ill at that time, and his wife was blind. The family was in

焦裕禄冒雪访贫问苦的素描画
A sketch of the scene of the visit Jiao paid to two needy villagers.

梁大爷问:"大雪天,你来干啥?"

焦裕禄说:"毛主席叫我来看望您老人家!"

梁大爷感动地说:"多谢毛主席他老人家操心啦!去年我们村遭了水灾,可副业搞得不赖,社员有吃有喝。别看俺家没劳力,可日子还过得下去。"老人说着,一行热泪流了下来,滴在两人紧握的手上。

焦裕禄和同志们商量后,随即救济梁俊才二十元钱。梁俊才接过钱感动地说:"在旧社会,我交不起租子,地主封我的门;如今,毛主席派干部冒着雪,亲自给我送救济款,我一辈子也忘不了!"双目失明的梁大娘听到这儿,摸索着走过来,双手上下抚摸着焦裕禄,说:"真是毛主席的好干部,真是毛主席的好干部……"

3. 改名叫"继焦"

1963年春节过后,红庙公社葡萄架大队社员张传德家徒四壁,连粮

dire need of help. On entering Liang's house, Jiao saw he was slumped helpless in his bed. Jiao shot to his bedside and then pressed gently against Liang's pillow.

"My dear old pa," feelingly Jiao crooned, "May I know how your illness affects you? Anything I can do to help?" Liang struggled feebly to raise his torso to a barely erect posture before he opened his eyes and asked, "Well, who are you?"

"Now, now, I'm your son!" replied Jiao affectionately.

"Why did you choose to come here in the blighting snow?" inquired Liang.

"You know," said Jiao, "It is Chairman Mao who urged me to come look you up."

"Oh, thank Chairman Mao for his concern about me," said Liang gratefully, "My wife and me did ok last year, though we, two, were poor and devoid of even a farm hand, and though a flood did bring calamity to our village last year. Anyway our village made it last year because our village's sideline production was rewarding." Tears trickled down Liang's cheeks. The two pairs of mutually clasped hands were sprinkled with the old man's tears.

Then Jiao went aside to consult his companions for advice on how much should be the alms to be offered to Liang. Soon twenty *yuan* were put into Liang's hands. The old man was deeply moved, saying, "In pre-liberation days, at the end of one year I failed to pay rents to my landlord. And he came to brutally block the door of my dilapidated cottage. Now Chairman Mao has dispatched his cadres to travel thus far in the heavy snow to my house to bring me the relief fund. This is what I would bear in my mind till I breathe my last." Liang's wife was quite aware what was going on, though she was blind. Now she groped to stumble to Jiao and began to stroke him off and on, while murmuring, "You're doubtlessly one of Chairman Mao's excellent cadres, indeed!"

3. The lad's name was changed to Zhang Jijiao.

Being singularly hard up, Zhang Chuande and his wife, two villagers living in Putaojia village in Hongmiao which was a rural district, were actually starved into abject beggary after the spring festival of 1963. The only alternative left them, if they wanted to survive, was to desert their homeland and struggle to stray to Xuzhou. They hoped they might live as vagrant beggars there. Thus, they trudged to Xuzhou. Shortly after they arrived there, the wife gave birth to a male infant. The name they gave to it was Zhang Xuzhou. An age-long custom with a lot of regions in China prohibits a woman to enter the home of any of her relatives' within a period of thirty

食都难吃上，思来想去，只好带着妻子到徐州一带逃荒要饭。到徐州不久，妻子生下儿子张徐州。在中国很多地方，自古有一种风俗：产妇不满月，不能进别人的家门。因无处可去，生下小徐州六天，张传德夫妇就带着孩子回到兰考家中。由于路途颠簸，小徐州得了黑热病。

一天，焦裕禄到红庙村走访，来到张传德家，看到小徐州奄奄一息，身旁还放着稻草和箩筐，孩子的娘坐在一边痛哭，焦裕禄一问才知道原来张传德夫妇二人没钱给孩子看病，准备等孩子断气后，将孩子用草裹了，装到箩筐里扔到乱葬岗上。焦裕禄走到小徐州身边，摸摸孩子的胸口，还有微弱的呼吸。焦裕禄当即给医院负责人写了一封便信，对张传德说："赶快把孩子送到医院抢救！"张传德拿着焦裕禄的信，带着孩子往县医院赶去。

焦裕禄随后到村大队部，又给县医院打了一通电话。县医院接到焦裕禄的电话后，非常重视，连夜组织抢救。小徐州已经瘦得皮包骨头，静脉难以确认，几位护士都不敢给孩子扎针，最后还是一位老护士在脚趾间扎下了针。这一夜，几班医生、护士轮流看护孩子。经过精心医治，小徐州的病情慢慢好转。

后来，焦裕禄再次来到张传德家探访，看到小徐州已健康长大。张传德感恩地说："这孩子能活下来，多亏了您啊焦书记。"焦裕禄说："现在是新社会，孩子才是咱国家的未来啊。"

焦裕禄去世后，为了纪念焦裕禄，继承焦裕禄的遗志，张传德将儿子的名字改成张继焦。张继焦长大成人后，到焦裕禄纪念园工作，守护着焦裕禄的陵园。

Chapter III An undrainable fountainhead of wisdom

days starting from the date when she delivers a baby. Such an age-long custom still prevailed in Xuzhou at the time both Zhang and his wife stayed there as vagrants. As Zhang and his wife were homeless in Xuzhou, she was not allowed to stay in any house immediately after her delivery and forced to stay in open air for six days in a row. On the seventh day as they found they were really at the end of their tether, they started on their home journey to Lankao. Of course, the homeward trek was more hellish than anything they had faced in their life. And the baby caught kala-azar.

It so happened that Jiao Yulu chanced to be in Hongmiao one day for visiting needy villagers there. On entering Zhang Chuande's cottage, Jiao's eyes were attracted to the dying baby lying on a cushion. A small pile of straw and a wicker basket were deposited beside the cushion. Zhang's wife was weeping bitterly by the cushion. Having inquired Zhang and his wife about what had happened to the baby, Jiao was told that as both the man and his wife were too hard up to pay for the medical treatment the baby was to receive, they had no alternative but to leave the baby to die without any treatment. The straw and the basket were to be used to pack the baby's remains in after the end of its life. Then its body would be carried in the basket to a specific spot in a remote dune, where remains of the poor were unceremoniously dumped to decay there. Jiao walked up to the cushion and softly touched the baby's chest. On finding out it was still breathing very weakly, Jiao instantly sat down and wrote a letter which was addressed to the head of a hospital in the county. Then he said to Zhang, "Now take this letter with you and immediately rush your child to the hospital for an emergency treatment. Quick!" Zhang Chuande complied.

Then Jiao rushed to the office of Hongmiao Rural District for using the phone there to ring up the head of the hospital. He told the latter all about the disease of Zhang Chuande's baby over the phone. The hospital head was duly alerted and promised to take good care of the baby. Then he went to get the required emergency treatment ready prior to the arrival of Zhang Chuande and his baby. The emergency treatment given to the little patient, after his arrival in the hospital, went on into the wee hours of the next morning. His shocking emaciation blurred veins in any part of his body and virtually frustrated attempts on the part of the nurses present in the emergency room to give him an intravenous drip until a veteran nurse ventured to try and finally succeeded in making the tip of a syringe needle pierce a vein between the baby's toes. Doctors and nurses on the night shift were very dutiful. Thanks to the

张传德抱着儿子张继焦参加焦裕禄的追悼会
Zhang Chuande took his son, Zhang Jijiao to Jiao Yulu's funeral service.

quality follow-up treatment, the baby recovered steadily and was discharged from the hospital in due course.

Later, when Jiao had a chance to go to Hongmiao Rural District, he made a point of going to look Zhang Chuande up. At the latter's home, Jiao found the kid was now taking a new lease of life. Tremendously rejoicing at his kid's condition and being grateful to what Jiao had done for his family, Zhang said, "We are indebted to you for Zhang Xuzhou's second lease of life!" ("Zhang Xuzhou" was the kid's given name at that time.) Jiao hastened to replied, "Oh, you don't say! The republic we're living in now, you know, is unquestionably antithetical to its antecedent. Therefore, our kids are, in their own right, entitled to quality therapeutic service because upon them the future of our nation hinges!"

Zhang Chuande had the name of his kid altered to "Zhang Jijiao" ("Zhang Jijiao" is English transliteration of the three Chinese characters "张继焦". The implied signification of the Chinese name is "following Jiao Yulu's example".) after Jiao's demise. That was for eternalizing Jiao's memory in Zhang Chuande' family. And the kid's new name was also meant for impelling him to lead a life truly worthy of Jiao Yulu's expectation of him. Later in his adulthood, Zhang Jijaio went to work as a functionary in Jiao Yulu Memorial Park, as his love of and gratitude to Jiao demands him to oblige the memorial park with his unreserved devotion and practically protective exertions.

4. The delivery to the needy of winter clothing, which Jiao did on one of those bitterly cold nights

A sizeable allocation, granted and delivered by the provincial authorities concerned, of relief winter clothing arrived in Lankao in the evening of January 16, 1963. The allocation was scheduled to be stored in a warehouse which was owned by Lankao Textile Company and situated at a suburban locale less than a kilometer away from the center of the county. On being intimated of the arrival of the relief material, Jiao immediately instructed his assistant to order all the colleagues working with the CPC County Committee to hurry to the said warehouse. They were expected to take part in distributing the relief winter clothing to the pauperized people in the county before the very night expired. Jiao himself was the first to come to the warehouse. He waited in its courtyard for others to arrive. Before long, all the colleagues involved assembled in the courtyard. Now firmly to them Jiao enunciated,

4. 雪夜送棉衣

1963年1月16日傍晚，上级拨给兰考的救济棉衣运到了位于城外一里多地的县纺织品公司仓库。焦裕禄得知此事后，让办公室通知所有机关干部都到纺织品公司仓库集合，把棉衣连夜发给群众。焦裕禄率先来到仓库院内，等人到齐后，他语气坚定地对大家说："同志们，天气冷吗？现在全县还有上万的农民兄弟没有穿上棉衣，怎么度过这风雪之夜？我们共产党员是为人民服务的，不能眼睁睁看着群众受冻，必须连夜把棉衣送到群众手中。不然，我们就对不起党，对不起我们的农民兄弟。"在他的鼓舞下，大家拉的拉、抬的抬，一直干到深夜1点多钟，才把1万多件棉衣基本发完，最后剩下的不足百件。

这时，焦裕禄对跟前的五个人说："余下的我们六个人包了，送到爪营公社去！"说完，他们就把棉衣装上架子车，出发前往爪营公社。

天冷路滑，一路上焦裕禄一边用力拉着车子，一边给大家鼓劲，累得满头大汗。几个青年见此情景都很感动，争着要拉架子车。一个青年恳切地说："焦书记，让给我们拉吧，您白天那么忙，晚上还拉车，太辛苦了！"

"The freezing weather is killing, isn't it? Comrades, there are around ten thousand needy people in our county are destitute of even the least winter clothing. How can they manage to survive the diabolic cold? It's obligatory for us, communists, to exert to the utmost to benefit the people. Can we now casually pretend to be blind to their sufferings, to their being tortured by the devilish weather? It's imperative for us to deliver all the relief winter clothing to all the needy in our county before the night is over. Otherwise, each of us is to be dubbed "a traitor to our Party" or "a foe to the poor". His clarion call kindled fervor in everybody in the courtyard. They launched into the arduous labor of carrying out the distribution of the relief material in an efficient and proper way. The initial wee hours of the next morning saw the bulk of the distribution task of delivering a little more than ten thousand pieces of relief winter clothing finished. By now there were less than one hundred pieces waiting to be conveyed where each of them ought to go.

Jiao agilely beckoned over the five young colleagues who stayed closest to him at the time and said to them, "As there are only less than one hundred pieces left to be delivered and as they are all destined to go to Zhuaying Rural District, just let the six of us handle this residual relief thingamabob and tell all the others to go home and have some rest, ok?" The five consented. Thus, Jiao and the five briskly had the less than one hundred pieces loaded to a gigantic cart and then started on their way in the direction of Zhuaying Rural District.

The frigid night and the slippery road imposed overfatigue on Jiao, as it was he alone who pulled the cart, with his five companions either shoving the cart at its back or going alongside the cart to give it some sideways pushes. Though being worn out and sweaty all over, Jiao exerted to encourage and cheer his five young companions up. By and by, they became softened and began to vie with Jiao and with each other to pull the cart. One of the young men said to him, "Oh, Secretary Jiao, do let us, the five young men, pull the cart. It's unfair to leave you so fagged out what with your too damned busy daytime and what with your having been pulling the cart so strenuously now! So, please do let each of us pull the cart in turn."

But Jiao wouldn't budge a bit and said, "Worn out am I? No. What fatigue now costs me is absolutely much and much less than what death did cost any of our revolutionary martyrs. Isn't that so? The fatigue we're now experiencing is not at all worth worrying about. Why is it obligatory for us to urgently pass the relief

焦裕禄紧紧拽着架子车，丝毫没有让的意思，说："辛苦吗？比起战斗中牺牲的烈士们，这点辛苦算什么！我们这么晚了还要送棉衣，为的什么？想想正在受冻的群众，你就再也感觉不到累了。这雪天路不好走，我拉惯了，比你们有经验。"

当前来迎接的爪营公社的干部看到焦裕禄时，吃惊地说："您怎么也来了！您身体不好，怎么还拉这么重的架子车？"

焦裕禄说："我怎么不能来？我就不能拉架子车？我们不是人民的上司，我们都是人民的勤务员，必须和群众同甘共苦、共患难。难道说我是县委书记，身体不好，在大雪天群众挨冻的时候，就可以在家安享清福吗？"

到爪营公社后，天已放亮，同志们看到焦裕禄脸色发白，左手不时地摁着肝部。公社的同志赶紧抱来柴火，准备生火让他暖和暖和。焦裕禄连连摆手制止："大雪天，群众缺少柴烧，我们千万不要随随便便将它烧掉。现在不是我们几个人的取暖问题，而是要赶快把棉衣送到群众手中。"说着，他又和公社干部分头带着棉衣去了群众家里。

material over to the poverty-stricken families? Just think of how brutally tortured by the damned cold weather those families are now! And you'd grow quite nonchalant of our exhaustion. The snowy night coupled with the treacherously glassy road does present some trouble. But, look here, I was inured to pulling a cart in such circumstances. Yes, on this score I believe I'm much more experienced than you."

Some officials working for Zhuaying Rural District hurried forth from their office to meet the approaching relief-winter-clothing cart and its escorts. On finding that Jiao was pulling the heavy cart, these Zhuaying men were genuinely astounded and yelled, "Why, is it so darned obligatory for you, as secretary of our CPC County Committee, to pull such a heavy cart for delivering the relief stuff here, what with your poor health?"

"On what grounds," said Jiao, "should I be exempted from the task of delivering the relief stuff here? On what grounds may I be spared from pulling a cart? Do you think I'm entitled to playing the role of a glamorous and presumptuous bureaucrat to wash my hands of any laborious task? All of us are without exception servants of the people. It is incumbent on us to share our people's tribulations and mirth. Do you think that I may be allowed to wallow in the snuggery of my hearth and home on the pretexts that I'm secretary of the CPC Lankao County Committee and that my health is delicate, while the needy people in our county are experiencing the deadly affliction the inclement weather imposes on them?"

When the relief-stuff delivery at Zhuaying was still in progress, there was already a glimpse of dawn. It was only with the peep of dawn that all the colleagues in Jiao's surroundings were able to notice that Jiao was very pale and that he pressed his left hand hard against the part of his chest where his liver was. Someone hurried to fetch some dried twigs from homesteads of inhabitants living in the vicinity of the rural-district office. Having gathered the twigs in the small courtyard of the office, they wanted to set them afire, so that the fire could give Jiao a little warmth. But when they were about to ignite the twigs, Jiao rushed to stop them, saying that the homesteads wherefrom the twigs had been fetched were also in dire need of them to cook their meals and keep their houses warm in such inclement weather. "We're not entitled," persisted Jiao Yulu, "to burn them at will. What we must focus our attention on right now is by no means whether anybody in this courtyard is upset by the cold, but whether the relief material can be conveyed to the needy more quickly."

5. 腾出自己的房子

焦裕禄在洛阳矿山机器厂任车间主任时，有一天，他正在看书，隐约听见一阵婴儿的啼哭，他循声找去，在更衣间看到一个嗷嗷待哺的孩子，他就把孩子抱到了办公室里。车工于秀敏准备给孩子喂奶时，发现孩子不见了，急得到处找。当她推开主任办公室的房门时，突然愣住了，只见焦主任一手端个水杯，一手拿个小勺，正在给孩子喂水，暖气片上搭着尿布。

焦裕禄说："我看孩子在哭，害怕孩子着凉，就把孩子放到这儿好了，这里安静，也暖和。"于秀敏非常感激焦裕禄。焦裕禄了解到，于秀敏不久前从外厂调来，两个月前生了孩子，因厂里新房没有盖好，他们一家仍住在离厂很远的东郊，生活很不方便，就把孩子带到工厂边哺乳边上班。

过了几天，焦裕禄把自己家向阳的17平方米的房间让给了于秀敏夫妇，并帮他们搬了家。但焦裕禄一家七口人，却挤在一间13平方米的小屋里，孩子们睡在地板上，角落里被各种书籍、工程图纸塞得满满当当。

Without more ado, Jiao turned to join some Zhuaying functionaries and helped them with expediting the distribution of the relief winter clothing.

5. He readily quit his comfortable homestead to accommodate the pressing need of his subordinate's family for a short-term settlement.

During his tenure in office with Luoyang Mining Machinery Plant as its director of a workshop, it so happened one day that he mindlessly overheard distant wails let out by a baby, while he was reading a book in his office. Considering the wails rather odd, he stood up and left his office, trying to locate the source of the wails. And he found out there was an infant left howling in a locker room which was vacant but for the little screaming creature. Then he took it to his office.

Now Yu Xiumin, a female lathe-hand working in Jiao's workshop, flew in hot haste to the locker room in order to give her baby a breastfeeding in time. She was shocked to find the locker room empty and instantly stormed half dazed out of it to search for the infant's whereabouts. But she was dumbfounded the moment she intruded into Jiao's office. There was Jiao, the workshop director, holding a warm cupful of water in his hand with a little spoon in his other hand. He was busy feeding the baby with water. And its diaper was spread over the hot radiator. Jiao said to her, "I saw it alone shrieking in the locker room and got worried that it might catch cold there. Listen, just leave it with me in this office as it is quiet and warm here." For Jiao's affectionate concern for the baby, she was grateful to Jiao. By and by, he learned that she had been transferred here lately and that she gave birth to the baby just two months before. Now that the construction of new residential buildings which were to be allotted to workers of Luoyang Mining Machinery Plant was not completed yet, the plant was unable, for the time being, to provide her and her family with temporary lodgings. Therefore, she and her family had to keep living in their original apartment which was in the east suburb of Luoyang and strikingly distant from the plant. This of course enmeshed her everyday life in a lot of troubles and impelled her to take the baby to the plant day in day out with her for giving it timely feeding and nursing.

Days later Jiao and his family voluntarily vacated the chamber which he and his family lived in till then and which measured 17 square meters and had a southern exposure. Then Jiao asked Yu Xiumin and her husband to move to live in the chamber he and his family had just vacated. At the same time, he help Yu and her

二、艰苦奋斗

1. 天下哪有这么大的床

1956年夏天,焦裕禄在洛阳矿山机器厂任基建科副科长时,负责修建一条金谷园车站直达洛矿建厂工地的临时公路。由于没有大型机械,材料短缺,当地施工条件也不好,修路成为一项困难重重、非常艰巨的任务。

修路指挥部设在一个仅有五户人家的小村庄,好几百名民工和干部都集中在这个小村里,临时搭的工棚也挤不下这么多人。焦裕禄提出把工棚让给工人,干部露天睡觉。他带头睡在工棚外,还风趣地说:"天下到哪里找这样大的屋,这样大的床?"

由于条件差、任务重,大家的情绪都不高。焦裕禄非常理解大家的心情,谁思想上有了"疙瘩",有了不愉快的情绪,他都主动去谈心。当他发现很多同志有畏难情绪时,便及时召开会议。他说:"要有全心全意为人民服务的思想和愚公移山的干劲,发愤图强,艰苦创业,自力更生,只有这样,困难才能被克服,艰巨的任务才能完成。"在他的鼓舞和带动下,大家都积极投入到修路的工作中。

有一段路正赶上三伏天修,天气炎热,有几个工人中暑了,焦裕禄及时让他们休息,又请来医生,并安排食堂为他们改善伙食。由于焦裕禄指挥得当,又时时关心工人,工人们精神振奋,干劲倍增,个个以饱满的热情投入到修路工作中,最终按时完成了任务。

husband with transporting their belongings. Jiao and his family — his household consisted of seven persons — now voluntarily moved to live in a room measuring only 13 square meters. In the circumstance, Jiao Yulu's children had to sleep on the floor at night. Every nook or recess in Jiao's room was stuffed tightly with books, periodicals, and schedule drawings.

II. Jiao's unswerving adherence to frugality in performing his official duty

1. "Have you ever slept in a gigantic bed like this?"

In summer 1956, to him, as deputy head of the capital-construction-work section of Luoyang Mining Machinery Plant, was assigned the task of organizing and supervising the construction of a highway between Jinguyuan Railway Station and the site where the developmental program of Luoyang Mining Machinery Plant was in progress. It was a highway for short-term use, or "a temporary highway". The task was really a hard nut to crack, what with the fact that the workforce assigned to build the highway was not equipped with indispensable, large heavy-duty machines and handicapped by very acute shortage of supply of materials of cardinal importance. Besides, the construction had to be carried out in a very unfavorable condition.

The "command post" in charge of running the temporary highway construction had no alternative but to have itself set up in a small village having only five households. The workforce, scores of hundreds strong men, together with the cadres had no alternative but to live for the time being in the small village. They set up all the makeshift tents that were available to them at the time in order to provide themselves with noticeably shabby shelter against the elements. But the number of the makeshift tents was too insignificant for the number of workers needing the shelter. Jiao came forth to announce that no cadre was allowed to pass a night under a tent. "No cadres here," said Jiao, "are allowed to have overnight lodging under a makeshift tent. They must sleep in open air, so that all the makeshift tents can be used by the workers." That evening he preceded the rest of the cadres to spread out his bedding in the field and in open air and jokingly said to others, "Have you ever been in an enormous bedroom like this? And have you ever slept in a gigantic bed like this?"

焦裕禄穿过的衣物
A piece of traditional Chinese clothing of Jiao Yulu's

焦裕禄穿过的鞋子
These are shoes all so tattered, but Jiao Yulu wore them nonchalantly.

As the workforce was very nastily equipped and as the construction was a very arduous and demanding exertion, the workforce was dispirited. Jiao fully comprehended how things stood and actively took the initiative in engaging those who got disturbed or incensed in a cordial and soothing talk, trying his best to allay them. On being aware that a considerable number of workers were overwhelmed with the excruciating physical labor and got increasingly resentful, Jiao arranged for all the workers to attend a meeting where he tried his best to encourage and arouse them, saying, "All of us ought to be sincerely and constantly mindful of the interests of the Chinese people. In exerting to the utmost to serve our people, we ought to follow the example of 'the foolish old man' who never budged a bit, as the legend tells us, in his determination to seize his goal. We need to boost ourselves with the toughest willpower in order to fortify our nation, to defy all manner of adversities in order to fashion a new future for our nation, and to never cherish the illusion that China can depend on godsends to make herself prosper and blissful. Look here, it is only by dint of self-reliance, indomitable determination, and unfailing resistance to adversity and setback that we can accomplish the construction of the temporary highway." Jiao's words were a powerful momentum to revive in the workers an explosive fervor, which rapidly transformed them into enthusiasts for the highway construction.

The dog days of summer 1956 saw construction of the temporary highway make headway very laboriously in a desolate, scorched landscape. Many workers were inflicted with sunstroke. Jiao took pains to provide them with adequate medical service and improved diet so as to ensure swift and comfortable recovery to them. Jiao's able and dutiful leadership succeeded in arousing fiery enthusiasm in the workers who strove to the utmost to accelerate the construction. Completion of the highway construction was not only on time but satisfactory.

2. Jiao invariably used very cheap lodgings and board whenever traveling at the taxpayer's expense.

It was deep in the night when the train that took him together with four colleagues to Beijing on an official business in winter of 1956 pulled up at Beijing Railway Station. The air was freezing. One of his companions said to Jiao, "Hey, shall we check into a chic hotel to mark our travel to the splendid capital of our great country?"

2. 出差住小旅馆

1956年冬天，焦裕禄和四位工作人员一同去北京出差。到火车站时已经是深夜了，寒气逼人。有人说："来到我们伟大的首都北京，该找个像样的旅馆住下。"

焦裕禄听后说："出差住什么地方还不是一样。"听了这句话，虽然大家嘴上没说什么，但心里还是想找个条件好的旅馆住。他们来到一个旅馆，进去一看，房间又黑、又窄、又矮，有几个同志就不高兴地说："这怎么住呀？"焦裕禄却沉重地说："同志们，我们的工作任务还没完成，哪能考虑自己呢？还是先完成政府交给我们的任务要紧。"

他们几位被焦裕禄说服了。但是一个房间只有四张床，还剩下一个同志怎么办呢？有的同志提议找一个单间让焦裕禄去住，被焦裕禄拒绝了。焦裕禄找来旅馆服务员，请他给加个床铺，服务员说："这房间不好加铺，给你另找个房间吧？"

焦裕禄说："把床临时铺在门口就行了。"

那服务员见他一脸认真的样子，只好同意了。

焦裕禄又耐心地对其他人说："现在国家正在搞建设，我们不能多开支旅费。"

在他们出差的日子里，焦裕禄和工作人员一起商量、研究方案，做好每天的工作计划。出差路程较远时，焦裕禄为了节省些钱，总是提前步行，能不坐车坚决不坐，有的同志说："坐车吧，反正回去报销。"焦裕禄说："报销用的也是国家的钱，不能浪费。能节约一分钱，就能为国家的建设增一份力量。"

"Do accommodations," curtly asked Jiao, "we get on a business trip make any difference to our carrying out our mission?" Though none of his companions chose to react to his query, yet all the same they craved mutely for plush accommodations. Then the five of them plodded casually into a hotel only to find its rooms poorly illuminated and cramped. One of them said fuming, "Do we deign to take lodgings here?" "Comrades," said Jiao feelingly, "none of us has so far done anything towards the fulfillment of our mission. Does it stand to reason that we'd let accommodations be our top priority? I believe and hope you will agree to prioritize our business over accommodations."

In the end, his persuasive efforts prevailed. But there was still a problem to be solved. Every room in the hotel was regularly furnished with four beds. But Jiao's group consisted of five people. That meant that one of them had to be excluded from the room the four took. Somebody proposed that Jiao alone go to occupy another room. But Jiao refused as that would of course increase the expenditure on their travel. And they now traveled at the taxpayer's expense. Thus, Jiao went to talk to a waiter, asking him to deposit an additional bed in the room they took. But the waiter declined on the ground that the room was already too cramped for four beds. "You can choose to occupy another room," the waiter claimed, "We do have rooms to spare just now."

"You can," persisted Jiao, "so deposit a bed in the corridor as to let it go alongside the wall and close to the door of this room, can't you?"

On observing how serious and stubborn Jiao looked, the waiter conceded though rather reluctantly.

Jiao turned around and said patiently to his companions, "Our nation is now all in for her reconstruction. It's quite indecent for us not striving to be very frugal with the travel expense."

In the duration they stayed in Beijing, Jiao made a point of arranging adequate consultation with his companions every day concerning the task and plan they were to accomplish. In the days they were in Beijing, Jiao or one of his companions had from time to time to run some errands. Sometimes, such an errand required him or one of his companions to go on a very long trip in Beijing. Of course, they could avail themselves of Beijing bus service when they needed to go on a very long trip in Beijing. But Jiao chose to go on such a very long trip on foot, rather than to avail

3. 老房子照样办公

焦裕禄在兰考时,兰考县委机关的大院坐落在一片低洼地上,地势低,屋里屋外十分潮湿,地下的盐碱不断地浸上来,砖面上不几天便会长出白色的碱毛。被子十天半月不晒,几乎都能拧出水来。在焦裕禄来兰考之前,县委机关的同志们就在酝酿搬家的事,有人还提出一个装修县委和县委领导办公室的计划。

焦裕禄得知后,向大家提出了一个问题:"坐在破椅子上就不能革

焦裕禄的办公室
This is a picture showing the office Jiao worked in.

himself of Beijing bus service simply for reducing their business trip expenditure, because he knew he was traveling at the taxpayer's expense. He chose to leave his hotel very early in the morning so that he could move over a strikingly long distance on foot to reach his destination on time. Some of his companions said to him, "Do take a bus and don't go on such a distant trip on foot, because all the expenditures on ineluctable bus fare are certainly to be reimbursed." "I know that," said Jiao, "but the reimbursement is made at the taxpayer's expense all the same. I don't want to waste taxpayers' money and do choose to be as frugal as I best can, so far as taxpayers' money is concerned. In this way I'd exert to the utmost to stick up for the reconstruction in our country."

3. "Does a rundown office building wield the magic of nullifying the efficiency of an office worker who works regularly in it?"

The compound occupied by the Lankao CPC County Committee sat in a swampy area during Jiao Yulu's tenure of office. Baneful humidity permeated every building in the compound inside out. Saline or alkaline moisture climbed upwards from underground miry strata to soak up everything above the ground. Surfaces of bricks were invariably covered with a white thin layer of crystalline alkali. If a piece of bedding was not sunned for a fortnight or so, water could be wrung out of it. In those years prior to Jiao's tenure of office here, CPC Lankao County Committee had been astir with initiatives to contrive a dislodgement of the committee from the rundown building sitting low in the swampy plot and to install it at a new site. Someone in the committee had even gone so far as to formulate plans and programs for giving the would-be county-committee building — and especially the would-be county-committee secretary's office — a lavish decoration.

After having assumed his office in Lankao, Jiao Yulu was given to understand how the committee had craved for a new county-committee building at a new site. Accordingly Jiao had to say something by way of revealing his reaction to the committee's craving. Thus, he came forth to pose the question: "Is it true that when a revolutionist is furnished only a tumbledown chair to sit down in his office, he is bound to quit the revolution for good? Just answer me this."

"Does a rundown office building," he continued, "wield the magic of nullifying the efficiency of an office worker who works regularly in it? Lankao hasn't succeeded so far in bringing about any change in its landscape. The local people have still to

命吗?"他说:"老房子也照样能办公。现在,兰考的面貌没有改变,还吃着国家统销粮,群众生活很困难,奢侈浪费的事情不能做。"在焦裕禄的带动下,兰考县委的同志们打消了装修办公室的想法。

4. 不到社员家里借被子

1963年3月,兰考县召开三级扩大干部会议,工作人员小张跟随焦裕禄去兰考县架子公社调查摸底,解决生产救灾问题。

来到架子公社时,天快黑了。他们找到公社的一位干部说明了来意,这位干部就领着他们两人前往架子公社公路北生产队的一个饲养室。住下后,焦裕禄就同饲养员聊起来。饲养员说这个生产队不到四十户人家,120人,现在实际在家的只有30多人,那些能走动的都带着自己的老婆孩子外出逃荒要饭去了。正谈着,生产队长送来了窝窝头和开水。

焦裕禄对工作人员小张说:"小张,开饭了,今晚吃的还是好饭呢!"

小张说:"什么好饭?不过是用苜蓿片磨成的面做的,一吃一硌牙,这哪是什么好饭?"

焦裕禄说道:"小张,你知道吗?就是这些东西,群众还经常吃不上!"听了焦裕禄的话,小张不再说什么,默默地吃了起来。

这时,焦裕禄又和饲养员攀谈了起来。饲养员告诉焦裕禄,几年前他的老婆饿死了,留下了一个小孩,今年才9岁,队里分的粮食早就吃光了,要不是喂养着这两头牲口,他早就带着孩子出去要饭了。现在,他养的这两头牲口,队里规定每天喂养不少于半斤料。可是老牛没奶,他得每天给小牛做一锅"糊糊儿"(用玉米面、面粉等熬成的粥),小牛要是喝不完了,他就跟孩子一人喝上一点。焦裕禄听了心情十分沉重,半天没有说话。

晚上,他们就住在饲养室的草屋里,没有被子盖,但焦裕禄也不让饲养员到社员家里去借被子,他说:"社员家里都很困难,咱们将就一

secure their survival by being given the privilege of consuming foodstuff, the price of which is markedly lower than the price prevalent with food markets in other parts of our country on account of the subsidy provided to our county by the Central Government. The basic living standards of people in our county are too low to allow us, public servants, to flirt with luxury." Jiao's cogent warning and his irresistible charisma were very powerful in eradicating the craving on the part of the county-committee functionaries for a new and luxuriously decorated county-committee building.

4. He was contented to nestle in straw bedding overnight, rather than inconvenience anybody in the village.

An enlarged conference of representatives of all the government functionaries in Lankao was to be called by Lankao County Administration in March 1963. Prior to the convention, Jiao traveled together with Zhang, his assistant, to do some inspection and investigation in Jiazi Rural District, intending to help the rural district with sorting out knotty problems impeding its efforts to proceed with natural calamity relief and boost local agricultural productivity. It was already deep into the twilight that Jiao and Zhang arrived at the district. They sped to the district office and met there a cadre. On learning their intention, the cadre led the two guests to a cattle raiser's hovel, which was the property of the district office and now occupied by the cattle raiser as his makeshift lodgings. The cadre told the two guests that the hovel now served as their temporary lodgings, too. Then the cadre left. So, Jiao and Zhang had to manage to settle in the hovel for the night. (There was no hotel or hostel in the district.) Before long, the raiser came back to his hovel. Jiao proceeded to engage him in a talk and was told that there were less than forty households containing nominally around 120 people in the district. Actually, there were only thirty odd people staying in the district, as the majority of the district's population deserted their native place to stray away in every direction. They moved away one family after another, trying to grab their survival in other provinces. They paused in their conversation when the head of the rural district appeared with loaves of steamed dough, which was made of pulverized stems of some wild plant and a kettle of boiled water. Jiao turned to Zhang and said casually, "Come, guy, this is a delicious supper."

"Delicious food!" exclaimed Zhang, "This stuff is made of crushed stems of

晚上吧。"小张很快睡着了，而焦裕禄在草堆上半躺半坐，思索着如何帮助群众渡过难关。

三、科学求实

1. 调度员要做到"四熟"

1959年春，洛阳矿山机器厂投产后，厂里任命焦裕禄担任调度科科长，负责全厂的生产调度工作。

焦裕禄查看机器运转情况
In the photo, Jiao Yulu is seen giving the machine a check.

alfalfa, see? What's horrible is that you've to crunch every mouthful of the stuff you chew. And you said the supper is delicious?"

"Look here, Zhang," said Jiao, "what you're ignorant of is that even such an unpalatable affair as alfalfa is not an easy acquisition as food stuff for the local people! Don't you see that?" Zhang was hushed and ate his supper mutely.

By and by Jiao resumed his chat with the cattle raiser who began to relate his own story. "My wife starved to death," said he, "just a few years back. My kid survives her and is now nine. The amount of foodstuff allotted me by the district office has long run out. I would have to leave here together with my son to become a vagrant but for the favor given me by this district office which now hires me as its cattle raiser." The cattle raiser was now held responsible for feeding a cow and its calf. His daily routine included cooking a potful of congee to feed the calf as the cow was unable to yield any milk. The congee was cooked with the grain which was supplied to him by the rural district office every day. Sometimes the calf could not eat up the whole potful of congee. The leftovers were godsend to him and his kid. They would eat the leftovers to allay their hunger. Macabre pungency of the cattle raiser's story gagged Jiao for a long time.

That night the three of them slept in the hovel, which was denuded of any bedding or cotton-wadded quilt. But Jiao barred the cattle raiser from going to the neighborhood to borrow some cotton-wadded quilts from villagers there. He said, "Villagers here are hard up. It isn't proper for us to inconvenience them. We're contented to nestle overnight in straw bedding in the fodder cubicle here." Zhang fell asleep before long. Reclining in a pile of straw, Jiao was ruminating on how to help the local people find a way to tide over the ongoing crisis.

III. One of Jiao's rules of behavior is: "Always strive to think logically and fulfill my duty faithfully, practically, and sensibly."

1. The prerequisite for one desiring to become a qualified scheduler is mastery of the four categories of information.

Luoyang Mining Machinery Plant went into operation at the spring of 1959. At that time, Jiao was installed as head of the plant's department of operational

一天，焦裕禄和一位调度员到车间了解生产情况，他问那位调度员："现在厂里提出日产卷扬机一台，你看完成任务的关键在哪里？"由于那位调度员不了解车间情况，一时答不上来。接着焦裕禄又指着一台卧式滚齿机旁边的一根中间齿轮轴问调度员："生产这根齿轮轴的主要工序有哪些？"调度员也答不全。焦裕禄意味深长地对他说："不做艰苦的调查研究，是难于取得发言权的啊！"

第二天，他向所有的调度员提出了一项要求：每个调度员对自己主管的车间必须做到"四熟"，即人员熟、设备熟、产品零件熟、能力负荷熟。

焦裕禄十分重视调查，他经常说："调查就是解决问题，调查能出办法。"他的小本子上画了许多零件图和统计数字，他对全厂各车间的设备，台台心中有数。每天他都到车间检查每一个生产环节，注意每一道工序的生产情况和存在的问题。在掌握了大量的第一手材料之后，才召开全厂的生产调度会，提出符合生产实际的意见，更好地协调了各车间的生产。

在一次调度会上，因调度组长何卓林没有做好准备，情况了解得不够，在会上任务安排不下去。他就用硬压的办法安排任务，结果和车间一位计调组长吵了起来，会议只好停止。

会后，焦裕禄领着何卓林来到车间，和工人开"诸葛亮会"。从下午1点一直开到4点，然后又去找上午和何卓林吵架的那个计调组长。焦裕禄首先说上午开会用压的办法不对，接着把了解的实际情况摆了出来，并提出了完成任务的具体方法、措施和时间要求，就这样顺利地把任务定了下来。何卓林站在一旁，看在眼里，服在心里。

从车间回来的路上，焦裕禄对何卓林说："一切实际工作必须向下做调查，没有调查，就没有发言权。老何，没有办法就该找群众做调查嘛，靠压是压不服人的。"

有一个时期，焦裕禄发现车间统计数字不准确，配套报表不及时，

scheduling. So he was held responsible for the plant's overall operational scheduling. Not long after he was assigned to the post, he went to a workshop. There he talked to its operational scheduler. "You must be aware," said Jiao, "that our plant has assigned to your workshop the task of producing one large winch per day. Well, what do you believe is crucial to accomplishing the task?" As the operational scheduler was very unfamiliar with the operation the workshop was carrying on, he was at a loss to provide Jiao with any answer. Then pointing at an intermediate gear shaft close to a horizontal hob machine, Jiao asked him again, "Do you know anything about the primary procedures needed for producing a gear shaft like this?" The scheduler was again nonplussed. Now Jiao said to him feelingly, "Failing to strive very hard to acquire sufficient knowledge of what is going on in your workshop would never be able to relieve you of the embarrassment you just felt or restore to you confidence and initiative when you have to confront any other inquirer."

The next day, Jiao laid down a rule for all the operational schedulers in the plant to observe. The rule stipulated: "It is incumbent upon an operational scheduler to be well versed in the following four categories of information: (1) personal data of all workers in his (or her) workshop, (2) a full knowledge of every machine in his (or her) workshop, (3) a full knowledge of every ingredient part of the product made in his (or her) workshop, and (4) a full knowledge of production capacity and safe load of every machine in his (or her) workshop."

He attached great importance to conducting investigation, repeatedly claiming, "To carrying out an investigation is to gain access to solving an issue and provide you with a key to a problem." Every page of his notebook is densely populated with statistics, figures, sketches or charts of parts or components. He was very familiar with all the machines in every workshop in the plant. He neither failed to inspect every workshop every day nor missed checking any important operational link, strictly supervising whether there was a sign of forthcoming trouble in an operational procedure. It was not until he had gathered enough firsthand information and statistics that he would call a plenary meeting, in which all the operational schedulers participated for assigning diverse tasks of production to each workshop of the plant, for providing each workshop with insightful suggestions, and for achieving operational coordination between workshops.

Once in the course of such a plenary meeting, He Zhuolin, a section chief

焦裕禄在洛阳矿山机器厂工作时的照片
Another snapshot of Jiao Yulu, which was taken at the time when he worked for Luoyang Mining Machinery Plant

心中有些纳闷，他感到调度工作的耳朵不灵、眼睛不明，这是致命的问题。这天，焦裕禄来到铸铁车间了解生产情况，车间主任蒋泉根在介绍生产情况时，有数字，有分析，还能说出零件的流动情况。他觉得很好，又逐一翻阅了计调组的台账和报表，发现他们实行了统计人员下现场，每日进行统计的方法，并且打破框框，创造了一种适合自己生产需要的新的配套报表。

焦裕禄激动地说："老蒋同志，好呀！你为全厂生产统计工作立了一大功，我要把你们的配套报表在全厂推广。"

在第二天的生产主任会上，焦裕禄把他们的报表给每人发了一份，大大表扬了他们一番。职工们都说，焦裕禄善于把群众的工作方法和智慧总结出来，推广出去。在三年的调度工作中，焦裕禄对全厂生产的关键环节都了如指掌，使调度科一跃成为全厂的先进科室。外国专家佩服地说他是一位了不起的中国人，工人和技术人员都说他是一部"活工艺"。

working with Jiao Yulu's department, presumptuously demanded all the operational schedulers to accept "the plant's overall scheduling program" which was actually arbitrarily concocted by him. Of course, his "program" was called into question at a session of the plenary meeting. Still He Zhuolin wouldn't budge. This ignited a furore in another section chief. What ensued at that session was a brawl between the two and that curtailed the session.

Later Jiao asked He to go with him to a number of workshops. There Jiao and He had a lot of consultations with workers. The consultations lasted three hours starting from 1 pm. Still later Jiao asked He to go together with him to have a talk with the section chief who had a brawl with He at that session. On meeting that section chief, Jiao was the first to talk, saying, "The way He Zhuolin forced all those who attended the plenary meeting to accept his 'program' is wrong." Then Jiao proceeded to expatiate to the other section chief on a newly drafted version of "the plant's overall scheduling program" which was formulated on the basis of the findings gathered from the several consultations conducted by Jiao and He with the workers from a number of workshops. The new version of "the plant's overall scheduling program" was accepted by the other section chief. So the disagreement came to an end. Though throughout the course of Jiao's conversation with the other section chief, He Zhuolin remained silent, yet admiration grew in him for Jiao Yulu's charisma.

After saying adieu to the other section chief, both Jiao and He sauntered homeward together. "Our effort to find solution to a problem," said Jiao to He, "must be preceded by an exertion to investigate, to gather necessary information, and to study. He who makes no investigation and study has no right to set forth his opinion or comment. When we find we are at our wits' end, just go into the multitude for conducting an investigation. It is totally useless to be presumptuous."

It so happened that for a few months in a row, the operational reports submitted by a number of workshops to his department were significantly impaired by inaccuracy. And some workshops failed to submit their supporting reports on time. This worried Jiao, because if his department which was held responsible for the plant's overall scheduling could not be provided with accurate and timely information concerning the plant's overall operation, that could be lethal to the plant. One day he went as usual to various workshops to inspect and examine how production plowed on in each of them. In cast-iron processing workshop, he ran into Jiang

2. 不蹲下去看不清蚂蚁

焦裕禄常说，不蹲下去看不清蚂蚁。到兰考任职后，他总是在处理完繁忙的公务后，走访群众，了解情况。一天晚上，焦裕禄走进了老饲养员肖位芬的饲养室。

"同志，进里边床铺上坐吧，这么晚了，你还没睡？"并不认识焦裕禄的肖位芬一边给牲口拌草，一边热情地向他打招呼。

焦裕禄往地铺上一坐，就与肖位芬聊了起来："老大爷，喂牲口很辛苦啊！"

肖位芬说："中华人民共和国成立以前，我受地主压迫，比起那年月，眼下给队里喂个牲口算啥苦？"

焦裕禄说："苦和苦不同啦！从前的苦，苦得没指望，如今的苦是先苦后甜，日子越过越好。"

他们俩谈了很久，焦裕禄才起身告辞。事后，肖位芬才知道，到牛屋跟他交谈的人竟然是县委书记。没过几天，焦裕禄又来探访肖位芬，这次他是来请教如何发展农业生产的。肖位芬激动地说："你是县委书记，跑到饲养室，跟我这喂牲口的商讨全县的发展计划，我是个大老粗，恁大的问题，我能拿个啥主意？"

焦裕禄说："改变兰考面貌，人人都有份。您见多识广，有生产经验，我是专门来向您老人家请教的。"

Quangen, director of the workshop. Then the latter took the initiative in reporting to Jiao in detail how his workshop was carrying on its production, providing Jiao with accurate and concrete information about how his workshop was faring. Jiang's report consisted of statistics, analyses, and even minute details of delivery of all the parts and components manufactured by his workshop. Jiao was gratified by Jiang's oral report. Then he proceeded to examine all the per-machine records and supporting reports drawn up by the workshop's planning and scheduling team. Now he was very much delighted to find out that a rule laid down by Jiang Quangen was strictly clung to in his workshop. According to the rule, it was obligatory for the statistician who worked with the workshop to come to the workshop every day to register and record all the relevant statistics. Besides, Jiang Quangen had formulated a new system of reports and supporting reports to replace the old and outdated system of reports and supporting reports. And the new system had a significant advantage over the old one.

On discovering all of this, Jiao was enraptured and said loudly to Jiang, "Oh, Jiang, my old pal, you've done something extraordinary in the interest of our plant's statistical management, statistical evaluation, statistical decision, and supervision by statistical means. I promise to recommend your new system of reports and supporting reports to all the other workshops in our plant."

The next day he called a meeting attended by directors of all the workshops. At the meeting he presented to each of the directors present a copy of Jiang Quangen's new system of reports and supporting reports and fervently extolled Jiang's accomplishment. It was the consensus of the plant's population that Jiao Yulu was an expert on pinpointing ingenuity of the common people and on propagating it. In the three years of his tenure as head of the plant's operational scheduling, he was an expert on all the key operations performed by the plant. It is he who succeeded in so nurturing the plant's operational scheduling department that it became one of the plant's advanced units. A number of foreign experts who worked for the plant admired him and viewed him as an extraordinary Chinese. Workers of the plant affectionately called him "an epitome of productive technology".

2. Modesty and humility provides an easy access to a treasure trove of knowledge and wisdom.

Jiao Yulu used to offer to others the advice: "Modesty can easily shear off your ignorance." Since he began his tenure of office in Lankao, he used to visit some

焦裕禄拜访过的饲养员肖位芬

This is Mr. Xiao Weifen, a cattle raiser in Lankao, to whom Jiao Yulu, as secretary of the CPC Lankao County Committee, repeatedly paid reverential visits simply for seeking advice from him in the matter of domestic animal husbandry.

ordinary people after his office hours, earnestly intending to know more about the county and its people. Late in one evening, he came sauntering down the road to the flimsy hovel occupied by Xiao Weifen, an aged cattle raiser.

"Hi," Xiao cordially greeted him, "it's deep into the twilight now. And you don't plan to turn in? Well, please get in my hovel and have a seat on my straw bedding, won't you?" The cattle raiser didn't know who the nocturnal intruder was and kept stirring the fodder in the trough for his animals. Promptly Jiao got in, casually plumped on the straw bedding on the floor, and began a chat with Xiao.

"Hey, buddy," said Jiao to Xiao, "I know keeping livestock is nothing but sweat and toil!"

"In decades," said Xiao, "prior to the establishment of People's Republic of China, I toiled under a landlord's thumb. But now I labor in the interest of our rural district. The intensity of hardship involved in the livestock keeping I'm doing for my rural district is actually negligible, if compared with that involved in the bestial way of livestock keeping landlords forced me to do in the past."

"The hardship involved in the livestock keeping in the past does differ from that involved in the livestock keeping you're doing now. The bygone hardship deprived you of even the least bit of hope for a promising future while the present-day hardship heralds a sweet future lying in store for you. Things are going to change for the better, mind you."

The two chatted for a long time before Jiao rose to bid the old man farewell. It was days later that the old cattle raiser was accidentally given to understand that the guy who dropped in at night to have a casual chat with him was none other than the top leader of the county administration. Days lapsed before Jiao came to visit the old cattle raiser again. This time Jiao came expressly for seeking advice from the latter in the matter of how to boost local farming productivity. Having understood the purpose of Jiao's second visit and being hardly able to curb his agitation, Xiao said, "Being the top official in our county, you deign to come to my haven for seeking advice about the development of our county from me, a funny, illiterate bloke! Oh, how on earth can I bring myself to intelligently concoct some great idea to cheer you up?"

"Look here," said Jiao Yulu soothingly , "striving to have the lot of Lankao change for the better is an effort everybody living in Lankao is obliged to share, isn't

肖位芬说:"咱这里的沙土窝,能种泡桐树,它挡风固沙,用处多;牲口也得多养,这是咱农民种庄稼的命根子;兰考的沙土地最适合种花生,花生秧又是喂牲口的好饲料。"焦裕禄听了,连声称赞这些都是好主意。后来焦裕禄把从群众中得来的建议总结为"兰考三件宝,泡桐、花生和大枣",在全县进行了推广。

又过了几天,焦裕禄再访牛屋。肖位芬一见焦裕禄,急忙说:"焦书记啊,你跑了一天,怎么不回去休息?这牛屋气味不好闻,咱们回屋里坐吧。"

焦裕禄进屋后,坐在地铺上说:"我也是农民出身,喂过牲口,今天我来是向您请教喂牲口的经验。"

肖位芬激动万分地说:"我没学问,恐怕说不出什么经验。"焦裕禄说:"只要有想法,就提出来。"肖位芬说:"农闲季节,号召社员多为牲口扫树叶。农忙季节,号召妇女儿童割青草。特别是夏季,要给牲口搭凉棚,不要让它们暴晒和淋雨。"

焦裕禄高兴地说:"喂好牲口也是农业发展的一条出路,您介绍的经验真是宝贵的财富。"两人又谈了一些问题,一直谈到半夜。

that so? Well, I know you do have very extensive knowledge about how things stand here, apart from your being markedly experienced in farming practice. That's why I make a point of coming to you to beg for your advice on how to formulate the plan for our local development."

Then Xiao talked deliberately, "You know Lankao is overspread with dunes which are best for growing paulownia. It's very powerful in not only thwarting the devastation gale-force wind inflicted on our arable land but preventing dunes from drifting. The tree is magically almighty, indeed! Besides, the scale of animal husbandry here ought to be appreciably multiplied. Improvements to our farming efficiency and livelihood hinge largely on the expansion of our animal husbandry. Moreover, the sandy soil in our county is sheer bliss to the growth of peanut. Stems and leaves of peanut after its fruit has been harvested are very fine fodder for cattle." A natural flow of compliments on Xiao's ingenious ideas poured out of Jiao Yulu. Extensive investigations and probes conducted by Jiao in his direct contacts with the local people induced him to realize that "paulownia, peanut, and date constitute the three wonders Lankao can pride itself on" .From then on, he addressed himself to energetically enlarging the planting in Lankao of the three "wonders".

Before long Jiao went on his third visit to Xiao's cowshed. When Jiao was in Xiao's presence, the latter hastened to exhort the former, saying, "Haven't you, Secretary Jiao, been kept very busy and hurrying here and there all day long? Isn't now the right time you go back home to have a little rest? My cowshed stinks. It really does! If you persist in having a chat with me, let us go to my hovel, ok?" Thus, Secretary Jiao was led to the old man's hovel and seated himself in the straw bedding on the floor. "Hey, pal," said Jiao, "Like you, I was born to a peasant's family and did livestock keeping too. I'm here now specifically for seeking your advice on how to keep livestock."

"I'm practically unknowledgeable on that score, you know," said Xiao, "I'm afraid I can't provide you with some worthwhile advice."

"That's all right," said Jiao, "just let me know if there is any idea which flashes across your mind and which you think may profit us in a way."

Xiao said, "Well, I think our county administration needs to urge our people to actively engage in gathering fallen foliage in slack spells from farming. Fallen leaves can serve as fodder to feed domestic animals. Our county administration can call

3. 先顾吃饭，再顾好看

1963年早春，正是栽种泡桐的大好季节。胡集大队规划在村南大面积种植泡桐树。一天上午，社员们都到齐了，大捆大捆的桐苗也运来了，只等下令就开始行动。就在这时，林业主任和大队支书在怎样栽种的问题上产生了分歧，各持己见，互不相让。

正好焦裕禄和几位工作人员一起骑自行车到胡集大队检查泡桐栽植情况，看到了上述一幕。正在那儿躺躺坐坐的群众一看焦书记来了，都站了起来，不约而同地说："焦书记来了，请他评评理吧。"

焦裕禄环视了一下周围的群众，问道："怎么啦？"社员说："意见分歧，不能统一。"焦裕禄问："什么分歧意见达不到统一？"

大队支书说："我觉得胡集既然是全县发展林业的重点，植树造林就得弄个样子给人家看看。栽植泡桐，要做到纵横成行，整齐划一，零星散植的泡桐苗，一律进行移栽……"

林业主任说："我不同意你这种栽法。俗话说，'人挪活，树挪死'，不能追求形式上的美观，应从生产实际需要出发……"

焦裕禄想了想，笑着说："你们说的都有道理，但我们想问题，要抓主要矛盾，眼下的主要矛盾，是渡荒救灾。发展泡桐，就要'先顾吃饭，再顾好看'。"他指着成捆的等待种植的幼桐苗说："这些桐苗往地里移栽时，要成排成行，便于将来机械化耕作。"他又指着散见于田地的单株独苗说，"这些苗就不要动了，不管成行不成行，先保证它活下去就行。三五年以后，泡桐成长起来了，风沙治住了，再考虑整齐美观的问题。"

"先顾吃饭，再顾好看"八个字，把大家伙说得心服口服，大家很快就开始干了起来。

upon local womanhood and teenagers to actively cut and store grass during busy farming spells while the local manhood is fully engaged in laboring in the field. Adequate shelter needs to be built — particularly in summer — for horses, sheep, and cattle to protect them from the elements."

Jiao was very much pleased with this new batch of good ideas from Xiao and said, "That successful animal husbandry constitutes a valuable branch of agrarian economy is certainly an indisputable truth. All the new ideas which you have the kindness to offer to me are a wealth of profitable information, indeed." The two of them continued to chat and discuss a number of problems the county was confronting till midnight.

3. What is of top strategic importance should be accepted as top priority.

Spring is the optimal time for planting paulownia saplings. Now that the executive of Huji village had laid down in advance a plan for planting paulownia saplings in a large plot of land to the south of the village, one morning in early spring 1963, able-bodied Huji villagers rallied in the plot of land as they had been called upon to, and cart loads of paulownia saplings had already been conveyed there and were ready for planting. Everything was ready, and villagers were just waiting there for the village executive to issue order for them to start the paulownia sapling planting operation. At this juncture, a debate occurred between two members of the Huji village executive. One member was the village's afforestation-management head, and the other secretary of the village's CPC branch. The debate focused on how the saplings should be planted. As neither debater would concede, the planting operation was held in check.

At this juncture Jiao Yulu and some of his assistants arrived at the scene. It was precisely for checking how the planting operation at Huji village was faring that Jiao and his assistants came here. They parked their bikes and proceeded to deal with the stand-off. All the villagers there who had been for the time being forced into inertia by the stand-off were now aroused by Jiao's arrival and shouted in unison, "Now let us listen to what Secretary Jiao is going to say about the dispute." Jiao looked meditatively around at the villagers before he asked, "What is this all about?" A villager replied, "A debate is going on here and neither debater is willing to concede!"

"What's the crux then?" asked Jiao.

"I'm of the opinion," said the secretary of the village's CPC branch, "that as Huji

焦裕禄下乡骑过的自行车
This is the bike Jiao Yulu, as secretary of the CPC Lankao County Committee, usually rode to remote rural areas in Lankao County for fulfilling his official duty.

焦裕禄在泡桐幼苗下留影
Jiao Yulu is seen standing by paulownia saplings.

village has now been officially proclaimed 'Lankao County's exemplary afforestation venue', it goes without saying that the planting of saplings ought to conform to a definite geometric pattern of layout so that all the planted saplings here tend to display an artistic vision. I mean saplings planted ought to be on a straight line not only breadthwise but also lengthwise. Not a sapling may be allowed to stray either breadthwise or lengthwise away from the straight line to which it belongs. Besides, there are scores of paulownia trees already growing sporadically all over this large plot which now we have allotted for growing new saplings. All the sporadically growing paulownia trees ought to be uprooted and transplanted somewhere else ...." But the afforestation-management head protested, saying, "I beg to object to your idea. As the saying goes, 'Displacement may bestow luck on a human whereas it means death for a tree.' Uprooting means death for all the sporadically planted sapling trees here. It's absurd to prioritize artistic vision over what agrarian productivity craves ..."

After musing for a while, Jiao smiled and said, "As I see it, neither of you is insensible. But what concerns us here and right now is this: we have to make sure in the first place what is our top priority. I believe the top priority we have to uphold and strive to pursue now is curbing the natural disaster. Of course, at the same time we should strive to provide our people in our county with sufficient relief so that they can safely tide themselves over the ordeal. In order to curb or even to subdue natural disaster, growing paulownia is of top strategic importance. We have to exert to the utmost to make the population of paulownia mushroom in as short a period of time as possible, because paulownia is a very powerful deterrent against natural calamity. At the same time, we should do everything in our power to avoid depleting the paulownia population. What is of top strategic importance should be accepted as top priority." Now Jiao turned around to point at the bundles of paulownia saplings lying about and continued, "I think when you are going to plant these saplings, each of them should stand at its proper spot. In other words, none of the saplings may be allowed to stray either breadthwise or lengthwise away from the straight line to which it belongs, otherwise, tractor-plowing will be out of the question in this large plot of land in the future." Presently he raised his arm to casually point to the widely scattered paulownia trees standing here and there in the area and said, "Don't bother to pull up these young paulownia trees now. Let them continue to grow where they do now. A few years later, the paulownia population is bound to mushroom to the

4. "贴膏药" "扎针"

1963年3月，焦裕禄查风源，来到兰考张庄村。在一眼望不到边的黄沙里，忽然看到一小片绿地。他赶紧找当地群众询问，得知这是村民魏夺彬母亲的坟地。

魏母的坟头在风口上，每年都会被狂风刮开，露出棺材。魏夺彬多次修坟，但却总是一次又一次被风刮开，找不到好办法。直到有一天他在村南挖河时发现，把沙土下面的淤泥挖上来盖在沙丘上，沙土就刮不起来了。他受到启发，第二天一早，便从河边挖来两车淤泥，把母亲的坟头封住，栽上草。打那以后，魏母的安宁再没被风沙打扰过。

焦书记听群众这么一说，眼前一亮，激动地说："这是一个重要的发现呀，一个人一个早上封一个坟头，我们运用人民群众的力量，100人，1000人，全县的几十万人，大干一年、三年，都采用淤泥压沙的方法，岂不能把这些沙丘变成锦绣？"

焦裕禄认真研究之后，带领群众在张庄搞试验。他们的做法是把地面一米以下的淤泥翻上来，盖住沙丘，近处没有淤泥就到别处找。然后再种上草，栽上树，或撒上树种。焦裕禄把这个方法总结为"翻淤压沙、育草封沙、植树固沙"，他还形象地把翻淤压沙称为"贴膏药"，把种草、栽树称为"扎针"。焦裕禄还给治灾的群众按工分（农村人民公社计算社员工作量和劳动报酬的一种尺度）分粮食。这样，很多外出逃荒的灾民开始返回家乡，参与治理"三害"。

沙土地"贴上膏药"，"扎过针"之后，经历了几场七级以上大风的考验，人们看到风沙锁住了，沙丘固定了，树木成活了。1964年1月27日，根据焦书记的建议，在张庄召开了全县治沙推广现场会，把张庄成功治沙的经验在全县沙区推广，焦裕禄用"吃别人嚼过的馍没味道"的求实作风，找到了一条治理风沙的新路子。到1965年，兰考已封闭沙丘34万亩，取得了"治沙战役"的基本胜利。

subjugation of natural calamity here. It is not until then that we would take it upon ourselves to reshape the layout of the paulownia population here in conformity with artistry."

Jiao's characteristically pithy comment, "What is of top strategic importance should be accepted as top priority" triggered not only enthusiasm but also confidence in the villagers. Now they were vying to get planting of saplings proceeding quickly and nicely.

4. Jiao Yulu's keen eye and keen sense

In conducting a survey in Lankao of the routes of movement of gale-force wind, he went to Zhangzhuang village in March 1963. When trudging into a seemingly boundless expanse of sandy and barren terrain, he suddenly caught sight of a small stretch of grassy land ahead. He was surprised and hastened to a cottage nearby. The villagers living in the cottage told him that the small grassy patch was the tomb of Wei Duobin's mother.

Wei Duobin was a villager. The tomb sat somewhere along the route of movement of gale-force wind. For years in the past, the thick layer of sandy dirt piled above his mother's coffin was completely swept away by the gale-force wind year in and year out. Therefore, in those years Wei Duobin had no alternative but to repeatedly carry load after load of new sandy dirt to cover her coffin up again and again until one day when he was digging deep into the bank of a river to the south of his village in order to widen the stream a bit. In the course of digging, he shoveled up from deep beneath the bed of the river tons of silt, which he had to spread and heap on a long stretch of the sandy bank and the brink of a dune. Before long he discovered to his surprise that wherever he had the sandy soil covered with the silt, the sandy soil remained settled down fixedly in spite of the vehement sweeping blasts of the gale-force wind. This intrigued him. The next morning he went to the river bank with a heavy cart. There he shoveled up a cartful of silt from the bed of the river and then pulled the cart to his mother's tomb. After he got a few cartfuls of silt to his mother's tomb, he overspread the tomb with the silt. Later he contrived to have some vegetation grow in the silt covering his mother's tomb. From then on, the gale-force wind could do nothing to rob the tomb of the sandy soil buried beneath the silt Wei had overspread there.

After listening to the villager's account of Wei Duobin's story, which sparked his

兰考开展"翻淤压沙"运动
Lankao people engaged themselves in blanketing the dunes in silt.

当年焦裕禄翻淤压沙使用过的锄头
The hoe used by Jiao Yulu at the time he took part in the campaign of "blanketing dunes in silt" in Lankao. This hoe is the only extant one of altogether 400 hoes used by all those who joined the said campaign.

keen sense, Jiao Yulu said excitedly, "What a significant discovery Wei Duobin has made! If a man can in the span of one morning cover a patch of sandy soil the size of a tomb, why, if we can induce one hundred, or one thousand, or even ten thousand able-bodied men to overspread silt a tomb size of a dune! If we can induce several hundred thousand able-bodied men to do this in the span of, say, one, two or three years, isn't it possible for us to have all the dunes in our county converted into fertile land?"

Afterwards he made an in-depth study of the method of "blanketing dunes in silt" as an important measure for combating the gale-force wind. Now a pilot project intended for "blanketing dunes in silt" was unleashed by Jiao Yulu in Zhangzhuang village. The specific method adopted by the villagers is like this: in case a dune is situated near a river (or watercourse), silt is to be fetched from underneath the bed of the river and carted to where it is needed for the blanketing operation. In case a dune is far away from a watercourse, silt is obtained by digging over one meter deep beneath the top layer of the sandy soil, underneath which is a subterranean stratum of silt or mud. Then silt or mud can be extracted therefrom to be used in blanketing operation. After a dune is blanketed in silt, vegetation and paulownia are to be introduced to populate the silt. Jiao Yulu summarized the method in the following words: "Silt must be successfully extracted to blanket a dune before vegetation and trees are made to populate the wrapping silt. Trees can eternally imprison the sandy soil under the layer of superimposed silt." Since the pilot project intended for "blanketing dunes in silt" was unleashed in Zhangzhuang village, villagers began to join in activities under the project. As Zhangzhuang was a disaster area at that time, food shortage was acute. Villagers there preferred actually foodstuff to cash as award for their involvement in the project. Therefore, Jiao opted for paying them in foodstuff. This served to attract a considerable number of villagers who had deserted the village earlier in order to seek their survival elsewhere back to the village to take part in activities under the project.

After the completion of the project in Zhangzhuang village, a number of visitations of gale, which was fiercer than grade 7 (by Beaufort wind scale) gale-force wind were experienced by the village, but the end result of the project remained intact. Now the villagers firmly believed that all the dunes in the village were thoroughly transfixed. That meant the village was from then on forever free

第三章 一本永远读不完的书

1963年春，兰考人民向沙害进军
In the picture taken in spring 1963 can be seen how laborious the Lankao people were in grappling with the bane of drifting sand dunes.

如今的张庄景象
This photo serves to show what the landscape in Zhangzhuang village is like now.

of onslaught of sandstorm and afforestation in the village continued to expand. Actuated by a proposal put forward on January 27, 1964 by Jiao Yulu for convening in Zhangzhuang village a meeting, to which all the rural districts and villages in the county were to send their representatives. The meeting was intended for showing to all the representatives how triumphant the pilot project, once put into force in Zhangzhuang village and intended for "blanketing dunes in silt", had turned out and also for calling upon the rest of the county to follow Zhangzhuang village as an example in actively taking effective measures to counteract the three banes. The initiation of the campaign to put the pilot project intended for "blanketing dunes in silt" into effect in Zhangzhuang village is indebted to Jiao Yulu's keen eye and keen sense that led him to descry the significance of the casual initiative on the part of Wei Duobin's effort to protect his mother's coffin from the devastative gale-force wind. Thanks to Jiao's keen eye and keen sense, Lankao County succeeded in blazing a trail to subjugating the three banes. The year 1965 saw Lankao have 340,000 *mu* of dunes blanketed in silt. This means a remarkable success in the county's counterattack against the three banes.

IV. Jiao's deeply ingrained sense of duty endowed him with courage, ingenuity, and insight.

1. His unusual astuteness as demonstrated in the way he enticed a neighborhood tyrant to forfeit his life.

In those years when Kuomintang ruled China, a district in Weishi County in Henan Province going by the name of Daying was notorious for it's a remarkably large number of such rotten human beings as wicked millionaires, gangsters, and Chinese quislings. Huang Laosan was at that time the most egregious example among those rotten human beings. In collusion with petty and medially-ranked Kuomintang officials and bullies living in his neighborhood, he perpetrated all manner of inhumanities and outrages, taking advantage of the wealth he had raked up and the clout he could wield. He was literal hell to Daying district. A mere mention of his name was enough to scare an ordinary inhabitant to turn pale right away.

It is in spring of 1949 that Jiao was appointed as administrative head of Daying district. Following his installation he conducted an extensive and in-depth

四、迎难而上

1. 智斗黄老三

尉氏县有个大营区,中华人民共和国成立前此地汉奸多、土匪多、财主多。其中有个土匪头目叫黄老三,他与附近一些伪县长、土匪等拉帮结派,仗着有权有钱,欺男霸女,为非作歹。当时在这一带,提起黄老三人们可谓谈虎色变。

1949年春,上级组织把焦裕禄派往大营区任区长后,焦裕禄走乡串户,经过了解得知,区里有个叫李明的,被黄老三抢了家里的20亩地,黄老三还掠走了他的妹妹。李明气不过,说了狠话,结果被黄老三打得断了气。万幸的是入殓时李明又活了过来,发誓要报仇雪恨。

得知黄老三作的恶后,焦裕禄找李明谈心,表明了要除掉黄老三的决心。李明咬牙切齿,请求加入除掉黄老三的队伍。焦裕禄就让他在民兵队里做通信员。

焦裕禄一面派民兵查访土匪下落,一面号召群众发放传单,张贴标语,宣传政府"抗拒从严,坦白从宽"的政策。果然,一些土匪喽啰前来区里投降。

土匪头目黄老三坐不住了,放出狠话:"今后谁再敢背叛我黄老三,抽了他的筋,扒了他的皮,连他的家人一个不留。"还声称要跟焦裕禄来个鱼死网破。

焦裕禄和民兵队开会商量对策。李明不解地问:"焦区长,为什么不赶紧捉住黄老三,一枪把他毙了?"

"杀了黄老三容易,他手下的土匪咋办?咱们要想办法,一个一个把他们揪出来,一网打尽。"焦裕禄说,"李明,今天是清明节,他可能要上坟祭祀,咱们先抓捕了黄老三,给他敲个警钟!"

于是,李明带上十几个民兵悄悄地隐藏在黄老三祖坟附近的树林

investigation and survey among the local inhabitants and learned that Huang Laosan succeeded in seizing twenty *mu* of arable land from Li Ming, a local inhabitant, apart from looting the latter's younger sister. Thus, to give vent to his hatred, Li Ming took to calling Huang spiteful names behind the latter's back. After having been intimated of this, Huang contrived to get Li Ming murdered by flogging him to death. But at the very moment when a coffin arrived for taking Li Ming's body to a cemetery, he revived. After his revival, Li Ming swore an oath to take revenge on Huang.

Having learned about all the harms Huang had inflicted on Li, Jiao Yulu went to call on Li and let the latter know that he was determined to bring Huang to justice. Being brimmed over with hatred against Huang, Li begged Jiao Yulu to accept him as a member of the team organized expressly for cracking down on Huang. Jiao agreed to have him enlisted, in the first place, in the local militia as a messenger.

Now Jiao deployed militia detachments for scouting and reconnaissance to discover the gangsters' hideouts and at the same time had the local people organized into a number of groups. These groups were to carry out the task of leafleting and putting up political posters which were for giving out information about the CPC's policy which stipulated that "those who own up are to be leniently treated, but those who don't are to get harsh treatment". As a result of the task energetically carried out by these groups, thugs, goons and some of Huang Laosan's followers flurried to the district's administrative head's office to surrender of their own accord.

That sparkled a last-minute, frenzied panic in Huang Laosan who now howled savagely to his followers, "Whoever dare to follow those traitorous villains' example and go give themselves up to the communist authorities, I'd as soon have them skinned and their hamstrings snipped. And I would even spare none of their folks." Then he contrived to intimate Jiao Yulu that he wanted to take the latter's life at the cost of his own life.

Jiao went to call a meeting attended by all the militiamen for formulating the optimal strategy for extirpating the Huang Laosan and his gang. At the meeting, looking at Jiao quizzically, Li Ming asked, "Why don't you cop Huang Laosan, the brute, and dispatch him right away?"

"It's easy for us to single him out and do him in," explained Jiao, "but how can we flawlessly round up his whole gang? Tact is needed in order to leave none of them a chance to flee. Well, Li Ming, today is the Qingming Festival, a day on

里，一会儿，黄老三果然来上坟了。

正当黄老三烧香磕头时，李明率领民兵一拥而上，把黄老三捉了。众人把黄老三押到了焦裕禄面前。

黄老三问："焦区长，你不是要与我交朋友吗？怎么又派人抓我呢？"

"请你来是为了向你打听点情况，"焦裕禄说，"今天我不杀你，你只要把附近的土匪名单告诉我，再告诉我你手下有多少枪，我就放你回家。"

黄老三一听："只要不杀我，这个好办。"

焦裕禄根据黄老三提供的名单把这些土匪抓了起来。李明觉得黄老三手下的土匪喽啰抓的不少了，便说："焦区长，我看差不多了，该找黄老三算账了吧。"

焦裕禄还是神秘地一笑，吩咐他先把乡长梁长运叫来。

过了一会儿梁长运来了，焦裕禄让他去把黄老三叫来，就说黄老三儿子来信了。

梁长运和黄老三走着说着，到了区政府大院。黄老三一进大院，焦裕禄突然脸色一变，立刻下令："把黄老三给我捆了。"

黄老三一听，吓得一迷瞪："焦裕禄，你跟我玩阴招是不是？你说我儿子来信了，叫我到区里，现在却又抓我，是何道理？"

焦裕禄说："你儿子在部队里为民杀敌，是人民解放军，你却在家残害百姓，你良心上过得去吗？上次让你交代的土匪还远远没有交代完，要想活命，就要坦白从宽，否则把你关进大牢！"

黄老三说："焦区长，我已经给工作队提供枪支，又供出了我手下的名单，也算是立功了。今后就不要再找我的麻烦了，否则兔子急了也要跳墙。"经过突击审讯，黄老三不得不又供出十几个土匪，交出数百支枪。

集中收网后，焦裕禄说："放了黄老三。"

李明怒道："现在黄老三身边的土匪基本上全部抓获了，还放了黄

which, as our custom demands, every local family ought to go to pay homage to the place where its ancestral remains are kept. Therefore, it is very likely that Huang is to go to his ancestors' tomb as his own way of observing this festival. Now we'd take advantage of such an occasion for arresting him. This may be counted as our initial measure to try to instill intimidation into him."

In due course more than ten militiamen were detailed to lie in ambush in a grove close to Huang's ancestral tomb, with Li Ming serving as their guide. As if not to fail his ambushes' expectation, Huang did in due course arrive at his ancestral tomb and then set about kindling incense sticks, planting the burning incense sticks before the tomb, and kowtowing to it. While he was doing his veneration, the militiamen led by Li Ming swooped on him abruptly. Thus, he was apprehended. The militiamen escorted him back to Jiao's office. When in Jiao's presence, he sought to go on the offensive by asking brusquely, "District Head Jiao, you have promised that you and me are to make friends with each other, haven't you? Why do you have me arrested now?"

"It's precisely for getting some information from you that you're now in my presence, see?" said Jiao, "You are not to be bumped off, provided that you've the kindness to inform us about names of all the evildoers in this area and its vicinity. Besides, just tell me the number of rifles, which are now in your possession. I will set you free, provided that you consent to do what I've enumerated."

"I'd readily," answered Huang, "do what you've just asked me to, so long as you'd spare me!"

What ensued was the militia's initiative to round up the whole lot of scum whose names were put on the list of Huang's followers. Weeks elapsed, and jails in Daying district were about to overflow with the newly captured jailbirds. Li Ming reckoned that by now all Huang Laosan's followers had been locked up. So he approached Jiao one day and said to him, "Administrative Head Jiao, I reckon we've completed the imprisonment of all Huang's followers. In that case, I think it is now time for us to square accounts with Huang Laosan." But remaining quiet, Jiao just smiled mystically. Before long he said to Li, "Would you please go to fetch Liang Changyun, the village chief, for me?"

Minutes later, Liang was in Jiao's presence. Then Jiao said to Liang, "Now, please go to bring Huang Laosan here. Just tell him that there is a letter for him from his

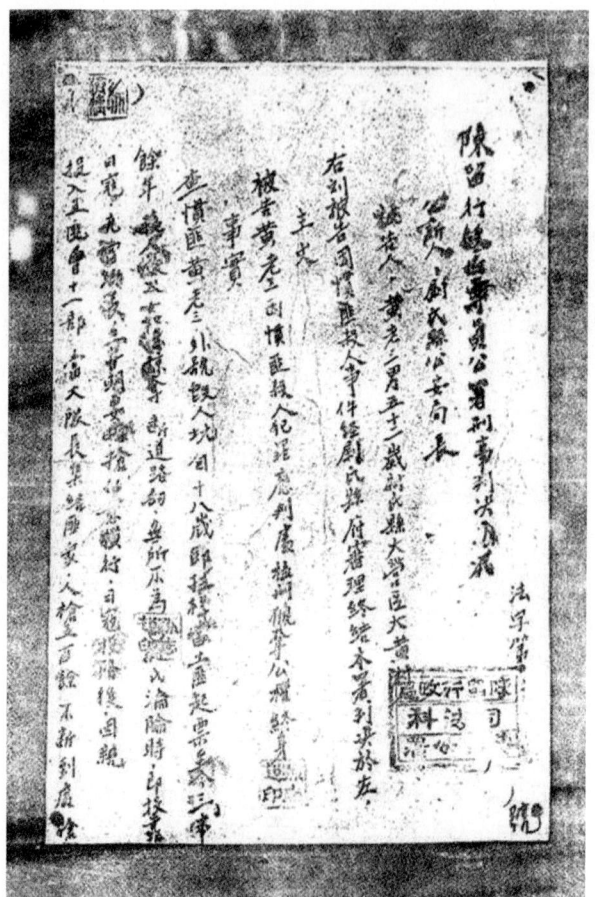

处决黄老三的刑事判决状

A photocopy of a verdict pronouncing a death sentence against Huang Laosan.

Chapter III An undrainable fountainhead of wisdom

son."

Accompanied by Liang and talking to him casually, Huang walked leisurely into the courtyard of Daying district office. On seeing Huang approach, Jiao suddenly yelled vehemently, "Now come to truss Huang Laosan up right away. Do!"

Quite taken aback, Huang let out a howl of anger. "Jiao Yulu," Huang shrieked, "so you've been tricking me! You allured me to come here on the pretext that there was a letter for me from my son. And now you've me tied up, why? Justify yourself if you can!"

"Your son," said Jiao, "have joined the People's Liberation Army and is now serving the people. But look at yourself! What you've been doing are all misdeeds to harm and torment the people. Don't you feel to have numerous deaths on your conscience? You didn't make a clean breast of what I required you to confess to me, did you? If you desire to have your life spared, confess honestly. Otherwise, imprisonment is what lies in store for you. Understand?"

"Administrative Head Jiao," said Huang Laosan, "I've provided your militia detachments with rifles and given away to you names of all my followers. You ought to register what I have done in your interest as my merits and stop from now on causing me any more trouble, ok? You know even a rabbit will go on desperate offensive, if it knows it has been brought to bay." But Jiao went to deliberately subject Huang to a series of highly intensified interrogations, and the latter was forced to give away names of ten odd gangsters and confessed that he still had hundreds of rifles cached in some secure storage.

After the last batch of Huang's followers was arrested and after his last secure storage of rifles was confiscated, Jiao gave the order that Huang be set free. This exasperated Li Ming who roared at Jiao in rage, "Since we have extracted from Huang all the information he can supply us, why on earth are we still going to leave him alive?"

"Of all the damned vermin now in our custody, Huang Laosan is the damnedest for sure. It's obligatory for us to render him perfectly convinced that his execution is indisputably what he deserves. Mind you, his presence here in Daying district office was engineered by the invitation we extended to him, rather than by dint of an arrest warrant. It is not appropriate for a Communist government to mess things up by ignoring moral or political principles and propriety."

老三，到底还有啥原因？"

焦裕禄说："黄老三是个大土匪，咱们要杀他，得叫他心服口服，咱是把他叫到政府大院的，又不是抓来的，作为共产党员应讲究原则，仁礼为先。"

黄老三被放后，扬言要卷土重来，有朝一日烧了区政府大院，自己当权。不久之后的一天深夜，黄老三率领一队人马，向区政府压来。焦裕禄和民兵早已得到了消息，布下了天罗地网，抓捕黄老三如同瓮中捉鳖。

公审大会上，黄老三被枪决了，大营区的老百姓欢呼雀跃，纷纷高喊："杀了黄老三，大营晴了天，睡上个安稳觉，吃上了心静饭。"

焦裕禄与群众庆祝剿匪反霸工作的胜利
Jiao Yulu and people in Daying district are celebrating the victory of campaigns against bandits, local tyrants and thugs.

After his release, Huang Laosan went to rant wildly that he was going to recoup what he had been deprived of, raving that he was going to set the building of the district office on fire one of these days and burn it to the ground and that he was going to be enthroned as new ruler of Daying district. Deep into one night, an armed rabble of hooligans led by Huang Laosan tried to launch a raid on the building of the district office. But the militia had already got wind of the attack and lurked in ambush. Thus, the rabble and Huang were laid siege to, disarmed, and arrested by the militia.

Later Huang stood a public trial and was sentenced to death. After the trial he was executed. Inhabitants of Daying district rejoiced at his execution, yelling rapturously,

"The sun turns even brighter,

As Huang Laosan, the villain, is no longer.

From now on each of our evenings or nights can be a perfect haven,

And each of our meals can best our vitality freshen."

2. The role he played in manufacturing the first of all the super winches ever made in China

During his tenure of office with Luoyang Mining Machinery Plant as its director of metalwork workshop No.1, he, as well as his workshop, was assigned in spring 1958 a pivotal mission that was "trial-manufacturing a double-drum super winch" which was expected to be the first of all the double-drum super winches to be manufactured in China. To carry out this mission, he and his workshop had to resolve a string of very difficult problems, such as lack of necessary equipment, shortage of technical know-how, nil prior experience. In the face of suchlike challenges, he valiantly chose to adapt his own way of living to the new circumstances given rise to by the new mission imposed upon him; namely, from thence forward he lived all day long in his workshop and refrained from going back home every night. Thus he worked laboriously in his workshop in daytime and held discussion or gathering with his colleagues in his workshop in evening or at night for reviewing what they had done in daytime. More often than not, such nocturnal discussion or gathering went on into the wee hours the next morning. But at the break of dawn he had to pull himself out of his makeshift bed which was a sizeable bench in the corridor in the second floor of his workshop and start his new day. For nearly sixty nights, on which

2. 新中国第一台大型卷扬机

1958年春，在洛阳矿山机器厂任一金工车间主任的焦裕禄，接受了一个重大任务：制造中国第一台大型双筒卷扬机。焦裕禄面前摆着一大堆难题：设备不全，技术不足，经验空白。为此，他开始了"以厂为家"的生活，白天紧张工作，晚上召开生产会议，凌晨2点才能休息。到了四五点钟，又开始新一天的工作。在制造卷扬机期间，他在二楼走廊的一条大板凳上睡了50多天。

卷扬机上有一种叫轴瓦的零件，按工艺规定，这种瓦上要浇注一层"巴氏合金"。传统手工浇注，不是出现气孔，就是黏合不牢，出了不少废品。这不但浪费了很多贵重的钨金，而且直接影响了工程进度。一个技术员说："这种人工浇注的轴瓦质量虽然不符合规定，但可以凑合着用，反正是试制品，凑合一下吧！"有人附和说："我们在外国实习时，这样大的轴瓦，他们也用手工浇注，质量也不能完全保证，咱们还能有什么办法！"

焦裕禄说："外国有的，我们要有；外国没有的，我们也要有。只要发扬自力更生精神，我们就能登上世界先进科学技术的高峰。这是我们厂试制的第一台大型卷扬机，我们交给国家的产品，一定要高质量，绝对不能凑合！"

为了解决技术难题，焦裕禄带领技术员查阅了大量国内外资料，并深入生产现场，向外国专家请教，与工人们研究措施，精心设计了切实可行的工艺流程。他还动手和工人一起操作，解决了整铸齿轮、烘装大齿轮等问题。

经过艰苦奋战，2.5米大型双筒卷扬机只用3个月的时间就试制成功了！在厂的外国专家也对此感到不可思议。"五一"国际劳动节那天，一金工车间红旗招展，锣鼓喧天，车间全体工人、干部将一台披红挂绿的自制卷扬机献给了人民的节日。2.5米大型双筒卷扬机的试制获得了成

the fate of the would-be double-drum super winch hinged, the sizeable bench served as his only bed.

A component going by the name of "bearing bush" is indispensable in a winch. But the bearing bush to be used in a double-drum super winch needs to be coated with Babbitt alloy. Conventional manual coating usually leads either to studding the coating with pores or to causing poor adhesion between the coating and surface of the bearing bush. A bearing bush with such poor coating can only be discarded as a waste product. This is precisely what happened to the process, in Jiao's workshop, of manually coating bearing bushes with Babbitt alloy. As a result, Jiao's workshop turned out an appreciable number of defective bearing bush. This brought about not just a considerable waste of tungsten-gold which is a precious alloy but also a direct impediment to achieving progress in their effort to build the super winch. One technician working with the workshop ventured to put forward his advice, saying, "Although all the flawed bearing bushes we have so far produced fail to meet the basic standards, yet they can be used as make-do things anyway, so long as the super winch we want to build is nothing more than a tentative initiative. Therefore, it is worthwhile to try to make these defective bearing bushes do." One technician came forth to second this advice by saying, "Together with some of our guys, I went on a field trip to a number of plants abroad. There Babbitt alloy coating of sizeable bearing bush was done manually too. Likewise, percentage of waste products resulting from the manual coating process was alarming. Therefore, I don't think it's possible at the present stage for us to fare better than our foreign counterparts."

"What can be manufactured in other countries," protested Jiao, "we should strive to render our country able to manufacture too. And what other countries are unable to manufacture now, we should strive to render our country able to manufacture it sooner or later. So long as we would unswervingly adhere to the policy of "Make our nation live solely on its initiative and resourcefulness", our nation is bound to negotiate the peak of science and technology. We're now trial-manufacturing a double-drum super winch. It's the first of its kind ever manufactured in our country. We're going to hand over our end-product to our country. Whatever we hand over to our country ought to be an excellent product, rather than a make-do affair that serves to fail our country's expectation."

Striving to the utmost to overcome technological impediment, Jiao organized

功，也填补了我国机械制造业的一个空白。

焦裕禄（前排左五）同苏联专家、工友在双筒卷扬机旁合影
This group photo shows the super winch trial-manufactured by the workshop, of which Jiao was at that time in charge. Workers of the workshop and experts from Soviet Union are seen standing in front of the machine. The one who is the fifth from the left in the front row is Jiao.

3. 暴雨中查水情

一次，焦裕禄到兰考县固阳公社了解灾情。当时天正下着大雨，他认为雨季正是探查水路走向的好时机，立即电话通知县委干部一方面带领群众排水防涝，另一方面查清水路。焦裕禄带领三名干部，背着干粮，打着雨伞，走进风雨之中。广阔的土地上积满了雨水，庄稼被水淹了。走进村庄，有些群众的房子倒塌了，雨水流向街头。焦裕禄和其他县里、乡里的干部立即投入抢险中，帮助群众牵牲口，搬粮食，修缮房子。随行干部一看水灾严重，痛心地说："庄稼全淹没了，今冬又是生活难关，这如何过呀？"

technicians to extensively search through technical literature originated either with China or with other countries for imbibing relevant technical knowledge, to closely survey the actual manufacturing processes going on in the workshop, to consult with foreign experts on some knotty technical issues, or to consult with some workers about some concrete measures to be taken or to be given up, until he succeeded in designing an excellent and feasible process flow. Then he joined his workers in operating the machines to put the process flow he had successfully designed into effect. Thus, he and his workers succeeded in solving problems that had frustrated their efforts to complete both gear casting and bull gear baking.

After three months of very arduous labor, the workshop, which Jiao was in charge of, succeeded in manufacturing a 2.5-meter double-drum super winch. Foreign experts who worked with Luoyang Mining Machinery Plant at that time rated the successful manufacturing of the super winch as an inconceivable undertaking. The day on which the workshop completed the building of the super winch was at the close of April that year. On May Day, the International Labor Day, Jiao's workshop was decorated with brilliant red flags. An especially composed fanfare punctuated by roaring drumbeats almost drowned the workshop. Its workers and staffers solemnly rolled the newly built super winch out of their workshop and announced that they offered the new machine as a gift to May Day. The machine was appareled in multicolor festoons and the successful building of the machine signified that a gap in China's spectrum of machinery building techniques was filled in.

3. Poor health was no deterrent to his fulfillment of duty.

Once Jiao was on his way to Guyang Rural District in order to conduct a survey of the tribulation left behind by the flood there. While he was trudging in a downpour, it suddenly occurred to him that raining can help the people who live in a lowland easily ascertain in which direction the rainwater that floods their lowland tends to flow. Jiao believed that as Guyang Rural District was in a lowland, its functionaries should avail themselves of rainy days to find out in which direction the rainwater covering their lowland tended to flow. Therefore, after Jiao arrived at the office of administrative head of Guyang Rural District, he immediately phoned up the government functionaries who worked for the CPC Lankao County Committee, on the one hand, to organize local inhabitants to dig additional ditches for draining the rainwater so as to prevent it from forming waterlogging and, on the

1963年春，城关乡群众在低洼易涝地区挖排水沟
The picture was taken in spring 1963. In it are shown villagers from Chengguan village working hard to ditch the alkaline lowland.

大队干部唉声叹气地说："唉，还得国家救济呀，这下又戴了一顶穷帽子。"

焦裕禄沉重地说："不要叹气，困难总会过去的。要因势利导，找好排水通道，挖好排水渠，为以后做好防洪准备。"

到了下午，雨下得更大了，焦裕禄的衣服几乎湿透，同行的干部关心他的病情，劝道："焦书记，您回去吧，前面都是水路，由我们去查，您保重身体。"

other, to avail themselves of the raining day to find out the direction in which the rainwater was most likely to flow. After having done the ringing up, Jiao asked three staffers to accompany him on a tour of inspection. Then he and the three staffers stepped outdoors into the rain, each carrying with him some solid food. Outside heavy rainwater was everywhere. The crops in the fields were mostly submerged. A considerable number of cottages in a village collapsed in the rain. Paths in the village were inundated. Then together with the cadres in the village Jiao immediately came to the villagers' rescue, helping them with herding their cattle to a safe place, retrieving their food and clothes from inside their battered cottages, or repairing their cottages. The village cadres who were together with Jiao at that time sighed in dejection and pain, "All the crops are inundated. This is a bleak prophecy of starvation in the coming winter! What can we do to survive?"

"Damned!" a cadre sighed and drawled, "none can grant us our survival unless the national authorities would allocate us some famine relief which is actually a disgrace in disguise, indeed!"

"But dejection," Jiao said gravely, "can lead us nowhere. Adversity cannot stay perennial. We should seek the way for turning the tables on the flood. We've to find out in which direction the stagnant rainwater can be induced to flow. Additional ditches should be dug to facilitate drainage of stagnant rainwater, and they can be improved for long-term use."

That afternoon the rain became heavier. Jiao's clothing was almost soaked through. The colleagues in his company knew about his very poor heath and were worried. "Secretary Jiao," they said to him, "you'd better stop wading along with us in the rain. The terrain ahead is apparently fit for ditching. Now you might as well retrace your steps and let us go along to deal with the terrain. We do really worry about your health."

"Please don't worry about my health. It's ok. I'm worried if I do not survey the terrain in person." Thus, all of them continued to wade along in the stagnant rainwater. The terrain was completely submerged, and nobody knew how deep the stagnant rainwater was. They had completely no idea where the terrain paths or roads lay, given the deep and turbid stagnant rainwater covering them. Jiao was the first to launch into the submerged terrain, wielding a long and tough sorghum stem as a probe for finding out how deep the rainwater was. At the same time he carefully

焦裕禄说:"我的身体是小事,我要亲自查看,才放心。"

前边积水成河,深不可测,四处无路,焦裕禄率先下河,用高粱秆探测积水的深浅,观察流向。他和干部们以及技术员们走村串户,顺着水流做标记,绘制了洪水流向图,掌握了防治内涝的详细资料。

4. 太行堤事件

黄河以"善淤、善决、善徙"而著称,兰考地处黄河中下游,黄河的决堤、改道使得兰考洪灾不断,也常常危及周边地区,尤其是紧邻的山东。兰考地势西高东低,每逢大雨,洪水自然东流到了山东省境内。兰考县的南彰和张君墓两个公社与山东省交界,边界上有几处重要的泄水口,形成了兰考洪水借山东之路入海的自然河道,常常给山东带来客水之患。为此,山东的曹县在边界处筑起一条百里长堤,取名太行堤,从此兰考的洪水不能向东流走。太行堤建成后,一遇大雨,兰考的水流不出去,东半县就遭水灾。兰考洪水要排出和山东曹县不让入境就成了两地矛盾的症结,两地为此经常发生纠纷。据说自明朝以来,两县为了一个"水"字,爷爷们拼过大刀,父亲们对过土炮,儿孙们架过机枪。

watched, trying to detect the almost invisible movement of the rainwater. Together with some village cadres and technician, he plodded along from one village to another, purposely leaving behind them a series of conspicuous marks, which were expressly for indicating the draining routes of various bodies of stagnant rainwater. Afterwards they were to map out, on sheets of paper, drainage diagrams of stagnant rainwater and flood, so that they could provide Lankao County Administration with detailed information for eliminating the bane of waterlogging.

4. Jiao's wisdom as demonstrated in the way he dealt with the Taihang Embankment Event

Being apt to form river channel sedimentation, induce embankment breach, and occasion channel migration was precisely what the Yellow River was notorious for. Lankao is situated between the river's middle reaches and its lower reaches. The river's frequent channel migration and embankment breach constituted the source of Lankao's consecutive calamities and often inflicted devastation on regions peripheral to Lankao, particularly some regions which were in Shandong Province. The elevation of the western part of Lankao is greater than that of the county's eastern part. The stagnant rainwater accumulated in Lankao naturally moved to its peripheral regions in Shandong Province. Both Nanzhang and Zhangjunmu, two rural districts in Lankao, verge on the boundary between Henan Province and Shandong Province. There were a few key drainage outlets, through which stagnant rainwater or flood in Lankao surged readily into Shandong and continued to rush therefrom until it reached its estuary in the eastern part of Shandong. Each time Lankao's stagnant rainwater or flood ran in a torrent into Cao County, which is a county in Shandong Province, a deluge victimized the county. Therefore, to block the deluge surging in from Lankao, Cao County constructed a colossal embankment measuring fifty kilometers long along the border between Cao County and Lankao County. The embankment now goes by the name of "Taihang Embankment". After the erection of the embankment, the stagnant rainwater in Lankao was deprived of its outlet which had previously unleashed it to run rampantly in Cao County. The embankment of course inflicted a flood on the eastern part of Lankao County. Therefore, Lankao's desire to dump its stagnant rainwater into Cao County and the latter's desire to block the inflow of calamitous water from the former were literally antagonistic. Confrontations between the two counties had lasted for over one

1963年，兰考遭遇了特大洪灾，南彰与张君墓两个公社洪水肆虐。兰考人准备破堤，山东人加固了堤防，双方集结了几千人准备武斗，情势紧张，武斗一触即发！

　　焦裕禄了解情况后，及时做出决定：一面发出通令坚决制止武斗，不准破堤放水；一面派县委工作人员前往曹县的上级机关山东菏泽地委汇报情况。去之前，有人说："兰考与菏泽不在一个省，不是一个专区，怎么个汇报法？"焦裕禄说："下级组织向上级组织汇报请示，是党的原则，为什么不能汇报？"于是，工作人员按照焦裕禄的意见到菏泽地委汇报了兰考洪灾以及南彰、张君墓两个公社的紧张形势。菏泽地委领导听后，非常重视，随后通知曹县，要求双方协商解决水患纠纷问题。曹县遂派工作组来兰考商定具体的治水方案。参加会议的是两县领导和水利工程技术负责人，曹县县委书记主持会议。两县的水利技术员都讲了各自的协调方案，但却因意见不同而争执起来。

millennium.

In 1963, an unprecedentedly mammoth deluge inundated Lankao. Both Nanzhang Rural District and Zhangjunmu Rural District were on the verge of being completely engulfed by the flood. Inhabitants of the two rural districts were desperate and readied themselves for promptly breaching Taihang Embankment. At the same time inhabitants of Cao County in Shandong Province did everything in their power to reinforce the embankment. The multitude having assembled on either side of the embankment was several thousand strong and equipped with weapons. A violent confrontation between the two armed multitudes was actually touch and go.

On being informed of the very precarious situation at the embankment, Jiao instantly announced an official ban on the attempt to resort to violence and an official ban on the attempt to breach Taihang Embankment to both Nanzhang Rural District and Zhangjunmu Rural District. In the meantime, Jiao dispatched his subordinate officials to the CPC Heze (Heze is the name of a prefecture in Shandong Province. Cao County was under the jurisdiction of Heze Prefecture.) Prefectural Committee for reporting to the secretary of the prefectural committee on the very tense situation along Taihang Embankment. Before Jiao's subordinate officials started on their travel to Heze Prefecture in Shandong Province, some functionaries in Lankao queried the appropriateness of the initiative taken by Jiao in sending his colleagues to the CPC Heze Prefectural Committee, saying, "As Lankao and Heze are neither in the same prefecture nor in the same province, does it stand to reason that Heze needs to involve itself in Lankao's affairs?" To such a query, Jiao gave the following reply, "The CPC Lankao County Committee is a unit on an organizational level lower than that the CPC Heze Prefectural Committee is on. The rule governing the set-up of the Communist Party of China dictates that it is obligatory for a party unit to report to another party unit which is on a higher organizational level. Therefore, it does stand to reason that Lankao reports the pertinent information to Heze." Thus, Jiao's subordinate officials rushed to Heze and reported the dangerous and riotous situation sparked by the calamitous deluge in Lankao County and Cao County to the CPC Heze Prefectural Committee. Being alarmed by the crisis, the prefectural committee attached great importance to it and immediately instructed Cao County to take the initiative in arranging for a parley between the two counties involved for seeking an appropriate solution to defuse

焦裕禄忙制止道:"咱们是来解决问题的,有话坐下来慢慢说。"

焦裕禄接着说,"我们虽然是两个省、两个县,但我认为根本利益不存在分歧。不论是华东局还是中南局,我们都应该服从社会主义全局;不论山东省还是河南省,都得实行'多快好省';不论菏泽专署还是开封专署,都要执行团结治水的总部署;不论曹县还是兰考县,都是党领导下的兄弟县。是不是这个道理?"

曹县那边很多干部点头认可。焦裕禄说:"你们很多同志可能不知道,我也是山东人。我老家是山东博山县,南下留在了河南,你们书记是我在南下工作团时的战友,我们一直是很好的朋友。在这个问题上,我既不会偏向河南,也不会偏向山东,咱们协商一个都能接受的办法好不好?"

the deluge crisis. Then a work team was promptly sent by Cao County to Lankao for working out a scheme that could effectively come to grip with problems arising from the monstrous deluge. Now attending the consultation held in Lankao were both leading officials of the two counties and leading technicians in charge of water conservation of the two counties. At the consultation, a leading technician of either side set forth a draft scheme. What ensued at the consultation was a collision of two diverse schemes for harnessing the deluge.

Jiao hastened to mollify the brouhaha by saying, "None of us comes here for a fracas. Each of us is here for grappling with the pressing issues confronting us. Now please do sit down and set forth your opinion in an amiable way! Please." Presently he continued, "As I see it, there isn't at all any conflict between the best interests of your county and mine. Although belonging respectively to the CPC Central Committee's East-China Bureau and the CPC Central Committee's Central-South Bureau, the two counties oughtn't do anything in direct contradiction to the basic interests of China, as a socialist country, as a whole. Neither Shandong nor Henan is allowed to stray away from the general political line of 'building socialism with greater, faster, better and more economic results'. Neither the CPC Heze Prefectural Committee nor the CPC Kaifeng Prefectural Committee is allowed to go against the general political strategy of 'solidarity and harmony be firmly upheld in sorting out complications arising from a severe flood'. Both Cao County and Lankao County are brotherly counties marching under the leadership of the Communist Party of China, aren't they? Ain't I right in asserting it?"

A considerable number of officials from Cao County who attended the consultation mutely nodded in acquiescence to what Jiao said. Then he added, "Probably many of the comrades from Cao County, who are present at this consultation have no idea that I myself am a native of Shandong Province. I hail from Boshan County in Shandong Province. I was quite a few years ago with the southward marching PLA which was at that time surging into South China to liberate people there from the Kuomintang regime. In the course of the PLA's southward incursion I was assigned to work in Henan Province, and from then on I have been staying in and working for the people of Henan Province. The current secretary of the CPC Cao County Committee was one of my colleagues when I was with the PLA many years back. He and I have been and still are on very good terms.

曹县方面的同志脸色缓和下来，大家开始继续商议。这时，曹县县委通信员进来说："兰考不少人上了太行堤，双方的群众要打起来啦。"

会议室的气氛又紧张起来。焦裕禄听后，和曹县工作组的人一起，赶到太行堤上，制止双方的群众。焦裕禄说："乡亲们，我是兰考的县委书记焦裕禄，今天来这里，就是和曹县处理水灾的问题，请大家保持冷静，大家都是从困难日子过来的，谁家都有儿有女。如果在此发生冲突，造成流血牺牲，你们的家人怎么办？"

焦裕禄接着说："我们都是共产党领导下的人民群众，都是平等的。两县的群众都是我的亲人。当下，两县已经开始商讨合作协议，共同处理太行堤问题，我保证第一时间解决水患问题，不会让大家遭受损失。请大家回去吧。"群众的冲动情绪得到缓和。曹县的县委书记也赶到了现场，劝阻了曹县的群众，双方暂时都熄了火、消了气。

随后，焦裕禄安排县委常委轮流在太行堤值班，每人24小时，防止发生事故。随后，他与曹县干部继续商议，双方初步达成了共识，成立了兰考、曹县治水联席会。最终，在国家水利部的协调下，双方签订了《关于兰考县与曹县拆除太行堤阻水工程的协议》，兰考、曹县两地的水患得到妥善解决。

Therefore, please rest assured that I wouldn't have a bias in favor Henan or Shandong in tackling problems involving the interests of either province. So would all of you who are present at this consultation please cooperate with me in thrashing out a scheme which is acceptable to both counties?"

Jiao's speech left all the officials from Cao County soothed and relaxed. Now all those present at the consultation started to renew the discussion. At this juncture a messenger sent by the CPC Cao County Committee intruded the conference hall wherein the consultation was in progress and declared, "A great multitude of Lankao inhabitants is assembling to Taihang Embankment. A massive throng of Cao inhabitants is also there and ready to meet the Lankao multitude with violence."

This again threw all those present at the consultation into a state of considerable agitation. Together with those present at the consultation, Jiao dashed to the embankment. There they tried to persuade the crowds from starting a reckless tussle. Jiao cried out, "Please listen to me, everybody! I'm Jiao Yulu, secretary of the CPC Lankao Committee. The ongoing consultation between representatives from Cao County and my county was seeking solutions to the flood problems but it had to adjourn right before we rushed here. We're determined to resolve the flood problems properly. I pray that all of you'd calm down now. All of you have been devastated by and are still experiencing the ordeal of the deluge. I believe all of you have to have the lives and safety of your family members taken into account. Once violence rages here to bring about deaths and wounds to them, do you think that can be rated as beatitude to any of your families? All of us are benefited by the nationwide leadership exercised by the Communist Party of China and welcome to the leadership. All of us are born equal. All of you, whichever county you live in, are my kith and kin all the same. For the time being, representatives from our two counties are consulting and discussing the proper scheme to be taken for dealing with complications on account of Taihang Embankment. Here I give you my word of honor that all the representatives from our two counties are striving to arrive as soon as possible at satisfactory solutions to the troublesome issues given rise to by the flood and that we'd do our best to spare you from loss to your property. Now I'd ask all of you to go back where you've come from." Jiao's speech was alleviating the hostility of the multitudes. At this juncture the secretary of the CPC Cao County Committee hurried to the embankment. He tried his best to pacify all the inhabitants of his

五、无私奉献

1. 给技术员送大米

焦裕禄到兰考后，发现泡桐能在兰考的沙土地上存活，可作为防风固沙的树种推广。为扩大种植规模，他十分重视泡桐的育苗试验。当时开展泡桐育苗的技术团队中大部分都是外地的年轻人，其中一个叫朱礼楚，是江西赣州人，从湖南林学院毕业后，分配到兰考做林业研究，是当时的高才生和高级技术人员。

朱礼楚是南方人，爱吃大米，而兰考当地主产小麦。从鱼米之乡来到风沙肆虐、"三害"严重的兰考，朱礼楚吃不饱穿不暖，水土不服，生活很不习惯。他女朋友到兰考看望他，目睹兰考恶劣的自然环境和艰难的生活条件后，劝他离开兰考。焦裕禄得知后，经常来找他聊天，询问工作生活上的困难。为帮助他解决吃饭问题，焦裕禄安排县委食堂的司务长把伙房里的米送过来，还每月把自己家的口粮给这几个技术员送去。

焦裕禄经常来看望这几位年轻的技术员。一次，焦裕禄问："你们是南方人，在兰考工作习惯吗？这地方怎么样？"

一位技术员直言："没有南方好，这里风沙大，生活苦，搞研究困难。"

焦裕禄点点头说："对啊！兰考是个风沙灾区，又连年受灾，生活是苦些，但这只是暂时的。兰考有这么多沙丘，只要我们大搞植树造林，进行农桐间作，风沙是能够被战胜的，生活也会好起来的。兰考有95万亩耕地，可以搞40万亩农桐间作，你们是泡桐研究者，到哪儿能找到这么大的研究基地呢！"

焦裕禄看着朱礼楚他们，又指着一棵泡桐说："这棵泡桐树，树干这样粗，树叶这样密，没有扎得很深的根是不行的。你们是南方人，远离家乡、阔别亲人，这是党的需要，只要在群众中扎下根，你们的工作就会像这棵泡桐树一样，根深叶茂。"

county. Therefore the enmity between the two crowds was ebbing away now.

Later Jiao took pains to arrange for members of the CPC Lankao County Committee to work on shifts throughout the twenty-four hours of a day to keep the embankment under close surveillance day and night to balk any attempt at renewing hostility on or in the vicinity of the embankment. Jiao urged to renew the consultation between representatives of the two counties. In due course a consensus view was formed among all the representatives involved, and a joint caucus was established to take charge of all affairs connected with the natural disaster of flood. Before long and through the good offices of the Ministry of Water Resources was signed between the two counties an agreement which went by the name of "Agreement between Lankao County and Cao County on Demolition of Taihang Embankment That Impedes Drainage of Flood". This led to a proper settlement of disputes between the two counties.

V. Jiao's selfless dedication

1. Jiao offered rice as his gift to technicians who used to eat rice as staple food.

A short time following his arrival in Lankao, Jiao came to realize the fact that Paulownia is fit for growing and flourishing in sandy soil. So he decided to enlarge paulownia growth in Lankao, because the tree has the capacities for both diminishing the strength of gale-force wind and stabilizing dunes. He attached great importance to the activity of experimental nursing for paulownia saplings because it was crucial to multiplying the growth of paulownia. There was at that time a team of forestry technicians at work in Lankao. Most of the team members were young people hailing from China's southern provinces. Zhu Lichu, hailing from Ganzhou, Jiangxi Province, was a member of the team. He graduated from Hunan Forestry Institute and was assigned after his graduation from his institute to Lankao to take up a post of silvicultural research in Lankao. He was an excellent student while studying at his institute and a gifted forestry technician while serving in Lankao.

As Zhu Lichu was a southerner, he preferred rice to wheat as his staple food. But wheat is the staple of Lankao's agrarian economy. Having left behind him his homeland which overflows naturally with products of husbandry, Zhu Lichu came to work in Lankao which had not only such sandstorms as were more frequent and

朱礼楚（右一）和另一位林业技术员在育苗基地工作
In the photo Zhu Lichu (on the right) is seen working in a sapling nursery together with one of his colleagues.

朱礼楚（右一）和林业技术员实地勘察林业发展
Together with his colleagues, Zhu (the first on the right) is seen doing survey in a field.

excruciating than people could manage to put up with, but also the three banes which were more destructive than could be imagined. Since his arrival in Lankao, Zhu Lichu had not for one day felt he was duly fed or properly clothed against the elements, just feeling wretched and out of place in Lankao in the face of all the inconveniences that were indigenous to Lankao. Once his girlfriend came to see him in Lankao. Having witnessed how inclement the climate in Lankao was and how nastily degraded his living conditions were here in Lankao, she persuaded him to quit Lankao. Of this Jiao was intimated in due course. From then on Jiao made a point of frequently seeking Zhu's company and was deeply concerned about Zhu's job and everyday life. Having learned that Zhu had trouble inuring himself to consuming flour as staple food, Jiao instructed the chief steward in charge of the Lankao-County-Committee refectory to manage to allot an extra supply of rice to Zhu. At the same time Jiao and his family members all strove to put aside a portion of their monthly food ration and meat ration and sent the saved portions as gift to other forestry technicians whom Jiao often went to visit in his spare time. Once in chatting with them Jiao asked, "As all of you are from the South of our country, do you feel it difficult to get inured to the living conditions in the North of our country? What do you think of the climate here in Lankao?"

"Lankao, as I see it," said a technician candidly, "is not so laudable a place to live in as any county in the South of our country. Here the sandstorm is simply outrageous. And the local living conditions are anything but enjoyable. Doing research in Lankao meets with impediments which are practically beyond our capability to overcome."

"Sure," said Jiao nodding, "Lankao is a place perennially plagued by gale-force wind and sandy soil. Natural disasters have befallen it for years in a row. The endeavor to grab livelihood here is certainly unusually trying. But I believe such a state of affairs here cannot be permanent. Let us exert to the utmost to have myriads of dunes in our county covered by paulownia forests so that we can have our crops intercropped with paulownia trees. That's the best way to keep gale-force wind at bay and to improve our living conditions. They are bound to be improved. There are in Lankao 950,000 *mu* of arable land. It'd be appropriate for us to allot 400,000 *mu* to intercropping crops and paulownia. You're all pioneering researchers specialized in the field of paulownia cultivation. You must be aware that beyond Lankao there is no

在焦裕禄和周边干部群众的关心支持下,朱礼楚慢慢坚定了扎根兰考、开展研究的决心。经过几番试验,他们终于研究出了耐干旱、耐盐碱,适合在兰考种植的泡桐树种,为兰考治理风沙做出了贡献。多年后,已是垂暮之年的朱礼楚接受电视台采访时说:"来到兰考我后悔,留在兰考不后悔。"

2. 公家的鱼不能随便要

焦裕禄刚到兰考时,看到县委机关北面有一个废弃的大池塘,他觉

1963年8月,工作人员在渔场打鱼

In the picture, taken in August 1963, are seen two workers fishing in a fishery.

place in our country where you can be provided with as amazingly large a research laboratory for paulownia cultivation as Lankao?"

Jiao Yulu gazed at the young technicians in his presence for a while and then added, while turning to point at a paulownia tree, "You see the paulownia tree over there? Its trunk is so thick and its foliage is so dense. This indisputably means that the tree has stricken its root very, very deep underground. All of you are from the South of our country. Now you stay very far away from your folks and hometowns. Of course, it is our Party that demands your presence here. So long as you'd mightily endeavor to strike your roots very, very deep into the local population, your research effort is bound to go as flourishing as that paulownia tree over there."

Thanks to the warm and touching solicitude and support showered on him by Jiao Yulu and all the people in his surroundings and having been exerting to have his own frame of mind undergo a gradual process of change, Zhu Lichu finally gave up his former plan of quitting Lankao for getting a research job elsewhere and became firmly determined to stay forever in Lankao and pursue forestry research for the rest of his life. From then on and together with his colleagues, Zhu succeeded in identifying a specific species of paulownia which is superior to any other species of paulownia in its drought-resistant and saline-alkali-resistant capacity. Therefore, the species of paulownia is particularly suitable to grow in Lankao. The identification achieved by Zhu and his colleagues of the paulownia species should be duly rated as a valuable contribution to Lankao. Years later when Zhu who was already in his dotage was being interviewed by a television journalist, the former said, "Although at the time I was in Lankao for the first time I thought Lankao a big disappointment, yet my disappointment vanished after I had settled down here."

2. Jiao told his children, "It's a taboo to take possession of anything that belongs to an institution or community."

Shortly after Jiao took up his official post in Lankao, he noticed that there was a large pond to the north of the county committee's building. It was a waste pond but belonged to Chengguan Rural District. And Jiao thought it economical and productive to turn the pond into a fish pond. Therefore, he offered his advice to Chengguan Rural District that they could develop fish husbandry by availing themselves of the pond. After the waste pond was turned into a fish pond, Jiao often strolled there when he was at his leisure. In a year when it was the fixed time for the

得里面可以养鱼,就建议城关公社投放鱼苗,把池塘建设成渔场。他经常在休息时间到渔场转转看看。到了渔场打鱼收获的季节,工作人员为感谢焦裕禄,也为了让身患肝病的焦书记补补身体,就装了10多条活鱼送到他家。焦裕禄的孩子们一见活蹦乱跳的鱼,喜欢得不得了,嚷着要吃鱼。

焦裕禄回家后,问清了来龙去脉,就对孩子们说:"这鱼是渔场的叔叔辛辛苦苦养大的,是集体财产,咱一家没去劳动,咋能白吃呢?如果大家都占公家的便宜,那公家的事还能办好吗?"他的一席话使孩子们明白了道理,大儿子焦国庆当即就把这桶活鱼又送回了渔场。

3."看白戏"与"干部十不准"

一天,夜已很深了,几个孩子都睡下了,唯独大儿子焦国庆还没回来。焦裕禄正要问,大儿子焦国庆从外面回来了,并兴奋地告诉焦裕禄他刚刚看了戏。焦裕禄问他谁给买的票。儿子焦国庆说:"我说自己是焦书记的儿子,检票的叔叔就放我进了门。"

焦裕禄听后眉头一皱,严肃地问道:"国庆,你看戏不买票,对吗?"

people of Chengguan Rural district to come to net the pond for catching marketable fish, they did come in time to the pond to do the fishing. It turned out to be a huge catch. As the people of Chengguan Rural District were not only grateful for Jiao's advice urging them to avail themselves of the pond for developing fish husbandry but also very much concerned about Jiao's hepatitis, they filled a pail with ten odd fish and sent it to Jiao's home as their gift to him. That day when the pail reached Jiao's home, both Jiao and his wife were not in. On seeing the floundering fish in the pail, his children were all enraptured, imagining that they were going to have palatable fish dishes on their table soon.

Later when Jiao got back home, he questioned his children about whence came the fish. Then he told his children, "These fish are end product of the arduous labor of the people of the rural district. They worked hard to feed the fish day in day out. Therefore, the fish are a portion of their community's property. None of our family members has ever joined them in feeding the fish. It's wrong for us to grab for ourselves anything that belongs to a community. It is a taboo to take possession of anything that belongs to an institution or community. In case a citizen be allowed to seize at will whatever belongs to a community or institution, can the latter grow unimpeded and prosper?" Jiao's didactic words enlightened his children. Promptly Jiao Guoqing (Jiao Yulu's eldest son) went to carry the pail with the fish back to the pond and returned them to the people of Chengguan Rural District.

3. Miscellaneous instances that are quite illustrative of Jiao's ethics

It was already deep into the night. Except for Jiao Guoqing, Jiao Yulu's eldest son, other children in the Jiao family had all gone to bed. His father was on the point of making inquiry about his absence from home, the boy popped indoors and excitedly told his father that he had just left the theater where he had watched the performance. His father asked him, "Who bought the ticket for you?" The boy said, "Why, nobody bothered to buy the ticket for me, see? I just told the ticket-taker, 'I'm Secretary Jiao's boy.' And I was admitted."

"What!" frowning, Jiao Yulu said gravely, "son, you went to see the performance at the theater, and you didn't buy a ticket? Don't you see you were wrong?"

"I'm merely a kid," replied Jiao Guoqing, "and nobody cared what I was there for."

"Now you know how to get an institution palmed off in a petty way and did

儿子焦国庆说:"我是小孩,没人在意。"

焦裕禄说:"年龄小就知道占公家的小便宜,长大了就会贪大便宜,这是很危险的!演员唱戏,是一种很辛苦的劳动,看'白戏'是一种剥削行为!"

儿子焦国庆听爸爸口气严肃,知道了问题的严重性,表示自己再也不去看"白戏"了。焦裕禄从兜中掏出两角钱,交给儿子,语重心长地教导他说:"从小就要养成公私分明的好品德,不要因为爸爸是县委书记,就要搞特殊。明天把钱送给检票的叔叔,向他承认错误!"

有一天,焦裕禄在兰考礼堂外排队买票,有人惊奇地问:"焦书记,你看戏也排队买票啊?"

焦裕禄笑呵呵地反问:"我怎么就不能排队买票?"他买了一张第27排的票,对号入了座。剧场负责人发现他坐得靠后,上前对他说:"焦书记,请到前排坐。"

焦裕禄说:"谢谢!我买的就是这一排的座。乡下群众轻易不进城,看戏的机会少,前排的位置应该让他们坐!"

it blatantly when you're so young. You're likely to do it in a big way when you're an adult. Isn't that a perilous future for you? An actor's career is really a very arduous career. You enjoyed yourself at the performance without recompensing the actors and actresses in any way. That's nothing short of an exploitation!"

From his father's harsh guttural tone, the boy became awakened to the seriousness of his misbehavior and assured his father that he'd never do such a thing again. Then Jiao Yulu fished out from his pocket a twenty fen note and handed it to his son, saying feelingly, "Do take pains while you're in your childhood to evolve in yourself the habit of drawing a clear-cut distinction between what is truly yours and what is not. Don't try to avail yourself of my official post as a means to grab some prerogative for yourself. Now go to sleep. Go to give the money to that ticket taker first thing tomorrow and admit to him that you were wrong in watching the performance without buying a ticket."

One day while Jiao Yulu was standing in a queue before the box office of Lankao Auditorium for buying a ticket to an opera, someone asked him rather curiously, "Why, Secretary Jiao, is it necessary for you to buy a ticket for admission to the performance?"

"Why, buddy," guffawed Jiao protestingly, "Is it absurd that I stand in a queue and wait for my turn to buy a ticket? No." When his turn came, he got a ticket, which gave him a seat in the 27th row in the auditorium. He entered the auditorium and took the seat. Before long, the head of the auditorium noticed that Jiao was in the auditorium and that his seat was rather distant from the stage. Then he went to Jiao and said, "Secretary Jiao, wouldn't you like to have a seat closer to the stage?"

"Thanks," answered Jiao, "but it's fine with me taking a seat in this row, as my ticket assigns me to this seat. Villagers seldom have opportunities to gain access to the urban area of our county. They are rarely provided with an opportunity for going to a theater. Therefore, it is only fair to them to let them occupy seats in those front rows."

The head of the auditorium said, "But there are seats in a front row, which are reserved exclusively for leading officials of our county. That's now one of the conventions of long standing with us!"

Jiao had heard of such a convention of long standing with the auditorium. There had been, in the long past, such a secretary of the CPC Lankao County Committee

剧场负责人说："前排有给县委领导留的位置，这是多年的老规矩啦！"

这个"老规矩"焦裕禄早就有所耳闻。有一位县委领导爱看戏，不但不买票，而且经常领一大群看"白戏"的，坐满第三排的座位。时间一长，群众便称坐这一排的人为"老三排"，称这位领导为"老三排排长"。想到这里，焦裕禄严肃地对这位负责人说："过去个别人兴起的'老规矩'不合理，应当废除。我们不能为了迁就某些人的坏作风而放弃原则，要处处为群众着想。"

从儿子看"白戏"，再到一些领导干部占据"老三排"，焦裕禄感到当前的机关作风出现了问题，干部搞特殊化的问题很严重。在县委会议上，焦裕禄带头对自己儿子看"白戏"的问题进行了自我批评，并提出要针对干部队伍中出现的一些不正之风和不良倾向制定《干部十不准》。

4. 划掉自己的名字

一天，兰考酒厂给焦裕禄送来四瓶酒。送酒的同志说："焦书记，这是咱厂里的新产品，送给您尝尝，请您提意见哩。"

焦裕禄说："我不爱喝酒，品不出好坏，喝了酒也说不出个所以然，不起啥作用啊！"

酒厂的同志说："您先尝尝，提不出意见就算了。"

焦裕禄看酒厂的同志执意要给，就说："那好吧，送到县委食堂，让大家都尝尝，都提点意见，不比我一个人尝强吗？"最后，又捎带说了一句："谁喝谁拿钱。"

由于人口多，焦裕禄一家的生活并不宽裕，但他从不要组织上的救济。1963年春节前，下乡的焦裕禄回到县委，看到墙上贴的福利救济名单上有他的名字，大吃一惊：这次救济的人怎么这么多，而且自己的名字还在上面？他随即找到机关党支部书记问是怎么回事。焦裕禄问："这次

as was morbidly besotted with opera. But never for once he bought a ticket whenever he went to a theater to enjoy himself. Besides, every time he went to a theater he invariably took with him a retinue of playboys, none of whom bought a ticket for admission to a performance, under the aegis of the secretary. Each time such a swarm of intruders swooped into a theater, they promptly monopolized the seats in the third front row. As such a practice of gratuitous occupation of third-front-row seats had lasted for a number of years, the local population thought it fit to bestow on each of these playboys the funny sobriquet "a third-row veteran" and confer on the freeloading secretary the nickname of "a third-row tycoon".

Now memory of these invidious past episodes in relation to the freeloading secretary flashed across Jiao's mind and prompted him to say to the auditorium head seriously, "The convention of long standing which was concocted in the past and has proved to be absurd needs to be abolished, because such a convention is antithetical to our principles. It's simply suicidal to gratify somebody's unvirtuous craving at the cost of nullifying our principles. What we should do is acting in the best interests of the ordinary people."

Afterwards Jiao continued to reflect on his son's way in inveigling himself into the theater and on the freeloading secretary's way in incurring the popular bestowal on him the epithet of "a third-row tycoon". Then he came to realize that something was veritably awry with the morality of a portion of the local officialdom, as the portion was obsessed with the greed for raking for itself as many prerogatives as possible. Later at a session of a meeting attended by all the members of the CPC Lankao County Committee, Jiao took the initiative in telling them about his son's misbehavior in wangling a gratuitous admission to the theater for enjoying a performance gratis. Then after he had criticized himself before his audience for his serious lapse from his duty as a father, he set forth a draft resolution drawn up by himself, which was intended for rectifying the wrong behavior and various demonstrations of erroneous mental outlook. And Jiao gave the draft resolution the title of "Ten Behavioral Taboos for Government Officials".

4. Jiao Yulu was an epitome of unselfishness.

Lankao Winery sent four bottles of wine as a gift to Jiao. The guy running the errand on behalf of the winery of bringing the wine to Jiao said to him, "Secretary Jiao, here are four bottles of a new product by our winery. We'd like to know your

豫剧中的焦裕禄

This picture shows a scene from Jiao Yulu, a dramatic work set to Henan opera. In the scene the actor (right) enacting Jiao Yulu is seen talking to a character in the opera.

appraisal of them after having tasted them."

"Oh, I'd say as I'm rather averse to wine, I can't be expected to give any appraisal of them. I don't think I can give any sensible comment on them, even if I drink them. Please spare me from drinking the wine!"

"Just taste the wine, ok?" the guy said persistently, "We don't mind whether you'd give us any comment."

Seeing that the guy from the winery was determined to leave the wine behind him, Jiao said, "Well, I see you're determined not to take the wine back to your winery. What about sending the four bottles of wine to the Lankao-County-Committee refectory, so that people who eat there can taste them and give their appraisals? That'd be much better than having me taste the wine alone, wouldn't that?" Before the guy from the winery was about to bring the bottles to the refectory, Jiao hastened to add, "Mind you, whoever is to taste the wine at the refectory has to pay for the wine he consumes. Got it?"

Jiao had a numerous family to support. Its finances were, therefore, pretty tensely stretched. But he never dreamed of receiving some relief from the county committee. Prior to the Spring Festival of 1963, after he had just got back from an inspection tour in the rural areas, he went to the county committee building. There he chanced to notice that there was a bulletin put up on a wall. The bulletin contained a list of names of those who were recommended as candidates for receiving a sum of relief fund from the government. Included in the list was Jiao Yulu's name. On seeing that his name was included in the list, he was stunned, as he had neither anticipated the inclusion of his name in the list, nor expected that the names included in the list could be so numerous. Presently he turned to hurry into the office of the functionary who was in charge of drawing up the name list, as he wanted to make heads or tails out of all this apparent turmoil. In the functionary's office, Jiao shot a query at him, saying, "May I know what the prerequisites are that make one eligible for receiving the government relief?"

The functionary answered, "The three prerequisites are (1) his or her family lives in a disaster area, (2) his or her family is hard up, and (3) he or she has submitted an application for relief …"

"But my family," said Jiao smiling, "doesn't live in a disaster area. And I've never submitted any application for the relief. Why is my name included in the list?" And

救济有什么条件吗？"

"家在灾区，生活困难，本人申请……"支部书记回答。

焦裕禄笑着说："我家既不在灾区，我本人又没有申请，为什么也有我呀？"接着，他又郑重地说，"发放救济款，不仅仅是几个钱的问题，要把它当成政治任务去做。要教育干部，对待生活上的困难，首先要依靠自己省吃俭用去解决。我们都有工资，不能两眼向上，坐等救济。"

晚上，焦裕禄召开了机关党员大会，他在会上说："兰考是个重灾县，人民的生产、生活都很困难。我们时时、事事应该首先想着群众。我们是共产党员，要'先天下之忧而忧，后天下之乐而乐'，宁肯自己苦一些，也不要随便要国家的救济。我们是县委机关，更应该给全县干部做榜样。"最后，他严肃地说，"给我的救济，我一分钱也不要。"

在他的带动下，有十几名同志表示不要救济。后来，机关福利委员会又重新评定了救济对象，重点照顾了八个最困难的同志。

presently he added sternly, "Drawing up a list of names of recipients of government relief isn't simply a process of accounting indispensable to distribution of the relief funds granted by the government. It is actually an operation laden with political and didactical significance. The relief fund is a means for enlightening our functionaries on the principle that severe family finances can be and ought to be shaken off by firm adherence to a frugal way of living, rather than by looking forward to the relief the government doles out. All the functionaries here are paid by the government. None of us should be blindly obsessed with the relief or grant from the government."

That evening Jiao summoned all the communist party members who worked with the county committee to a meeting and stressed to his audience that since Lankao was a heavily inflicted disaster area, the Lankao people were experiencing very trying hardship in seeking their survival and in exerting to revive their farming. We, as communists, ought to put our people's best interests before anything else all the time. "We, as communists," he added, "ought to anticipate any troublesome prospect for our nation before the populace can come to realize it and never to feel relaxed and at ease unless our nation's prosperous future is faultlessly secured. I'd rather let my family experience a few years of penury than ask our government for some relief. We ought to set an example for the people of our county to follow suit, since we are working with our county's CPC committee." Minutes elapsed before he added in all seriousness, "I refuse to accept the government relief granted to me."

Then following his example, nearly a score of those attending the meeting whose names had been included in the list of government-relief recipients stood up to signal their renunciation of the government relief. Consequently a new list of names of government-relief recipients was released. Included in the new list were names of only eight recipients, of whose families survival was truly at stake.

第四章

历久弥新的精神

Chapter IV

Jiao Yulu's tremendous bequest to us

焦裕禄去世半个多世纪了，和过去相比，现在的兰考发生了翻天覆地的变化，即将于2020年和中国其他地区一起进入小康社会，中原大地呈现一片欣欣向荣的景象。当前，中国已经成为世界第二大经济体、世界第一大出口国和第二大进口国，中国的经济发展已成为拉动世界经济增长最重要的引擎之一。在科技、经济高度发达的今天，为什么还有这么多群众自发地拜谒焦裕禄烈士陵园，还有这么多作家写焦裕禄的故事，还有这么多媒体宣传焦裕禄精神？因为时代在发展，社会在进步，人民对物质生活和精神生活的需求在提升，人民对公平公正的社会环境和清正廉洁的干部队伍有更高的期待。习近平主席说过，希望通过学习焦裕禄精神，为推动党和人民事业发展、实现中华民族伟大复兴的中国梦提供强大正能量。焦裕禄为公职人员树立了很好的榜样和很高的标杆，他的精神历久弥新，永不过时。

一、教育了公职人员，争做为民、务实、清廉的表率

焦裕禄精神是中国公职人员的一面镜子。国家主席习近平曾说："我们这一代人都深受焦裕禄精神的影响，是在焦裕禄事迹教育下成长的。我后来无论是上山下乡、上大学、参军入伍，还是做领导工作，焦裕禄同志的形象一直在我心中。"5年内，习近平3次来到兰考县，要求公职人员把焦裕禄作为标杆，"深学、细照、笃行"，努力做焦裕禄式的好干部。

近年来，中国涌现出一大批与焦裕禄相关的书籍、文章、诗词、歌曲、电影、电视剧、话剧等文艺作品，这助推了焦裕禄精神的传播。很多公职人员为了更直观地了解焦裕禄的事迹，纷纷来到焦裕禄工作过的地方——兰考县，拜谒焦裕禄烈士墓，参观焦裕禄同志纪念馆、焦裕禄开展翻淤压沙试验并取得成功的地方张庄、围绕焦裕禄树立的"四面红旗"而建设的展览馆、毛主席视察黄河的兰考东坝头、焦裕禄组织开展

A mythically stupendous change has taken place in Lankao in a span of more than half a century since Jiao Yulu left us. It has officially announced that the county is scheduled to access, in 2020 together with most counties in our country, the status of "a moderately prosperous society in China". This will make the Central-China Plains shine more brilliantly than ever. Currently China emerges on the international socioeconomic horizon as the world's second hugest economy. Moreover, our country is currently both the world's largest exporter and the world's second largest importer, not to say that China's economy is among the world's most powerful economic leverages to boost the international economic growth. Why, given the current progress made by humankind in science and economic development, are there so stunningly large multitudes of people going of their own accord to pay homage to Jiao Yulu's grave? Why so huge a number of writers engaging themselves so fervently in telling and retelling stories about him? And why so extensive a range of national and international media showing so intense an interest in the moral and spiritual legacy left behind by him? The answer is this: Our nation is looking forward to a better social environment where justice and equality have a stronger grip on the social fabric and where all government officials are conscientiously ethical and talented, thanks to the enlightenment our nation has acquired, as a result of the great improvement made in the spheres of both material life and cultural life. President Xi Jinping has this to say of late, "I hope the enthusiastic movement urging our people to learn about and follow Jiao Yulu would supply a very powerful and positively-oriented dynamic to bring about the realization of 'Chinese dream' which can not only promote both our Party's cause and our nation's cause but also enable our nation to achieve her rejuvenation. A convincing example and an indubitable benchmark was set by Jiao Yulu for all government officials to follow or to strive to attain. In no circumstances his tremendous bequest can go devalued.

I. From Jiao, all government staff can learn how to serve the people in an unselfish and pragmatic way.

Jiao Yulu's personal morality can serve as an impeccable assemblage of moral standards for all the government officials in our country to adopt. President Xi Jinping said, "Mentality of the contemporary Chinese living in mainland China

2015年4月21日，中央党校省部级干部培训班在"焦桐"下学习
A training course for provincial and ministerial leaders was run by the Party School of the Central Committee of CPC in 2015. On April 21 that year, a class was in progress in an open plot inside a paulownia forest.

政府干部在张庄学习
A training course for government officials is seen in progress in Zhangzhuang village.

has inevitably been influenced in one way or another by Jiao's personal morality. Essentials of the fabric of the present-day China's moral instruction, or even didactic instruction, have been borrowed from Jiao's virtuous life. Jiao's ethical visage had never for an appreciable moment eluded my mind in any of such stages in my life as the span of years when I was sent to work in remote rural areas, or the span of years when I was a university student, or the span of years when I served in the PLA, or the span of years when I took up an official post." In five years Xi visited Lankao for three times. It is his pressing craving that all functionaries in our country should take closely after Jiao. Xi urges each of them "to learn about Jiao Yulu studiously, to find out the concrete differences between Jiao's personality and his (or her) personality, and to faithfully follow Jiao's virtuous example". Xi demands that every government functionary should mold himself (or herself) into an exemplary functionary like Jiao.

Recently in our country there has been a gushing output of publications, essays, poetry, songs, movies, TV series, and dramas extolling Jiao's life. This strongly impels the propagation of Jiao's morality. Motivated by their desire to view in person or to see with their own eyes the very scenes, where Jiao devoted his life to the best interests of our people, a rapidly increasing number of functionaries have come to Lankao, traveled there to pay homage to his grave, or visited Jiao Yulu Memorial Hall or some other sites, which are of relevant interest. For example, Zhangzhuang village in Lankao is precisely one of such interesting sites. It is the very place where Jiao started his experiment with the method of "blanketing dunes in silt" and finally succeeded in validating the method. The museum hall, which has been designated as its name "the Four Red Flags", is also one of such interesting sites. Apart from the interesting sites referred to above, Dongbatou in Lankao is also one of such interesting sites, because Chairman Mao visited Dongbatou during his inspection tour that swept along the Yellow River. The paulownia tree nursery is an interesting site too, as it is indebted to Jiao for its establishment.

1. From Jiao can be learned what is meant by "sense of duty".

Our government exists with the sole objective of providing our people with its wholehearted service. In other words, what our government strives to the utmost for is to serve the people wholeheartedly. And this is precisely what Jiao's ethics boil down to. "What filled his heart to the full was the best interests of the people. And what was totally absent from his mind was his personal interests." That is the way

泡桐育苗试验的基地，等等。

1. 学习焦裕禄精神，能够教育公职人员尽职尽责、服务群众

全心全意为人民服务不仅是政府的根本宗旨，也是焦裕禄精神的本质。"心中装着全体人民，唯独没有他自己"是焦裕禄为民情怀的鲜明体现。焦裕禄临危受命，担任兰考县委书记，不是为了做多大的官，而是为了解救受苦受难的群众，为兰考人民谋福祉。焦裕禄作为县委书记，虽事务繁杂，却经常下乡访贫问苦。他以人为本，把群众的事放在第一位，想群众之所想，急群众之所急。焦裕禄之所以深受群众爱戴拥护，根本原因就在于他把自己当作人民群众的儿子，努力为人民办实事、办好事。他常说："共产党员应该在群众最困难的时候，出现在群众面前，在群众最需要帮助的时候，去关心群众，帮助群众。"

2. 学习焦裕禄精神，能够教育公职人员尊重规律、求真务实

注重调研、寻找科学方法、制定有效策略是焦裕禄带领兰考群众成功治理"三害"的重要法宝。他常说，"干部不领，水牛掉井"，"吃别人嚼过的馍没味道"。为摸清灾情，他带领调查队跋涉5000多里，全县149个大队他跑了120多个，察灾情、找办法，做出治理"三害"的科学决策。他冒着大雨查看水情，摸清洪水流向；他在饭点时下乡，看看各家的烟囱是否冒烟，进而判断群众是否缺柴；在群众家吃派饭（指派农户给临时来村工作的干部所提供的饭食）时，他经常端着饭到牛栏等群众聚集的地方，与群众聊天。这些做法充分体现了从实际出发、尊重客观规律的科学态度。

Jiao's everyday cogitation worked. It is when Lankao had sunk into a life-or-death crisis that Jiao was entrusted with the task of wringing back Lankao people's survival from the natural calamity. He went to Lankao to take up his office merely for retrieving the people there from being starved or frozen to death. The dream of being promoted in due course to a higher official position never occurred to him. What motivated him to stay rooted in Lankao was to rake in as much material and cultural blessedness for the local population as possible. His everyday work, as secretary of the CPC Lankao County Committee was strikingly burdensome and time-consuming. But he managed to very often go on foot for a long distance to remote villages. There he visited the poor or the wretched. He was one who tried his best to make the service rendered by the government totally populace-oriented. Protecting interests of the populace was his top priority. Cravings and worries of the populace constituted his sole concern. That the populace adored him and rallied around to help him was solely due to his boundless love of the populace. He would exert to the utmost to serve the populace. He often told his colleagues, "A communist ought to be with the populace whenever the latter meet with trouble or are in dire need of help."

2. From Jiao Yulu can be learned what is meant by "adherence to truth and objective law which is independent of man's will".

To beat the three banes that had raged in Lankao for centuries, he had his own strategic line to follow for carrying on the different stages of the campaign step by step with the full participation and close cooperation of the Lankao populace. His strategic line consisted of three components. They are (1) carrying out a researching inquiry coupled with an in-depth study, (2) experimenting with diverse tentative methods in order to find out the pragmatic one, and (3) finalizing the formulation of the core strategy. Besides, he made a point of effectively activating all the government functionaries in Lankao to sincerely molding themselves into capable public servants devoted to the populace. Apart from being unselfish, a government functionary needs to be sensible, intelligent, and resourceful. He often said to his colleagues, "If a functionary is not clear-headed, the portion of the multitude staying in touch with him is often gratuitously nipped!" And he would often, offering advice to his friends, say to them, "You can get nowhere, just presuming or pretending you are able to step into anybody's shoes."

To carry out a researching inquiry or doing a thorough investigation in Lankao,

第四章 历久弥新的精神

外国代表团到焦裕禄同志纪念馆学习
Guests from all over the world are seen in the photo touring Jiao Yulu Memorial Hall.

3. 学习焦裕禄精神，能够教育公职人员严于律己、清正廉洁

作为一个县的主要领导，焦裕禄没有利用职务之便帮助女儿到政府单位上班，而是让她自谋生路，去酱菜厂卖酱菜。政声人去后，丰碑民心上。焦裕禄的行为诠释了共产党员的清廉，教育感染了公职人员，也赢得了人民和政府的信赖。腐败是国际社会共同面临的难题和挑战。习近平主席执政以来，铁腕反腐，严扎制度笼子，党中央出台了"八项规定"，颁布了《中国共产党党内监督条例》，修订了《中国共产党纪律处分条例》，全国人民代表大会制定了《中华人民共和国监察法》。政府规定，禁止新建楼堂馆所，控制"三公"经费，"打虎""拍蝇"同时出手，并要求公职人员以焦裕禄等先进人物为标杆，做清正廉洁的干

he often had to traverse a long distance on foot. Probably he had trudged on foot in Lankao for over 2,500 kilometers. He had been to more than 120 villages in the county for carrying out his inquiry and investigation. No devilish downpour could bar him from rushing out to the dangerous spots where individuals or households were in desperation or badly in need of rescue. It is in inconceivably inclement weather that he repeatedly waded into torrential floods to find out the directions of their drainage. Often during his sojourn in a village and when lunchtime was drawing near, he would saunter around to find out which chimneys in the village did not spew any smoke. Thus, he could get to know which households in the village had run out of either foodstuff or faggot as fuel for cooking and therefore must be now bogged down in starvation. Then he would hurry to procure help to them. As there was no hotel or inn in any village in Lankao, he had to eat meals given him by villagers when he had to stay in a village for a fairly long time. But he did not choose to eat a meal at a table with the household. Having got whatever foodstuff given him, he would stroll outdoors with his meal in hand to some cowshed or any place where he could get in touch with various individuals in the village. This is usually the way he ate a meal in a village. He desired to gather more information from a wide range of people he could manage to get in touch with, because he wanted to know about the truth and be pragmatic.

3. From Jiao Yulu a government functionary can learn how to suppress egoism and keep his hands clean.

Jiao did not allow his daughter to be appointed to a lucrative and snug post in a government office, because he did not want any of his kin to avail himself or herself of his position as top leader of the county. He ordered her to seek employment elsewhere on her own. Finally she got a job with a mill producing assorted pickles. Although Jiao is now no more, Lankao people can never forget him. His honesty and selflessness serve to illustrate a plain, honest communist's outlook on life and teach all the government functionaries how they should act to fulfill their official duties. A functionary who would live and work for the people in the way in which Jiao Yulu did is bound to be honored and trusted not only by the Central Government but by the whole nation. Nowadays corruption is a cancer sweeping across the international community and has posed to it a challenge. In China radical measures have been taken by the Central Government to extirpate embezzlement and graft since

部，在中国逐步形成不敢腐、不能腐、不想腐的有效机制，这一系列举动得到了中国人民的支持和世界各国的赞誉。

4. 学习焦裕禄精神的主阵地——焦裕禄干部学院

为了能让公职人员集中、有序、系统、专业地接受教育，更好地发挥焦裕禄的榜样引领作用，政府创办了焦裕禄干部学院。焦裕禄干部学院于2013年7月建成，8月开班运行。学院位于兰考县城东北部，一、二期共占地310亩，总建筑面积8.8万平方米，主要包括学术中心、报告厅、教学楼、剧场、行政楼、宿舍楼、餐厅及其他附属设施，可同时容纳700人住宿、1000人培训学习。培训时长3—10天不等，开设有课堂教学、现场教学、音视频教学、互动教学、体验教学、廉政教学等。学院建成6年来，已承接各地各级各类培训团队近3000个，培训学员超过16万人次。

焦裕禄干部学院正门
The front view of the academy's campus

President Xi Jinping was at the helm of the state. Procedural loopholes have been systematically unearthed and mended. The Central Committee of the Communist Party of China has proclaimed in a row the eight-point decision on improving Party and government conduct, the "Rules Governing Inner-Party Supervision", and the "Rules Governing Disciplinary Procedures". Then "Law of Supervision" was proclaimed by the National Congress of People's Representatives. Consequently, the latest fad with the nationwide officialdom in China for erecting chic and exquisite halls, guesthouses, memorials has been checked. Various forms of encroachment upon government funds or public funds have been uncovered, liquidated or repaid. An unusually large number of both embezzlers and grafters, large or petty, have so far been called to account and severely punished. Then the CPC Central Committee has recently come forth to give to the officialdom in China the clarion call that all of them should model themselves faithfully on Jiao Yulu, so that they can be expected to become truly free of corruption, selfishness, and arrogance. Now the officialdom in China is experiencing a transformation which has the magical power of first making the officialdom definitely scared of flirting with embezzlement or graft, then turning it completely imbecile in the face of an embezzler or grafter, and finally cultivating in it an ingrained resentment against an embezzler or grafter. What the Communist Party of China is doing to guillotine corruption in China is acclaimed and supported by the Chinese people and applauded by the international community.

4. "Jiao Yulu Executive Leadership Academy", the principal venue which is particularly favorable to fulfilling the craving for learning about Jiao Yulu

Jiao Yulu Executive Leadership Academy is an educational institution financed by the government. Its objective consists in popularizing to the greatest extent Jiao Yulu's moral influence and in providing government functionaries in China with the optimal circumstances where they can receive an ethical instruction that is systematic, intensive and professional. And what is unique with the academy is that the ethical instruction it offers is devised on the basis of Jiao Yulu's morality. According to the "Constructional Project Formulated for Jiao Yulu Executive Leadership Academy", completion of the project needs to undergo three stages. So far two stages have been completed. The second stage was completed in July 2013. In August the same year the academy was put into operation, even though the third stage has not been completed so far. Located in the northeastern part of Lankao, the academy's floor

学员在焦裕禄干部学院教室学习

A class is seen in progress in the academy.

area is, when its third stage of construction is completed, to be 88,000 square meters. On the campus, after the academy has completed its third stage of construction, there will be academic centers, lecture halls, teaching buildings, theaters, office buildings, dormitories, canteens and accessary facilities. The academy's residential capacity is for accommodating 700 trainees. The capacity of its teaching buildings is for taking in 1,000 trainees. Duration of its regular training can last for 3 to 10 days. The types of training or teaching it can now provide include classroom teaching, on-site teaching, teaching using audiovisual aids, interactive teaching, a learning-through-practicing way of teaching, and teaching focusing on the subject of how to defeat corruption. In the last six years the academy has received around 3,000 teams of trainees whose number is over 160,000 person-times.

5. "Jiao Yulu Spirit is definitely going to be universally permeating.

Positive deeds that are of tremendous historic significance leave behind them, as a rule, eternally indelible memories and influence. A spirit or personality that is a splendid and specific manifestation of noble-mindedness is naturally guaranteed safe conduct into or out of any country in the world. Reports of myriads of manifestations of noble-mindedness of Jiao Yulu started to gush out of Henan Province and permeated the entirety of China after his demise. Then from China they have been now circulating through the world. In 1966, after having gone through the news report "Jiao Yulu, the Paragon of All Secretaries of CPC County Committee in China", Ho Chi Minh, president of the People's Republic of Vietnam, was deeply moved. At that time President Ho Chi Minh who was already seventy-six, promptly composed — availing himself of his nom de plume "Linong" — an article bearing the title "The Experience People's China Has Attained" which was carried by *People's Newspaper* in Vietnam. In his article President Ho Chi Minh describes admiringly and respectfully Jiao Yulu as a specimen of millions of exemplary cadres successfully trained by Chairman Mao Zedong and CPC. Jiao Yulu was exemplary, so President Ho Chi Minh conceived, as a secretary of a CPC county committee, who devoted himself wholeheartedly to serving the people. In fulfilling his official duty as secretary of CPC Lankao County Committee, he worked selflessly, bravely, and judiciously, did his utmost to carry on his missions frugally, and was constantly amiable and kindhearted. He was capable and resourceful, so that he could successfully lead the local people to eradicate the three banes of waterlogging, sandstorm coupled

大学生在"焦桐"下学习

A training class for university students is seen in progress at a venue surrounded by clusters of paulownia trees.

5. 焦裕禄精神走向世界

先进事迹世代相传，伟大精神跨越国界。焦裕禄去世后，他的事迹从河南传到全国，又从全国传到世界各地。1966年，76岁的越南民主共和国主席胡志明读到《县委书记的榜样——焦裕禄》一文后，深受感动，随后以"黎农"为笔名，在越南《人民报》上发表了题为《中国经验》的文章，赞扬焦裕禄是中国共产党和毛泽东主席教育出来的成千上万出色干部之一，是模范县委书记，在担任兰考县委书记期间，以共产党人克勤克俭、不怕艰苦、不图名利、全心全意为党和人民服务的品德，领导群众制服风沙、内涝、盐碱三害。他还总结了焦裕禄的四种精神，号召越南干部学习焦裕禄。

据记载，焦裕禄的事迹被报道后，先后有新西兰、日本、几内亚、印度、老挝、柬埔寨、苏联等国家的大使、官员、记者、民间人士来兰考参观考察。1968年，越南驻华大使馆率团来到兰考，参观焦裕禄同志

with drifting dunes, and saline-alkaline land. In his article President Ho Chi Minh called upon all cadres in Vietnam to strive hard to learn from all Jiao Yulu's virtuous qualities.

It has been reported that ever since the amazing profusion of press reports on Jiao Yulu's life and career was transmitted worldwide, there has been a continual and unabated stream, from all over the world, of visitors to Lankao. Among them were ambassadors, government officials, reporters and individuals. They hailed from countries such as New Zealand, Japan, New Guinea, India, Laos, Cambodia, the Soviet Union. In 1968, a deputation sent by the Vietnamese Embassy in China and headed by the Vietnamese ambassador in China visited Lankao. It came to see Jiao Yulu Memorial Hall and paid homage to Martyr Jiao Yulu's Grave and to the monument erected in his honor, being bent on imbibing the moral heritage left behind by Jiao Yulu. The deputation made a point of looking in on Jiao Yulu's wife and offspring.

Ms. Shirley Wood, is one of the visitors to Lankao from the United States. She graduated from Michigan State Agricultural College. After coming to China and working as a teacher at Henan University, she went to visit Lankao and was moved with admiration and awe at Jiao's life and career. Thenceforth twice she induced her mother to pay visit to Lankao. At that time her mother was a member of the standing committee of World Peace Council. After the visits her mother wrote an article enumerating her reflections on Jiao Yulu's ingrained humanistic approach to the populace. Moreover, she took a large number of pictures of Jiao's life and career. Later she sent both her article and the pictures to the standing committee of World Peace Council.

With the initiation in China of Reform and of the move to unseal the door previously closed to the outside world, impediments to travel into or out of, or within China have been steadily done away with. Of course, this has helped trigger off an unending flow to Lankao of individuals, government officials, scholars and students from all over the world. In 2016, an assemblage of diverse overseas Chinese who, numbering fifty in all, lived respectively in twenty-three countries (such as USA, Singapore, Australia, Switzerland) proceeded to Lankao where these overseas Chinese addressed themselves to observing, studying and soaking up inspiration their expedition to Lankao offered them. Generally speaking, they were tellingly touched.

1968年夏越南代表团参观焦裕禄纪念馆
A delegation from Vietnam is seen visiting Jiao Yulu Memorial Hall.

越南驻华大使和焦裕禄的家人
In the photo are shown Vietnamese ambassador to China and members of Jiao Yulu's family.

Mr. Cui Shijie, an overseas Chinese living in Singapore, said rather bluntly, "Jiao's life and career is inconceivably uplifting though heartrending and should be reckoned part of the spiritual and moral wealth peculiar to the Chinese nation. All the leading government officials in mainland China ought to be herded to Lankao to see in person all that the place is to show them, so that they can be prodded to discard that portion of their outlooks, which has already stagnated into mental detritus. They should let themselves be obsessed with the sincere concern for the wellbeing of the local population. A secretary of a CPC county committee or an administrative head of a county carries an astounding lot of clout endowed to him or her by the Central Government on behalf of the Chinese nation. Thus, he or she is let to possess the marvelous magic of wielding the totality of resources in the county, the governance of which he or she is entrusted with. What is he or she going to do with the magic? Is he or she going to turn the totality of local resources into a lever to boost the living standard of the local people? To improve the local infrastructure? Or, to prop up local reconstruction? Don't let your tenure of office be warped into a self-wrought curse to blight or disgrace your official career or life. Do everything utterly in the interest of the local population, and they will never let your name slip from their reminiscence."

Ancestry of Mr. Hu Changqiao, an overseas Chinese now living in California, was native to Kaifeng, Henan. In his childhood he was frequently taken to Lankao. This time he was very favorably impressed with what he saw in Lankao and feelingly gave the following comment, "This time I notice in Lankao all the avenues, streets and alleys have been broadened. Sightly buildings and apartments are everywhere, presenting a winsome urban scene. I believe Jiao Yulu spirit is at bottom of all these transformations. New factories are booming. Modern residential quarters are mushrooming. Urban traffic facilities are redoubling. Development in present-day Lankao is more than amazing. However scrupulously have I this time applied myself to tracing the vestige of old Lankao, but failed to find out any. At least it is so in the urban area. I know such a brilliant metamorphosis as Lankao has experienced is solely indebted to Jiao Yulu spirit. The Lankao people are ambitious and daring and have now convinced the world that their aspirations were not at all hollow brouhaha in the face of macabre natural disasters and deadly ecological environment. And the aspirations of the local people have all successfully turned into reality."

Zheng Xitao, an American of Chinese extraction, was a member of the

纪念馆，拜谒焦裕禄烈士墓和遗像，学习焦裕禄的事迹和精神，并看望了焦裕禄的夫人和子女。在来兰考参观的外国友人中，还有一位原籍美国的吴雪莉女士，她毕业于美密歇根州立农学院，到河南大学任教后，她专程到兰考参观，被焦裕禄的事迹所感动，遂两次邀请其母亲——时任世界和平理事会委员，来兰考参观。吴雪莉的母亲参观后，写了一篇学习感想，拍摄了与焦裕禄相关的照片，发往自己工作的世界和平理事会。

改革开放后，交通条件日益便利，来兰考学习考察的国外友人、政府官员、留学生络绎不绝。2016年，一个来自美国、新加坡、澳大利亚、瑞士等23个国家和地区的50名海外侨胞考察团走进了兰考。在参观学习、实地考察后，他们深受震动。

来自新加坡的华人崔世杰坦言："太感动了，这是我们全体华人的财富，我们现在所有的领导干部都应该到兰考来看一看，转变自己的观念，要想着老百姓。一个县的县委书记、县长，国家和人民给了你这个权力，等于把这个资源全给了你，让你来执掌这一个地方的时候，你能为老百姓做什么，为老百姓想一想，怎么样改善老百姓的生活，怎么样把这个地区给搞好，你为官一任，你就要做出你的成绩来，老百姓会记得你的。"

另一位祖籍河南开封、年幼时常来兰考的美国加州华人胡长桥感慨道："这次回来后看到兰考的路也变宽了、房子也变漂亮了，正是焦裕禄精神鼓舞了兰考人民。从工厂的建设，还有老百姓的住房，以及道路的建设，都大大提高，我到兰考以后已经认不出来了，这都是焦裕禄书记的精神鼓舞着兰考人民。过去我们都说，兰考人民多奇志，敢教日月换新天，确确实实这一点已经做到了，以前所喊的口号，现在我看确实已经换了新天。"

在焦裕禄同志亲手种植的泡桐前，美国华人郑西涛不禁眼圈泛红，他告诉记者："今天最大的收获就是对"老百姓"这三个字有了更深一

assemblage, referred to above, of diverse overseas Chinese who came to visit Lankao in 2016. On the occasion he walked to the paulownia tree — fondly called "Dear Jiao's Paulownia" by the local people — which was planted by Jiao Yulu with his own hands, he could not help lapsing into a lachrymose mood and getting pink-eyed. And in an aside to a reporter, he said, "The most significant piece of knowledge I have acquired today is the full and final dimensions of the purport conveyed by the Chinese term 'lao bai xing'. The unfailing central concern of Jiao Yulu, as secretary of CPC Lankao County Committee, was nothing but the issue of how the impoverished get on with their everyday life. It is only such a cadre as is motivated with the same moral leverage as that Jiao was motivated with who can be impeccably dubbed a qualified cadre. And it is only a qualified cadre who can induce the people to loyally rally to the Communist Party of China. I reckon I can fully grasp the motive of the CPC Central Committee in consistently calling upon all the communists in China to concentrate on improving everyday life of the impoverished. Incessant acquisition of improvement in everyday life is precisely the most intense concern of all the ordinary people of a nation."

Around 300 elite statesmen and diplomats from more than thirty countries came to Lankao in June 2019. They were there to see for themselves how Lankao underwent the radical change and what was at its bottom. Their activities there were densely studded with spontaneous symposia serving as venues for these guests to compare notes and come up with consensus. Simplice Mathieu Sarandji, executive secretary of Mouvement Coeurs Unis and ex-premier of the Central African Republic, commented, "It is incumbent upon a political party to cement and strengthen a next-of-kin tie with the people in its country. In order to provide the populace with adequate opportunities for equally sharing all the gains of development in China, it is of vital importance for CPC to inculcate all its members with an initiative in upholding the basic interests of the populace above anything else."

"CPC has been very successful," so commented Samphanh Phengkhammy, member of the Central Committee of the Lao People's Revolutionary Party and vice-chairman of the Laotian Parliament, "in speeding up the fortification of its ideological and political fabric. To attain such a goal, the strategy adopted by CPC is characterized by a wonderful dovetailing the party's sturdy efforts at enlightening the

层的认识。焦裕禄每天关心的是最穷的老百姓的吃和穿，所以这样的干部才是真正的干部，才能真正得人心，我觉得这就是为什么现在中央一直提这个，多少代都提这个，这才是老百姓的福祉。"

2019年6月，30多个国家近300名国外政党领导人与代表来到兰考，实地考察交流后，代表们感触颇多，产生共鸣。中非团结一心运动全国执行书记、前政府总理萨兰吉·桑普利斯·马蒂尔说："政党应该与人民保持血肉联系。为了实现让基层人民共享发展成果的目标，教育党员干部是有高度重要性的。"在老挝人民革命党中央委员、国会副主席宋潘·平坎米看来，中国共产党"打开大门搞党建，把主题教育和对外宣介相结合"的做法极具"创造性"，而其中关注的"清正廉洁"对一个政党有生死存亡的意义。

二、鼓舞了广大群众，自力更生实现了农业丰收

历史上，兰考地处黄泛区，自然条件极其恶劣。只要黄河涨水，就会引发洪涝灾害。退水之后，黄河水携带的泥沙冲积过的区域，会逐渐成为盐碱地。春夏之交风大的时候，黄沙漫天飞舞，严重的时候会破坏庄稼。这就是兰考内涝、风沙、盐碱"三害"的形成过程。

1. 焦裕禄带领群众开展生产自救

初到兰考的焦裕禄看到兰考群众风雪之中拖家带口外出逃荒。当时全国都处在困难时期，兰考要改变现状，单依靠国家救济是不行的，必须自力更生。面对内涝、风沙、盐碱"三害"，焦裕禄没有退缩害怕，而是向大自然宣战。他知道一个人的力量是有限的，便号召班子成员和政府干部迎难而上，依靠群众、发动群众，同自然灾害进行顽强斗争，努力改变兰考贫困面貌。

Chinese people and the party's vigorous efforts at providing the world with enough information about the recent domestic development in China. The strategy should be rated a work of genius, as it sophisticatedly enshrining the virtue of 'ingrained indifference to personal pecuniary gain'— a virtue on which the survival of a political party hinges."

II. The moral bequest left behind by Jiao is blossoming in Lankao.

In the past century Lankao was geographically included in an inundation-prone region in China. The region generally went by the name of "the Yellow River inundation region". It was a natural-calamity-prone zone with very inclement climate. Whenever there was a flood coursing through the Yellow River, Lankao was bound to suffer either from inundation or from waterlogging. After a flood left Lankao, the alluvium left behind by the floodwater was the best generator of saline or alkaline top soil to spoil the fertility of arable land. In days between spring and summer in a year the gale-force wind was simply lethal. It could sweep the sand skyward to blur visibility in daytime and stifle the crops. Lankao was endowed with the three banes: waterlogging, sandstorm coupled with drifting dunes, and saline-alkaline land.

1. How Jiao led the Lankao people to snatch a bumper harvest in 1963 from the jaws of natural disasters without recourse to any help or relief from the outside world.

From 1961 to 1963, China's national economy was at its lowest ebb since the foundation of the People's Republic. It is in 1963 that Jiao was appointed to the post of secretary of the CPC Lankao County Committee. Shortly after he took office in Lankao, he was shocked by the massive exodus of Lankao natives from their homeland to seek survival elsewhere than their birthplace. But his intuitive understanding told him that as China's national economy was at that time even worse than in bad shape, it was out of the question that securing the survival of Lankao population could depend on any help from some quarters beyond Lankao. The possibility of Lankao's survival could rest solely with the inconceivably strenuous endeavor on the part of the Lankao population. And he knew that! He knew there was absolutely

焦裕禄关于发展农业、渡荒救灾的讲话
This is a photocopy of the printed text of a speech delivered by Jiao Yulu. The speech dwells on issues in relation to development of agricultural economy, control of natural calamity, and government relief to disaster areas.

　　经过艰苦的调查、测量和实践，他们采取了植树造林、翻淤压沙、广修水渠、排涝泄洪等一系列措施。与此同时，鼓励群众发挥主观能动性，发展牲畜养殖和粮食种植。当时，兰考县韩村只有27户村民。1962年秋天，因遭受了涝灾，每人只分到不到一斤的红高粱穗。在全县开展生产自救的带动下，群众说，"摇钱树，人人有，全靠自己一双手"，提出不要国家救济，靠割草卖草养活自己。这年冬天，他们割了27万斤草，养活了全体社员，养活了8头牲口，买了7辆架子车。焦裕禄得知后，号召全县向他们学习，学习"韩村的精神"。

　　在焦裕禄的带领下，在干部群众的共同努力下，兰考县治"三害"工作成效显著。在他去世后的一年时间里，兰考人民"挥泪继承壮士志"，齐心协力，把三年前焦裕禄倡导制订的改造兰考大自然的蓝图变成了现实。历史上一直缺粮的兰考，于1965年实现了粮食自给。全县2574个生产队，除300来个队是棉花、油料产区外，其余的全部有了自己的储备粮。

no alternative left to the Lankao people but to hope against hope that a desperate fight might extricate them from the impasse. Therefore, Jiao was not daunted by the three banes, facing them without flinching. He knew it was idiotic to plunge into the battle single-handedly. Therefore, he had, first of all, to have both all members of the CPC Lankao County Committee and all the government functionaries working in Lankao rally firmly around him. It is only with the wholehearted backup from all his colleagues that he could go forward to mobilize the local population to engage in the campaign aimed at changing Lankao's fate. In due course, his preliminary efforts aimed at forging tenacious solidarity among Lankao inhabitants and functionaries carried the day.

Thenceforward he focused his attention on the practical jobs of pushing ahead with investigation, in-depth study, formulation of plans, and experimentations until the time when the local population saw it fit to start extensive afforestation, carry on blanketing dunes in silt, and build a neat network of watercourses for draining stagnant floodwater. With all these stupendous achievements, they did not at all feel gratified, so they sought to develop animal husbandry and raise the quality and quantity of grain production. In autumn 1962, only 27 households kept staying put in Hancun village in Lankao without attempting to flee to the outside world for seeking livelihood. At the end of that year, the dole given to each person of the 27 households in the village was only less than 0.5 kilogram of red sorghum ears, thanks to the deadly waterlogging that had killed all the crops grown in the village. However, villagers of Hancun won their survival all on their own in 1963. They said proudly, "Nobody is literally resourceless, so long as he has hands and brains." They opted for in 1963 cutting green vegetation and preserving it as fodder which could be sold in the next spring to cattle raisers in neighboring counties. In winter of 1963, they reaped 135,000 kilograms of vegetation, which were all well preserved and sold in spring next year. The money from the sale was more than enough for buying food to ensure the survival of all villagers of Hancun. They used a little portion of the money to buy seven handcarts. Moreover, they also ensured the survival of eight oxen in their village. They confidently announced that they needed no relief from any quarters. On learning the acts of real heroism displayed by Hancun villagers, Jiao Yulu promptly and warmly acclaimed them and called upon all Lankao population to follow Hancun villagers' heroic acts.

兰考县东坝头乡黄河滩区万亩麦田

A glimpse of the 10,000 *mu* of wheat field in the vicinity of Dongbatou village in Lankao. The village is situated on a long stretch of beach land along the Yellow River.

兰考县小宋乡东邵岗一村初具规模的蔬菜种植大棚

In an expanse of level field in Xiaosong village in Lankao, a vegetable husbandry set-up is seen taking shape. In each oblong plot with plastic sheeting shelter is grown vegetable for marketing.

Marvelous achievements had been made by the Lankao people in their campaign to conquer the three banes. The success is indebted to the fruitful and powerful cooperation between the local people and government officials under the leadership of Jiao Yulu. In the year following his demise, Lankao people continued to make concerted effort to put into effect the program which had been endorsed and recommended by Jiao Yulu three years earlier and which was intended for changing Lankao's environment and climate for the better. Until 1964, Lankao had been suffering food shortage. But the county no longer experienced food shortage in 1965. At that time, there were altogether 2,574 farming teams in the county. Around 300 teams were engaged in growing cotton and oil crops. The majority of the 2,574 farming teams were unanimously engaged in growing grains and each of them had already established its own grain depot exclusively for storing its grain reserve.

2. Agriculture in the present-day Lankao

Now under the jurisdiction of Lankao County Administration, there are 6 villages, 7 towns, 3 avenue communities, and 454 rural communities with a population totaling 850,000. The county measures 1116.2 square kilometers, of which the arable land measures 785.8 square kilometers. The county's total grain output for 2018 was 569,000 tons. There are altogether six categories of "agrarian-produce base" established now in Lankao, and the six categories are wheat, corn, paddy rice, peanut, cotton, vegetable. Lankao has now been registered among China's top one hundred grain-producing counties and among China's top one hundred oil-crops-producing counties on the strength of both its high grain output and its high oil-crops output. Lankao has now been cited by the Central Government as "one of China's bases for marketable grain production". In 2018, over 10,000 *mu* of arable land in the county were used for growing honeydew melon, and 40,000 *mu* for growing sweet potato, and 150,000 *mu* for growing quality peanut, 10,000 *mu* for developing economic forest. Now in developing animal husbandry in Lankao, efforts have been stepped up to establish the so-called "5 + 1 set-up" which encompasses the breeding of chicken, duck, cattle, sheep, and donkey with the production of forage grass in tow. Besides, in Lankao are now rapidly developing such trades as private farm, rural professional cooperative.

2. 兰考县当前农业发展情况

目前，兰考县辖6个乡、7个镇、3个街道、454个行政村（社区），总人口85万，总面积1116.2平方公里，其中耕地面积785.8平方公里。2018年，全年粮食总产量56.9万吨。种植业方面，建有小麦、玉米、水稻、花生、棉花、蔬菜六大农产品生产基地，其中粮食、花生、油料产量居全国百强，是全国商品粮基地县。2018年，新发展蜜瓜1万多亩、红薯4万多亩、优质花生15万亩、经济林1万亩。养殖业方面，着力打造鸡、鸭、牛、羊、驴和饲草"5+1"产业体系。与此同时，家庭农场、农民专业合作社发展势头迅猛。

三、带动了文化旅游，引领了文化观光基地集群

50多年后，兰考今非昔比。如今的兰考是绿色的海洋，良田万顷，绿树成荫。近年来，兰考坚持每年植树1000万棵，全面推进环城绿化、

兰考泡桐花盛开的季节
Blooming paulownia trees are lending glamor and glory to Lankao.

III. Development of cultural undertakings and tourism and creation of a series of cultural-touristic interests in Lankao

The present-day Lankao is diametrically different from the Lankao that existed more than five decades earlier. The former is now bobbing gently about in a sea of green foliage, surrounded by an expansive periphery of green and lush fields studded with cluster of forests. Each year of the last decade saw more than 10,000,000 trees added to Lankao's numerous forests. The endeavor to develop an afforestation for encircling the entire county is in full swing. Also in progress are such endeavors as developing ecological afforestation and special economic forest along thoroughfares and watercourses. This is to give Lankao an extra afforestation measuring 78,300 *mu* in all. Completion of all these afforestation programs can offer to Lankao an arboreal coverage, the size of which is 30.15% of the total size of Lankao. When the time comes that Lankao has attained such an arboreal coverage, the county will be registered as "one of China's landscaped counties" and ranked among Henan's arboreally-superior counties. Now the short spell overlapping spring and summer in a year can witness a riot of pink and purple that is bred of paulownia blooms — a riot of colors that glamorizes and mystifies Lankao.

Lankao receives annually tens of thousands of visitors from all over the world now. They are here for visiting Jiao Yulu Memorial Hall, because they want to see with their own eyes what he achieved in his lifetime and intuitively feel the magic of his morality. Over three million visitors came to Lankao in 2017 to initiate for the county a mammoth billow of cultural tourism which pivoting on disseminating the quintessence of Jiao's personality and outlook on life. The interests serving to prop up the cultural tour include "Jiao Yulu Memorial Park", "Dear Jiao's Paulownia", "the Yellow River Scenic Zone", "Zhangzhuang village", "Lankao Cultural Exchange Center", and "A Venue Which Helps You Understand Jiao Better by Enabling You to Do What He Actually Did in His Life". Now in Lankao has forged a chain of touristic industry which consists of the following links: (1) cultural sightseeing, (2) program of "professional-ethics education for government functionaries", (3) industrial demonstration and emulation, and (4) folk culture.

1. Jiao Yulu Memorial Park

The park, roughly 91.7 *mu* in size, is situated on a dune, which is to the north of

廊道、河道生态林及特色经济林建设，完成绿化面积7.83万亩，使得兰考林木覆盖率达到30.15%，被评为国家园林县城，被纳入省级森林城市序列。当年焦裕禄领着兰考人民种植的防风固沙的泡桐林，春夏之交，粉紫色的花盛开，已成为兰考最美最浪漫的风景。

现在，每年都有成千上万的人从世界各地慕名而来，参观焦裕禄同志纪念馆，感悟焦裕禄精神的魅力。仅2017年就有300多万人来兰考参观，兰考迎来了红色文化旅游的春天。以宣传焦裕禄精神为核心，依托焦裕禄纪念园、焦桐、黄河、张庄、兰考县文化交流中心、焦裕禄精神体验教育基地等一系列文化旅游观光基地，兰考形成了由参观旅游、干部教育、产业观摩、民俗文化等组成的旅游产业链。

1. 焦裕禄纪念园

焦裕禄纪念园位于兰考县城北黄河故堤沙丘上，占地面积91.7亩，由

焦裕禄烈士墓
Martyr Jiao Yulu's Grave

the urban area of Lankao and forms part of the embankment to an ancient channel of the Yellow River. In the park are "Martyr Jiao Yulu's Grave", "Jiao Yulu Memorial Hall", "Monument to the Revolutionary Martyr", and "Dear Jiao's Paulownia". The construction of the grave was actually completed in 1966. Renovation has been done twice to the grave which is now placed under state protection as one of China's key cultural relics and has been designated as one of the key bases in China for educating people in patriotism. Built of white marble, the grave has a marble monument erected on its altar. On the monument is an inscription, which reads "Martyr Jiao Yulu's Grave". A stone wall stands at the rear of the grave. On the wall is an inlaid golden inscription which reads, "A Life Given up in the Interest of the People Is a Life Eternally Glorified. Mao Zedong". The inscription is in Mao Zedong's hand.

Construction of Jiao Yulu Memorial Hall, which measures 2,100 square meters and is a three-storied structure, was completed in April 1994. Affixed to the museum's wall is a plate bearing its name, which consists of eight Chinese characters and is done in Jiang Zemin's handwriting.

Monument to the Revolutionary Martyr, which was erected in May 1993, is 19.64 meters tall, bears an inscription in Mao Zedong's handwriting. The inscription reads "A revolutionary martyr is immortal". The figure "19.64", as used here to designate the length of the monument measured in meters, is actually meant to signify the year 1964, in which Jiao Yulu passed away. Party and state leaders such as Jiang Zemin, Hu Jintao, Xi Jinping came to visit Jiao Yulu Memorial Park. At a series of important conferences, President Xi Jinping stressed that Jiao Yulu's ethics should be observed as moral norm for our people and that every government functionary should strive to emulate him and repeatedly check his or her morality against Jiao Yulu's. Given the prevalent political ambience in China, which is laden with an enthusiasm for expediting nationwide economic and political reform, government functionaries in every part of China desire to come to Lankao for learning more about Jiao Yulu and drawing from his life and achievements inspiration that can provide them with political revitalization. Visitors from all over the world are, like the Chinese people, intrigued by Jiao Yulu's life and career and eager to come to China to more deeply understand what Jiao Yulu's ethics are like.

2. Dear Jiao's Paulownia

In the middle of March 1963, when Jiao was doing physical labor, together

焦裕禄烈士墓、焦裕禄同志纪念馆、革命烈士纪念碑和焦桐林组成。其中，焦裕禄烈士墓始建于1966年，之后两次重修，是国家重点文物保护单位、全国爱国主义教育基地。墓体由汉白玉砌成，墓前竖立有"焦裕禄烈士之墓"大理石碑，墓后屏风上刻有毛泽东题写的"为人民而死 虽死犹荣"。焦裕禄同志纪念馆于1994年4月建成，建筑面积2100平方米，上下三层，馆名为江泽民题写。革命烈士纪念碑于1993年5月建成，碑高19.64米（纪念焦裕禄同志1964年逝世），碑体正面镌刻着毛泽东书写的"革命烈士永垂不朽"。党和国家领导人江泽民、胡锦涛等都曾亲临纪念园瞻仰拜谒。特别是国家主席习近平，多次在重要会议上强调，要以焦裕禄精神为标杆，见贤思齐，反复镜鉴。在此影响下，中国各地区各层级的干部组团前来学习，接受教育，也吸引了其他几十个国家和地区的代表团来此寻找中国这位县委书记身上独特的魅力。

2. 焦桐

焦桐——焦裕禄当年亲手种下的泡桐树
In the middle of the photo stands Dear Jiao's Paulownia. The tree has grown out of a paulownia sapling which Jiao Yulu planted with his own hands.

with a crowd, in the field, he planted with his own hands a paulownia sapling. Later the sapling shot up vigorously. After he passed away, the local people fondly gave the sapling a pet name "Dear Jiao's Paulownia" as a way for honoring his memory. And the pet name sticks. Now the sapling has grown into a towering tree measuring 24.6 meters in height. Its maximum girth is roughly 5 meters, which can be barely enclosed by three adults with their stretched arms linked together. Now the tree is looked upon as a sacred image of Jiao Yulu's morality and also as a totem of the supreme verve unique to the Lankao population.

3. Zhangzhuang village

There are, in the river channel of the Yellow River, nine bends as the river flows eastward into the sea. The village is four kilometers to the east of the last bend in the river channel of the Yellow River. Once the village was the severest "wind gap" through which gale-force wind stormed into the interior of Lankao. The village sat entirely on dunes. It is the very place where Jiao Yulu discovered and finally confirmed the validity of the method feasible for fighting the three banes. After years of strenuous application of the method to blanketing dunes in silt, the village is now completely devoid of dune. All arable land in the village is richly fertile, rather than saline or alkaline. On March 17, 2014, Xi Jinping carried out an official inspection in the village and asked the leaders in charge of administrative duty there to pay special attention to helping the impoverished families in the village and to start in the village such kinds of farming or husbandry as were most compatible with the village's actualities, so that villagers' income could be enhanced appreciably. Thus villagers in Zhangzhuang began to concentrate on developing the industry of tourism in rural areas and also on developing animal husbandry by taking advantage of the "anti-poverty loan" granted to the village by authorities concerned. At the end of 2016, the village economy of Zhangzhuang was officially recognized as "having got rid of even the least tendency towards impoverishment". Recently the village has succeeded in securing the investment from Aojite Biotechnology Co., Ltd. (which is a listed company) to build a factory in the village. Besides, having been also built in the village are (1) a grand museum bearing the name of "Four Red Flags Museum", (2) a training center for rural cadres, and (3) a restaurant bearing the name of "Zhangzhuang in My Dream", not to say such a tourist set-up as "Pastoral Relaxation". All these developments contribute immensely to the village's economy.

焦桐是焦裕禄在1963年3月中旬带领群众治理风沙灾害时亲手栽下的一棵泡桐树。兰考人民亲切地称它为"焦桐",以寄托对焦裕禄的怀念之情。如今,这棵树已经长成一棵参天大树,树高24.6米,树围约5米,三个成年人伸开双臂才能勉强合抱一圈。这棵树成了焦裕禄精神的象征,成了兰考人民神圣的精神图腾。

3. 张庄村

张庄村位于"九曲黄河"最后一弯东4公里处。这里曾是兰考最大的风口,沙丘遍布。这里也是焦裕禄找到治理风沙灾害办法并取得成功的地方。经过多年努力,这里的流沙地如今变成了肥沃的良田。2014年3月17日,习近平主席来这里调研指导工作,叮嘱当地干部要关心农村贫困家庭,因地制宜发展产业,促进农民增收。在张庄人的努力下,村里开

张庄村貌
A glimpse of Zhangzhuang village

Consequently the village has been repeatedly cited by authorities concerned as "a Civilized Village in China" and "One of Henan's Civilized Villages".

4. Lankao Cultural Exchange Center

The center, measuring 450 *mu* in size, sits in the northeastern portion of Lankao's urban area. Within its precincts are Lankao Exhibition Hall, Liu Xian Memorial Hall, and Jiao Lin Memorial Hall. Lankao Exhibition Hall is over 1,000 square meters in size. Accompanying all the exhibits on display are elaborate commentaries, captions, diagrams, pictures, and statistics. Everything is properly in place. High-tech audio-visual devices are employed for enhancing the impressiveness of the exhibition, so that Jiao Yulu's life, career, and instructive undertakings are very well highlighted. Visiting the demonstrative paulownia forest tends to implant a "nostalgia" in a visitor's mind — a "nostalgia" that would urge him (or her) to come back to the demonstrative forest again and again. The wild exuberance of foliage and florescence in the forest is an epitome of the paulownia-dominated landscape unique to Lankao.

5. The Yellow River Scenic Zone

The scenic zone runs alongside the Yellow River and is in Dongbatou village in Lankao. The tourist interests in the zone include: (1) "Memorial Pavilion to Chairman Mao Zedong" who came to this village once in 1952 when he conducted an official inspection tour along the Yellow River, (2) "a trip on board a train" — a small train which is pulled by a steam locomotive bearing the name "Mao Zedong Locomotive", (3) "houses lived in by Lankao inhabitants in the year 1952". Now the scenic zone has become the largest tourist venue in Lankao, which offers a very wide range of touristic interests.

The tourist train there takes its tourists to cruise a landscaped belt stretching five kilometers alongside the Yellow River.

"Houses lived in by Lankao inhabitants in the year 1952" is actually a very faithful reproduction of those houses which existed in the village in 1952 at the time when Chairman Mao conducted his inspection along the Yellow River. In the reproduction are preserved historical relics that are related to Chairman's inspection and the reproduction is supplemented with some decorative devices that tend to arouse in tourists an empathy with the original inhabitants who once occupied those houses.

The Yellow River Scenic Zone is complete with such services as lodging,

兰考四面红旗馆
A glimpse of Four Red Flags Museum

始发展乡村旅游，通过扶贫贷款干起了种植养殖。2016年底，张庄摘掉了贫困的帽子。目前，张庄村引进上市企业奥吉特生物科技股份有限公司，建成了四面红旗馆、农村干部培训中心、"梦里张庄"餐厅、农家乐等旅游观光项目，取得了良好的经济效益。张庄村先后获得了"全国文明村镇""河南省文明村"等荣誉称号。

4. 兰考县文化交流中心

兰考县文化交流中心位于县城东北，占地450亩，主要建筑有兰考县展览馆、刘岘纪念馆、焦林纪念馆等。兰考县展览馆建筑面积1000多平方米，通过翔实的文字、丰富的图片、科学系统的数据以及高科技的声光电技术，展示了焦裕禄的生平经历和感人故事。泡桐林观摩区里泡桐树

catering, conference hall. Tourists in the scenic zone may engage themselves in the following activities: RV camping, self-service barbecue, picnic, children's paradise, and theme photo exhibition.

6. A venue which helps you understand Jiao better by enabling you to do what he actually did in his life

The venue stands to the south of Zhangzhuang village. It is in the village that Jiao started experimenting for the first time with the method of "blanketing dunes in silt". Within the venue the original physiognomy of all the dunes is kept intact. Measuring 120 *mu* in size, the venue is divided into the following four enclosures: (1) " 'Do-what-Jiao-actually-did' enclosure", (2) " 'Do-what-Zhangzhuang-has-done' enclosure", (3) " 'Experiencing-the-activity-of-checking-up-a-wind-gap' enclosure", and (4) " 'Farming-related-culture' enclosure".

Primary activity unfolded in the 'Do-what-Jiao-actually-did' enclosure consists of organizing visitors to do the physical labor in the way Jiao did when he was alive in leading the then Lankao people to conquer the three banes. This is for enabling visitors to relive Jiao's feelings and empathize with him.

In the last few years, culturally-oriented tourism in Lankao has been faring so promisingly that it now plays the role of a pioneer in spearheading the county's economic development. The bastion of Lankao's culturally-oriented tourism is able not only to faithfully reproduce the real scenes and actualities in which Jiao struggled valiantly, perspicaciously, and tenaciously to repel the three banes but also to tangibly further swell the influence of Jiao Yulu's behavioral ethics in our age. Therefore, what the bastion of Lankao's culturally-oriented tourism is actually doing is having the county's cultural resources metamorphose into such an advantage as to lend impetus to the county's economic growth. Consequently socio-economic development in Lankao is accelerated. Moreover, the expansion of culturally-oriented tourism is rapidly providing the local population with more and more opportunities for them to get jobs that do not at all require them to quit their hometown.

IV. The emergence in Lankao of a brand-new and unique industry — the musical instrument industry

Jiao Yulu's own observation enlightened him even more than half a century ago,

兰考县文化交流中心
A glimpse of Lankao Cultural Exchange Center

毛主席视察黄河纪念亭
Memorial Pavilion to Chairman Mao Zedong

when conducting preliminary investigation into paulownia as a tree species, on the fact that growth of paulownia is impaired neither by saline or alkaline soil, nor by the gale-force wind and, moreover, improves the fertility of the land. Therefore, he strove to the utmost to afforest Lankao with paulownia. This brought about a significant improvement in the county's ecological environment and a remarkable development of the county's forest industry. After he passed away, Lankao people, having not for one day forgotten about what Jiao had called upon them to continue to strive for, succeeded in the 1980s in creating in the county both 684,000 *mu* of farm-crops-and-paulownia intercropping fields and 51,500 *mu* of agroforestry.

1. How the fact that the timber of paulownia grown in Lankao is an excellent good material for producing the soundboard used exclusively for manufacturing China's folk musical instrument came to light.

The rapid afforestation in Lankao of Paulownia has been promoting the extensive use of its timber. Thus, furniture and, later on, implements, such as bellows, were made of its timber. Still nobody had thought of using paulownia timber for manufacturing musical instrument until the occurrence of an accident.

It so happened that in the middle of 1980s Mr. Zhang Liangen who, being at that time working with Shanghai Folk Musical Instrument Factory, was a past master at manufacturing *pipa*, a Chinese folk musical instrument, came to visit Lankao and was hosted by a villager. As the villager's wife was cooking in the kitchen, she had to pull the bellows in the kitchen off and on. Mr. Zhang was astonished by the sounds emitting from the bellows because they were rather mellifluous. He was intrigued and wanted to know from the villager what kind of timber the bellows were made of and was told that they were made of timber of paulownia grown in Lankao — paulownia which wouldn't have been so extensively propagated in Lankao but for Jiao Yulu's influential promotion. Then Mr. Zhang said to his host, "I promise you the timber of paulownia's perfect for manufacturing soundboard to be used in a folk musical instrument." The host was first stirred and then resolved to find means for converting the paulownia timber into a musical instrument. From then on he traveled far and wide for seeking the proper way to realize his resolution to turn paulownia timber into an excellent material for making folk musical instrument. He invited from Shanghai Folk Musical Instrument Factory such personages as celebrated expert in the manufacturing of Chinese zither, technical consultants, to

黄河湾风景

A glimpse of the Yellow River Scenic Zone

郁郁葱葱，花草绽放，兰考县"泡桐之乡"的美誉名不虚传。

5. 黄河湾风景区

兰考黄河湾风景区紧邻黄河，位于兰考东坝头乡。风景区内有毛主席视察黄河纪念亭、"毛泽东号"蒸汽小火车、兰考1952民宿等，现已成为兰考最大的综合观光旅游区。蒸汽小火车专为游览观光打造，乘坐小火车能够欣赏沿途5公里黄河风景区。1952民宿在保留1952年毛主席视察黄河时原有历史遗迹的基础上增加了仿古感的内饰装潢，内有民宿、餐饮中心和会议中心。风景区内还有房车露营、自助烧烤、野炊、儿童乐园、主题照片展厅等。

come to Lankao to give him advice on how to best realize his resolution. Thus he pioneered the establishment of a factory that would focus on the use of paulownia timber for producing Chinese folk musical instrument. His name is Dai Shiyong, the first entrepreneur in Lankao who successfully pioneered the business, in Lankao, of making folk musical instrument with paulownia timber. The folk musical instrument factory he established at that time in Lankao was the largest of its kind in the county.

In 1992, Ministry of Light Industry arranged for a team of experts to conduct a survey which covered ten odd regions in China. With respect to Lankao, experts concerned have made the following comment, "Given that Lankao is situated across the ancient river channel of the Yellow River and overlaps the margin of the northern-China dry climate and that of the southern-China humid climate, and given that its soil is mainly saline, alkaline, and sandy, timber of paulownia tree grown in Lankao is characterized by its commendable textural density or porosity, tough resistance to distortion, good resonance and sound transmission, and good air permeability. There-fore, as the timber is excellent in acoustic quality, it is suitable to be used as material for making the soundboard of a folk musical instrument."

2. A survey of the present-day folk musical instrument industry in Lankao

The development of the industry in Lankao has been in progress for three decades. The entire population of Guyang, a town in Lankao, is now engaged in developing cultural undertakings, which include manufacturing folk musical instrument and producing and processing varieties of soundboard and various accessories used in folk musical instrument. There are in Guyang altogether 106 enterprises working in the line of cultural undertakings. Of the 106, 13 are appreciably large enterprises which provide more than ten thousand jobs to the local population. The annual total output of the 106 enterprises includes more than 400,000 pieces of folk musical instrument and more than 500,000 sets of soundboards and musical accessories. The annual total value from the production of the 106 enterprises is five hundred million *yuan* (rmb). In the folk-musical-instrument market in our country, the three brand names of "Hongyin", "Zhongzhou", and "Sanhao" are now officially recognized as outstanding trade names for folk musical instruments manufactured in Henan Province. The newly modified modulatory Chinese zither bearing the brand name of "Hongyin", which is on the market only recently, is a product with state patent. "Hongyin" is now developing

6. 焦裕禄精神体验教育基地

焦裕禄精神体验教育基地位于张庄村南,这里是当年焦裕禄翻淤压沙首个试验地。基地在保留当年沙丘风貌的基础上开发,占地120亩,包括焦裕禄精神体验教育区、张庄治沙体验区、查风口探流沙体验区、农耕文明体验区等。焦裕禄精神体验教育基地主要以实地参与的方式,让体验者感受焦裕禄书记当年带领兰考人民治理"三害"时战天斗地的革命精神,加深对焦裕禄精神的感悟和理解。

近年来,红色文化旅游观光产业已经成为兰考一个新的经济增长点。兰考县红色文化旅游观光基地群不仅再现了当年焦裕禄在兰考战天斗地的场景,也推动了焦裕禄精神在新时代的兰考发扬光大。文化资源优势转化为经济发展优势,推动了兰考经济社会的发展,带动了当地居民就地就近就业,增收致富。

学员在基地开展翻淤压沙体验劳动

Government staff are seen doing physical labor in the "Do-what-Jiao-actually-did" enclosure.

cooperation with "Dunhuang" (a brand name associated with an enterprise based in Shanghai), and other thirty-odd famous brand names such as "Longyin", "Junyi", "Huazhong", "Dahe", "Jiaotong", "Mingyun" in producing new varieties of folk musical instrument. Xuchang village, which functioned as origin of the industry of folk-musical-instrument in Guyang town, has now been officially cited by Henan Provincial Administration as "an exemplary pioneer not only in finding ways to fight off impoverishment" but also in rejuvenating the village economy by developing culturally-oriented tourism. By availing itself of the resource in the form of paulownia timber, Lankao has been developing its furniture-and-building-material industry and is now concentrating its effort on establishing a household industrial park which will be rated as the largest of its kind in Asia, when its construction is completed.

Now 90% of soundboard for folk musical instrument sold in all markets in China is manufactured in Lankao. The county is officially recognized as one of the four major producers in China of folk musical instrument. The Chinese zither, *pipa*, and *liuqin*("*Liuqin*" is the Chinese name for a Chinese folk musical instrument.) made of timber of paulownia grown in Lankao are famous not only in China but in other parts of the world. They have been exported to more than ten countries and regions including the United States of America, Canada, Malaysia, Singapore. Lankao people are grateful to Jiao Yulu, because he not only was successful in ridding the county of the natural disasters but also bequeathed to the county an inexhaustible green wealth in the form of paulownia. Now the dulcet music from instruments made of timber of paulownia grown in Lankao is resounding all over the world.

V. Lankao's success in poverty reduction encourages the rest of China to follow suit, and inspires the international community to strive to build a community with a shared future for mankind.

World history can vow to testify to the fact that the problem of how to cope with the scourge of impoverishment has been unfailingly riveting to itself intense attention of the entire human race. And the problem remains today, as it has ever been remaining thus far, the hardest nut to crack for mankind. Therefore, elimination of impoverishment constitutes the loftiest goal humanity hungers for. In the first

学员在基地参加活动
A joyous scene at an enclosure

四、做强了特色产业，助推兰考民族乐器走向世界

50多年前，焦裕禄调查"三害"时，发现泡桐具有耐盐碱、挡风压沙、改良土壤的作用，遂在全县大范围种植，改善了生态环境，推动了林业发展。几代兰考人在焦裕禄精神的感召下继续奋斗，20世纪80年代末期，全县农桐间作达到68.4万亩，农田林网5.15万亩。

1. 兰考泡桐适合做民族乐器音板的发现过程

随着泡桐树的大量种植，木材产量逐年增加，桐木也被做成风箱等很多产品使用。那么桐木可用于制作民族乐器的音板是如何被发现的呢？这里还有一个传奇的故事。

two decades following the establishment of the People's Republic of China, Chinese people, being still under the oppressive yoke of penury, toiled inconceivably hard in order to shed it. Now we see that our people are getting themselves adequately fed step by step and comfortably kitted out. Even before his death in 1964, Jiao Yulu had already seen Lankao rid itself of primary symptoms of poverty. The year 1978 saw China initiate her grand programs of reform and opening up. From then on, the Central Government has been carrying on projects that serve to systematically eradicate indigence on a large scale. Thus in a period of over three decades, more than seven hundred million rural population were unshackled from a hand-to-mouth existence. This is something, which cannot but astound the international community. What is particularly worth mentioning is the fact that having made a comprehensive and in-depth survey of China's actual conditions, the Central Government has put forward the first centenary goal, which focuses on "elimination of poverty from Chinese territory". To be specific, by the term "elimination of poverty" is actually meant the attainment of two objectives: (1) full effectuation of the plan for curbing impoverishment, and (2) full effectuation of the plan for irrevocable elimination of poverty and backwardness. Moreover, the Central Government has announced that "absolute impoverishment" must cease to exist in China from 2020 onwards and that no families in our country be not fairly well off from 2020 onwards.

1. How Lankao sloughed off its indigence.

Dilapidated thatched cottage was the primary form of habitation for the Lankao population over half a century ago. Of course, none of that sort of slum thing is still in sight there now. Lofty buildings and numerous neat and attractive apartment structures have densely populated the county. In the past, "Lankao" was synonymous with indigence for the people living in the eastern part of Henan. In 2002, Lankao was included by the Central Government in the list of the counties in China, which were eligible for receiving the most serious concern and the largest possible relief from authorities concerned. At that time, Lankao population was recorded at 850,000, of which 773,000 lived in the county's rural areas. In a survey conducted in 2014, it was recorded that the county consisted of 454 administrative villages. Of the 454 villages, 115 were badly poverty-stricken and combined to have an impoverished multitude amounting to 77,350. The primary causes leading to the sheer poverty the impoverished multitude wallowed in were these: chronic and serious illness,

第四章 历久弥新的精神

兰考民族乐器发源地——徐场村
This photo offers a glimpse of Xuchang village. It is the place of origin of folk musical instrument industry in the county.

20世纪80年代中期,上海民族乐器厂著名的琵琶制作大师张连根在兰考一个农家做客,听见农家主人厨房里烧火做饭的风箱发出来的声音甚是好听,询问后得知风箱原材料竟是焦裕禄带领兰考人民种植的泡桐。张连根告诉男主人泡桐是制作民族乐器音板的绝佳材料。男主人听完后,便萌生了把木头变成乐器的想法。他发扬"三顾茅庐"的精神,走南闯北,把上海民族乐器厂著名古筝制作专家及相关的技术顾问请到了兰考,走上了用兰考泡桐制作民族乐器之路。这位兰考人就是兰考民族乐器的创始人——代士永,后来建成了当时兰考最大的民族乐器厂。

1992年,中国轻工业部组织专家对全国十几个地区进行考察,专家认为,兰考处于黄河故道,又位于干燥的北方和潮湿的南方交界地带,盐碱沙地长出的泡桐木质疏松度适中,不易变形,共鸣度高,透音性、透气性非常好,具有优良的声学品质,适宜做乐器音板。

severe physical disability, natural calamity, and being devoid of able-bodied laborer or rudimentary technical knowledge. Of course, there were cases of bereaved old people and bereaved young children who were left no means to ensure their survival. In 2014, the CPC Central Committee set in motion a new nationwide movement which was intended for further sharpening in all communist party members in China the awareness of endearing themselves to all ordinary Chinese people. In the initial stage of the movement, President Xi Jinping solemnly announced that he officially designated Lankao County as "a county eligible for his special concern". Once in the course of his official inspection in Lankao, he made a point of demanding government functionaries there to particularly take care of the poor households in the county. In addition, he demanded those functionaries to systematically provide the rural population with guidance so that they could develop such industries as were most congruous with their local resources. In response to President Xi's demands and also to the expectation of the Lankao people, the CPC Lankao County Committee has solemnly proclaimed its promise which is: "The CPC Lankao County Committee promises to work dutifully and efficiently to eliminate poverty in Lankao in three years and make all the families living in Lankao attain fairly well-off living conditions in seven years."

Being true to its own promise, the CPC Lankao Committee has been ever since exerting to the utmost to provide the Lankao population with proper guidance which focuses on eliminating poverty from Lankao. Members of the county committee have been vying with one another in serving the people in the same way as Jiao Yulu did in his lifetime and endearing themselves to the people in the same way as Jiao Yulu did in his lifetime. With regard to the phrase "full effectuation of the plan for curbing impoverishment", President Xi has laid down an accurate definition and required members of the Lankao County Committee to act in strict compliance with the definition he has laid down for the phrase. Now members of the Lankao County Committee have vowed to act accordingly and guaranteed "to leave out none of the poor families in Lankao". These members are determined to proceed strictly with the effectuation of both the plan for curbing impoverishment and the plan for irrevocable elimination of poverty and backwardness by striving to be impeccable in (1) their nomination of the poor families which are to receive support and relief from the government, (2) their determination as to what kind of help and relief is to be

学员在参观兰考民族乐器加工过程

Visitors are seen closely watching in a workshop how a folk musical instrument was processed.

2. 当前兰考民族乐器产业的发展情况

经过近30年的发展,如今兰考堌阳镇全镇从事文化产业(民族乐器、乐器音板及各种乐器配件生产加工)的企业106家,其中规模较大的乐器企业13家,从业人员1万多人,年产销各种民族乐器40多万把,音板及配件50多万套,年产值5亿元。乐器品牌中的"弘音牌""中州牌""三好牌"民族乐器被评为河南省著名商标,弘音牌新型转调筝获得国家专利产品,还与上海著名商标"敦煌牌"以及龙音、君谊、华中、大河、焦桐、鸣韵等30多个知名品牌合作。堌阳镇民族乐器的发源地徐场村也成为以民族乐器生产实现脱贫致富的先进村,乡村振兴的文

given to a specific poor family, (3) their formulation of different schemes respectively for diverse poor families, (4) their allotment of relief fund, (5) their different and specific personnel arrangements respectively for different villages, and (6) the content of their reports submitted to their superiors with respect to the effectuation of the two plans specified above.

To effectuate the two plans, members of the county committee have so far taken the following specific measures:

In order to mobilize all the local government set-ups to take the initiative in energetically plowing ahead with the effectuation of the two plans, members of the county committee have enunciated and strictly adhered to the principle that all the superiors must set a good example for their subordinates to follow suit. It is not at all an easy job to win the battle against poverty in Lankao, given an appreciable percentage of the Lankao population was at that time in dire poverty. Therefore, all the government officials in Lankao have to act in rigorous compliance with the spirit of Jiao Yulu's oath: "I'd stick at nothing and fight to accomplish it even at the cost of my life, since I'm determined to thoroughly reshape Lankao's physiognomy!" All the officials in Lankao are expected to act in compliance with Jiao Yulu's catchphrase: "A revolutionist should behave like a hero when confronting adversity." It is of vital importance that superiors should set a good example for their subordinates to follow suit. Moreover, formulation of a plan or program must accord well with pragmatism. A leader of a CPC set-up or of a government agency must know perfectly not only what his own official duty and responsibility are but also what his subordinates' duties and responsibilities are and cling unswervingly to all CPC and government principles and policies. In a word, it is important that all government officials should be reminded to actively reinforce their sense of duty. Lankao County Administration has already publicized the following two documents: "2014 — 2016 Program for Intensive Effectuation in Lankao of the Move to Curb Impoverishment" and "Propositions Concerning the Three-Year Intensive Effectuation in Lankao of the Move to Irrevocably Eliminate Poverty and Backwardness". The concrete measures now having been adopted by Lankao for implementing the two documents just specified include the following:

(1)Each member of the county committee is assigned to take charge of a definite number of towns and villages so that all the towns and villages can be more readily

中国·兰考民族乐器学术交流会开幕式
The opening ceremony of the Lankao Assemblage for Academic Exchange among Players of Chinese Folk Musical Instrument

外国友人在兰考县徐场村弹奏以兰考泡桐为主要原材料制作的古筝
A visitor coming to Xuchang village in Lankao from beyond China is seen playing a Chinese zither. The instrument is made of timber of paulownia grown in Lankao.

benefited by the help and guidance the county committee is able to give them. Each member of the county committee should strive to set a good example for the heads of the towns and villages, which he is assigned to take charge of, to follow suit.

(2)Various kinds of work teams are to be dispatched respectively by diverse agencies of the county administration, all the town administrations, and all the village administrations to the counterparts (respectively on town level and village level) of such work teams so that a tie of cooperation can be built up in a dovetailing or interlocking fashion between the two of them to facilitate the implementation of the two documents specified above. Each work team is composed of one to three agency staffers. Members of a work team must temporarily leave their respective governmental set-ups and go to live in a village or town where they are sent to keep up the tie of cooperation with the respective counterparts of their work teams, because it is only after a member of a work team has temporarily left the governmental set-up to which he (or she) is affiliated and lived away from the urban area of the county that he (or she) can really focus his (or her) energy on implementing the two documents specified above. Except for a holiday or for holidays on a row, a member of a work team is not allowed to stay away from the village to which he (or she) is assigned to keep up the tie of cooperation.

The CPC Lankao County Committee puts a great deal of stress on both accuracy and perfectness in implementing the plan for curbing impoverishment. Prior to the initiation of any practical measure aimed at curbing impoverishment, so the CPC Lankao County Committee instructs, a work team should apply a strict "means test" to every family in the village which the work team takes charge of. Then from the findings of all the means tests already made, the work team can identify and put on official record all the families in the village, the standard of living of which is below the poverty line set by the state and which are eligible for receiving support and relief from the state. Such findings as collected by numerous work teams in regard to poor families or individuals in villages all over China are to be reported to the state large databases in our country. The central authorities concerned together with regional or local administrations concerned are to make detailed analyses of big data supplied by various state large databases so that they can formulate, on the basis of their analyses, national standards for categorizing different types of impoverishment, different types of curbed impoverishment, and different kinds and quotas of support

化旅游村。得益于桐木等林业资源优势，兰考县也发展起了家具建材制造产业，正在建设亚洲最大的家居产业园。

目前，全国90%的民族乐器音板产自兰考县，兰考县也成为中国四大民族乐器生产基地之一。用兰考泡桐制作出的古筝、琵琶、柳琴已名扬海内外，远销美国、加拿大、马来西亚、新加坡等10多个国家和地区。兰考人民感恩焦裕禄，他在治理兰考"三害"的同时，也为兰考人民留下了取之不尽的绿色财富，把美妙的"泡桐之韵"传播到了全世界。

五、推进了减贫事业，为构建人类命运共同体做出了有益示范

从人类历史发展进程来看，贫困问题始终伴随着人类发展的步伐。当今世界，贫困问题依然是世界性难题，消除贫困是人类梦寐以求的理想。中华人民共和国成立后，在一穷二白的情况下，中国人为摆脱贫困进行了艰苦卓绝的奋斗，逐步实现了温饱。焦裕禄当年在兰考就是解决贫困问题。1978年中国实行改革开放以来，政府实施了大规模扶贫开发，使7亿农村贫困人口逐步摆脱贫困，取得了举世瞩目的伟大成就。特别是2013年以来，中国政府从国情出发，把脱贫攻坚作为实现第一个百年奋斗目标的重点工作，致力于精准扶贫、精准脱贫，提出了2020年全面消除绝对贫困、全面建成小康社会的宏伟蓝图。

1. 兰考的脱贫实践

在兰考，50年前很多群众居住的简陋茅屋现在已经被一栋栋高楼大厦和一排排特色民居所取代。回首过往，兰考在豫东地区一度是贫困的代名词，2002年被确定为国家扶贫开发工作重点县。2012年全县总人口85万，其中农村人口77.3万人。2014年建档立卡时，全县454个行政村中，

and relief to be delivered to poor families by the government. A work team is to work in close cooperation with the village administration to determine what kind and quota of support and relief is to be granted to which poor family in the village by first checking the family's specific living conditions against the relevant national standard. There are altogether 12 patterns of support and relief now prescribed by the Central Government: (1) the minimal subsistence grant, (2) the five-item insurance grant, (3) grant for ensuring children's education, (4) grant for habitation repair, (5) grant for acquisition of insurance, (6) subsidy for a migrant laborer, (7) emergency grant, apart from five other patterns. Generally speaking, thanks to the twelve patterns of support and relief, now living conditions of people living in villages in Lankao are very much improved, because they can safely ensure against hunger, inclement weather, children's being slumped in illiteracy, and unavailability of basic medical care.

The CPC Lankao County Committee attaches great importance to persistently setting reform and innovation in motion. Being not gratified with the social progress induced by the implementation of the 12 patterns of support and relief granted to numerous poor families, now the CPC Lankao County Committee has introduced three additional patterns of support and relief, which are "elimination of poverty on the industrial front", "elimination of poverty on the financial front", and "elimination of poverty in the realm of social life". Now the altogether 15 patterns of support and relief combine to blossom into a very powerful poverty-elimination conglomeration which generates (1) a mutually-promoting mechanism between industry and employment, (2) universally favorable financial sustenance, and (3) warranted impoverishment curb, that operates on the basis of the 12 patterns of support and relief which can relieve our society of any social upheaval. Moreover, the CPC Lankao County Committee is doing everything in its power to mobilize all sorts of social institutions in the county to take part in the social movement to curb impoverishment, calling upon all the entrepreneurs and advocates of philanthropic undertakings to join the cause of impoverishment elimination in Lankao. At the same time, the county committee makes every effort to educate the poor families in diligence, self-confidence, and self-respect.

The CPC Lankao County Committee exerts itself to the utmost to uphold the principle that whatever policy it formulates or whatever practical measure it takes is philanthropically-oriented. In pushing ahead with its plan for curbing

贫困村有115个，贫困人口77350人。这些贫困户大多是疾病、残疾、遭遇灾害或者缺技术、缺劳动力等造成的。还有一部分是孤寡老人、孤儿，没有经济来源，生活不能自理。2014年，在全党开展的第二批党的群众路线教育实践活动中，习近平把兰考县确定为自己的联系点。他视察兰考时，要求当地干部要关心农村贫困家庭，因地制宜发展产业，促进农民增收。为此，兰考县向习近平和全县人民做出"三年脱贫，七年小康"的庄严承诺。

为了摘掉贫困县的帽子，兰考以脱贫攻坚统揽全局，认真践行"学习弘扬焦裕禄精神，做焦裕禄式的好干部，做人民群众的贴心人"的要求，严格按照习近平精准扶贫的一系列要求，以"脱贫路上不落一人"的标准，做好贫困群众的救助工作，努力做到扶贫对象精准、措施到户精准、项目安排精准、资金使用精准、因村派人精准、脱贫成效精准。在实践中，主要有以下几个做法：

在组织发动上，兰考坚持以上率下。兰考贫困人口多，贫困程度较深，打赢脱贫攻坚战不是轻松的工作。在脱贫攻坚战中，兰考公职人员坚持以焦裕禄为榜样，学习他"拼着老命大干一场，决心改变兰考面貌"的韧劲和"革命者要在困难面前逞英雄"的决心，做到领导带头、干在实处、走在前列。从县委书记到乡镇党委书记到村支书，作为各级脱贫攻坚工作的主要责任人，一级一级压实责任、落实政策、解决问题，不断强化担当意识。政府组织制定了《兰考县2014—2016年扶贫攻坚规划》《兰考县三年脱贫攻坚工作的意见》等文件，采取县级领导干部联系分包乡镇制度，发挥示范带动作用。要求县直乡镇各单位各部门派出若干工作队，一对一分别与全县所有贫困村建立帮扶对接机制，各工作队（1—3人）脱离原单位工作、离开县城，投入全部精力到乡村开展扶贫，除节假日外，在村里吃住。

在扶贫政策上，兰考坚持精准精细。帮扶开始前，兰考县要求各工作队对全村农户进行调查摸底，从农户中筛选出收入低于国家贫困线且

impoverishment or its plan for eliminating impoverishment, the county committee would never for a moment deviate from bigheartedness. Members of the county committee have vowed to model themselves on the way Jiao Yulu endeared himself to the populace, on Jiao's unbreakable willpower to fulfill his duty, and on Jiao's endurance of all sorts of hardship and fatigue in carrying out his mission, in order to benefit all the poor in the county and help those among the poor, who have the potential to create a business of their own, to rapidly build it up. Members of the county committee are raring to help those among the poor in the county, who are able to do some physical labor, get employed as soon as possible. The survival of those among the poor in the county, who can neither create a business of their own nor do any physical labor, is guaranteed by the county committee. Moreover, the county committee is very earnest in instilling into the poor the desire for behaving with honor and dignity, so that they can have the impetus to work for their own survival, because there are a lot of jobs which require only very light physical exertion such as forest or park ranger, household cleaner.

President Xi Jinping has propounded his theory on the most efficient way to curb or eliminate impoverishment. Now Lankao has been plowing on, being guided by President Xi's theory and inspired by Jiao Yulu's verve, to campaign against impoverishment. Accomplishments made in this connection by the CPC Lankao County Committee are conspicuous, thanks to the zealous participation in this drive by all the social institutions in the county. All the Lankao population and government functionaries have been jointly exerting to introduce innovations into the curbing-impoverishment movement. At the same time they have laid emphasis on pushing ahead in a pragmatic manner. By the end of 2016, 69,591 native people had been steadily lifted out of indigence. There were altogether 7,046 native penurious people still waiting to have their hardship alleviated. The comprehensively estimated incidence of impoverishment was 1.27% by the end of 2016. The rate of public recognition stood at 98.96%. An assessment made by an official inspection of the estimated incidence indicates that the statistics just referred to above can well meet the "poverty alleviation index" prescribed by the State Council Leading Group Office of Poverty Alleviation and Development. Therefore, Lankao County has been officially announced to have been lifted out of impoverishment in March 2017. Lankao is the first of all the poverty-stricken counties in Henan that has shaken itself

符合国家扶贫标准的农户或贫困人口，进行标记，实行建档立卡管理。在帮扶政策上，国家和当地政府根据收集的贫困户情况大数据，进行分析研究，统一制定分类标准和帮扶标准。各村工作队和村委会根据村内每个贫困户的家庭收入、贫困程度、致贫原因等情况，对比政府标准对贫困户进行帮扶。帮扶内容有低保金、五保金、教育救助、医疗救助、危房改造、保险、外出务工补贴、临时救助等12项。通过救助，总体上让群众实现"两不愁、三保障"（不愁吃、不愁穿，保障义务教育、基本医疗和住房）。

在资源整合上，兰考坚持改革创新。在12项扶贫政策的基础上，兰考县还创新了产业扶贫、金融扶贫、社会扶贫等多种方式，探索出了一个产业与就业双向驱动，普惠金融支持，12项扶贫政策兜底保障的有效扶贫模式。兰考县还汇聚社会各方力量，倡导企业家、社会爱心人士等参与扶贫，同时发动贫困户自力更生，通过劳动获得帮助。

在扶贫理念上，兰考坚持以人为本。在扶贫中，兰考深刻践行以人为本的发展理念，以焦裕禄对群众的那股亲劲、抓工作的那股韧劲、干事业的那股拼劲为困难群众做实事、办好事、解难事，帮助能发展产业

兰考县稳定脱贫奔小康誓师大会

In the photo is shown a rally in progress in Lankao. The rally was for pledging Lankao people's effort to steadily eliminate poverty and attain a good standard of living.

free of penury.

2. What the present-day Lankao is like.

There are now three key industries propping up the Lankao economy: the industry of furniture plus timber processing, the industry of intensive processing of food and farm & sideline products, and some strategic industries that have newly emerged. Having been newly admitted into Lankao are the following enterprises:

(1) Hengda Home Furnishings Alliance with a total investment amounting to 10 billion yuan,

(2) Foxconn with a total investment of 6.8 billion yuan,

(3) an amalgamation of food processing businesses, which is spearheaded by both Lankao Zhengda Food Co. Ltd and Lankao Wellhope Animal Husbandry Co. Ltd.

Apart from the three enterprises, Lankao has generously accepted the following strategic industries that have newly emerged: Henan Mu Tong Environmental Protection Industry Co. Ltd and Guangda Environmental Energy (Lankao) Co. Ltd. The two enterprises are pioneering businesses. The presence of the two businesses in the urban areas of Lankao helps noticeably and reliably boost the county's comprehensive strength. The county's GDP for 2018 exceeded 30 billion *yuan* which is 8.1% up, compared with that for the previous year. The per capita disposable income of the urban population and of the rural population rose in 2018 respectively to 25,029 *yuan* and 11,910 *yuan*, which were respectively 8.5% and 9.2% up, compared with the statistics of the previous year. The growth rates of all the major economic indicators for the year 2018 were above Henan's average growth rates of the same year.

3. The significance of the successful elimination of impoverishment in Lankao, when viewed from the perspective of the global-poverty-alleviation initiative and also from the perspective of the initiative to build a community with a shared future for mankind

Location of Lankao is geographically at the center of the Central-China Plains. Lankao's socio-economic development can be regarded as emblematic of that of the Central-China Plains. The way in which Lankao struggled to achieve its elimination of impoverishment epitomizes the way in which more than 400 indigent counties in China had done. The experience Lankao has acquired in its most trying exertion

的困难群众发展产业，有劳动能力但不能发展产业的帮助其就业，不能发展产业也不能就业的实施兜底保障。另外，坚持扶贫与扶志相结合，激发贫困家庭和贫困人口脱贫的主观愿望和内在动力，发动贫困群众通过应聘护林员、保洁员等社会公益岗位而取得相应报酬。

在习近平精准扶贫理论的指导下，在焦裕禄精神的鼓舞下，在社会各界人士的参与下，兰考公职人员和群众干字当头、开拓创新、稳扎稳打、务实重干，扶贫工作取得显著成效。截至2016年底，全县共脱贫69591人，剩余贫困人口7046人，综合测算贫困发生率1.27%，群众认可度98.96%，经检验评估，符合中国国务院扶贫开发领导小组办公室的脱贫指标。兰考县于2017年3月正式宣布脱贫，成为河南省贫困县中首个脱贫的县。

2. 新时代兰考的发展面貌

现在的兰考，围绕家具制造及木业加工、食品及农副产品深加工和

兰考县城面貌
A glimpse of one of the urban areas in Lankao

to free itself of impoverishment can serve as an inspiration and enlightenment for regions which, though being still in the thrall of penury, seek to release themselves and are in the process of formulating a poverty-alleviation policy or strategy or of figuring out what a path to take for reversing the trend of impoverishment. News media outside China have made a point of stressing the fact that China has set a good example for the world in booting penury outdoors. It is indisputable that Lankao does shine brilliantly in China's great endeavor to sweep penury outdoors. The number of the poor in China was registered at 98.99 million in 2012 and reduced in six years to 16.6 million in 2018. The average annual reduction of the number of the poor in the span of six years stands at 13 million. Statistics from the World Bank show that of every one hundred people in the world, who have been proclaimed each year as having been lifted out of poverty, 70 odd are Chinese. China has been doing laudably enough to uphold the great cause of lessening poverty's grip on the world population. Sami kamhawi, deputy editor of *Al-Ahram*, an Egyptian newspaper, voiced the opinion that winning the battle against poverty not only concerns China's own development, but also has a huge impact on the international community, as China's success means the elimination of absolute poverty in a country that accounts for one fifth of the world's population, and is bound to provide other countries with very valuable experience.

In June 2019, a delegation jointly dispatched by political parties in a number of countries came to visit Lankao with the intention of vetting the way Lankao struggled to successfully slough off its destitution, misery and degradation. None of the delegation members could refrain from heaping earnest praise and commendation on the miraculous exploits accomplished by the local people. Simplice Mathieu Sarandji, executive secretary of Mouvement Coeurs Unis and expremier of the Central African Republic, gave a wistful comment, saying, "The significance of the exploratory initiative in achieving rural vitalization cannot be too highly appreciated indeed, because how to bring about a successful rejuvenation of agricultural economy is an issue of global concern — an issue which is of cardinal importance not only for China but also for all the countries in Africa and in Asia. Nowadays agricultural policies already formulated by some governments have been proved futile in revitalizing the flagging rural economy in those countries where there have been torrential peregrinations of peasants to urban areas. This is a factor to

兰考县城面貌

Another glimpse of an urban area in Lankao

战略性新兴产业 3 个主导产业，先后引入了总投资100亿元的恒大家居联盟产业园、总投资68亿的富士康，培育了以兰考正大食品有限公司、兰考禾丰牧业有限公司为龙头的食品加工产业集群，同时大力发展战略性新兴产业，相继引进河南沐桐环保产业有限公司、光大环保能源（兰考）有限公司等行业龙头企业，为增强县域综合实力打下了坚实基础。2018年，全县GDP（国内生产总值）突破300亿元大关，同比增长8.1%。城镇、农村居民人均可支配收入分别达到25029元、11910元，同比增长8.5%、9.2%。各项主要经济指标增幅均高于河南省平均水平。

3. 兰考脱贫实践对世界减贫事业及构建人类命运共同体的价值贡献

兰考地处中原，在区域和经济发展上有一定的代表性。兰考的脱贫实践是2016年以来中国400多个贫困县脱贫的缩影，兰考的脱贫经验也将为其他未脱贫区域制定扶贫政策、选择扶贫路径提供参考和借鉴。正如外媒所言：中国是世界脱贫的典范。兰考无疑是这项伟大事业中一颗

trigger off 'grey economy' in those countries. So far as the Central African Republic, which is my country, is concerned, the experience acquired by Lankao in its effort to rejuvenate its agricultural economy can be of inestimable value for my country."

Samphanh Phengkhammy, member of the Central Committee of the Lao People's Revolutionary Party and vice-chairman of the Laotian Parliament said, "The specific experience gained by Zhangzhuang village (The village is the very place where Jiao Yulu started his experiment with the method of 'blanketing dunes in silt' and finally succeeded in validating the method.) is in essence 'the master key' that serves to undo all the sealed doors to the treasure trove of rural prosperity in all the developing as well as all the under-developing countries all over the world. I firmly believe that what with the powerful leadership exercised by the Lao People's Revolutionary Party of and what with valuable experience and information supplied to us by our Chinese comrades, the Laotian people are bound to shake themselves free of the fetters imposed on them by impoverishment as soon as possible." Mr. Falcao, chairman of the European Democratic-Student Union, seeming to be intrigued by and becoming engrossed in the diverse dimensions to the magic wielded by the specific schedule having been adopted by the Chinese Central Government for achieving its goal of "elimination of poverty from Chinese territory", has this to say, "Successful elimination of absolute poverty from China by 2020 should be rated as a stunningly phenomenal feat unprecedented in the history of mankind's endeavor to put an end to impoverishment. It is a milestone of an extraordinary exploit aimed at refashioning the fabric of global economy." A member of the delegation was deeply impressed by the streamlined method, adopted by the Chinese Government, of "using innovated or improved farming techniques as a lever to curb impoverishment and multiply the poor peasants' income". "Such an approach to alleviating the scourge of impoverishment," said he, "is very enlightening because it readily leads us to perceive that one of the practical and simple measures for weakening the proneness to a mass exodus from the rural areas to urban areas on the part of such a portion of the rural population as has been made surplus because of farming-technique innovation or improvement is helping the poor peasants redouble their income."

Curtailment of impoverishment in a country is a very trying and formidable

耀眼的星。6年来，中国贫困人口从2012年的9899万减少到了2018年的1660万，连续6年平均每年减少贫困人口1300万。根据世界银行统计，全球范围内每100人脱贫，就有70多人来自中国，中国为世界减贫事业做出了积极贡献。埃及《金字塔报》副主编萨米·卡姆哈维表示，打赢脱贫攻坚战，不仅关乎中国发展，对国际社会也将产生巨大影响，因为中国的成功意味着占世界五分之一人口的国家消除了绝对贫困现象，势必为其他国家提供重要经验。

2019年6月，来兰考参观的国外政党代表考察团了解了兰考县脱贫致富的实践后，都交口称赞。中非团结一心运动全国执行书记、前政府总理萨兰吉·桑普利斯·马蒂尔感叹乡村振兴具有重要的世界意义："非洲国家的大部分居民都生活在乡村，而一些政权所出台的政策并不能很好地促进乡村发展，当村民跑到城市谋生，同样会出现'灰色的经济'。河南一个小乡村的经验，可能对于我们的国家来说，都是值得学习和借鉴的。"老挝人民革命党中央委员、国会副主席宋潘·平坎米认为张庄村（焦裕禄当年找到治理风沙办法的地方，现为兰考县的一个脱贫示范村）脱贫致富的经验"为全球扶贫减贫事业提供了金钥匙"。他说："我坚信有老挝人民革命党的坚强领导，有中国同志的宝贵经验，我们也必将早日摆脱贫困状态。"欧洲民主学生会主席法尔考则留意到了中国特殊的脱贫攻坚时间表，他说："到2020年消灭绝对贫困，这在全球减贫史上，都是具有里程碑意义的大事。"还有政党代表捕捉到了"技术扶贫"的细节——"我们看到中国通过技术的革新让农业人口脱贫致富，这种发展模式让我们了解了如何把生产技术解放出来的劳动力留在农村地区。"

减贫事业是一场大考，少则一两年，多则数十年，涉及经济、政治、文化、社会方方面面，涉及政府各部门和各行各业，是以政府为主导帮助农民摆脱贫困、实现小康的具体工作。其工作的难度，时刻考验着公职人员的作风、能力、素质和心态。做好扶贫工作，需要公职人员

endeavor. Its fructification may take one year, two years or even decades and calls for joint strenuous exertions put forth by economic, political, cultural, sociological circles, not to say all government agencies concerned, all industries, and all trades. The government should take the lead in pushing ahead with the trying and formidable endeavor of curtailing impoverishment, which consists of making practical efforts intended in the first place for releasing the poor in the rural areas from dire penury and then for helping them find ways to attain fairly well-off living conditions. The formidable endeavor to curtail impoverishment is very challenging to a government functionary and can serve as a touchstone to gauge his (or her) sense of duty, ability, personality, and frame of mind. To fulfill his (or her) duty in carrying out a specific mission relevant to the formidable endeavor of curtailing impoverishment, a functionary needs the fervor to motivate himself (or herself) to work unselfishly and untiringly, the intelligence to make himself (or herself) work efficiently, and the patience to make his (or her) task fructify in the end. The influence of a good example is almighty. The morality which Jiao Yulu behaved in accordance with is a good example that has exerted its influence to motivate the Lankao population to come to grips with impoverishment curtailment. The success secured by the Lankao population in eliminating impoverishment serves to vindicate both Jiao Yulu's morality and the inspiration and enlightenment his morality can give to the international community.

Eradication of absolute poverty throughout the world by 2030 constitutes not only the top priority of the UN sustainable development goals but also the foundation on which to build the community with a shared future for mankind. Now China is to precede the UN by ten years, as she is to eliminate impoverishment throughout the country in 2020. By the end of 2015, there were across the world still 736 million people living in absolute poverty. The majority of them lived in countries and regions in sub-Saharan Africa, India, and Latin America. These underdeveloped countries and regions are similar to China in many respects, though there are significant differences between them and China. The experience acquired by China in her efforts to curb and finally eliminate impoverishment, particularly the strategy and practical measures adopted by a county in China to bring about alleviation of poverty can be of pragmatic use for some underdeveloped countries or regions in the world.

2019年6月国外政党代表考察团参观焦裕禄同志纪念馆
In the photo are shown members of a delegation, jointly sent by a number of political parties in various countries, visiting the Jiao Yulu Memorial Hall in Lankao. They traveled there in June 2019.

用精神去砥砺,用任务去发动,用耐心去落实。榜样的力量是无穷的,焦裕禄精神鼓舞了新时代兰考的脱贫事业,兰考的成功脱贫也彰显了焦裕禄精神的恒久价值和世界价值。

2030年消除极端贫困是联合国可持续发展目标的首要任务,也是构建世界命运共同体的基础,而中国即将提前10年于2020年完成这一目标。截至2015年底,全世界仍有近7.36亿极端贫困人口,主要分布在撒哈拉以南的非洲、印度和拉丁美洲等国家和地区。这些欠发达地区与中国在国情上存在相同之处,也有很多不同。中国的脱贫经验尤其是县域地区脱贫攻坚的做法,对世界贫困地区的减贫事业有重要参照意义。

世界是个地球村。中国消除绝对贫困已经进入了尾声,但不能独善其身,更应兼济天下。兰考脱贫的经验可以为其他国家的贫困治理工作提供借鉴,如发扬焦裕禄精神,实行公职人员驻村帮扶机制;强化政

The world is actually a global village. Although the campaign in China to rid herself of absolute poverty is about to take a curtain call, she is certainly not contented with what she has done to benefit her own people. China is determined to do something in the interest of the international community. The experience which the Lankao people have accumulated in the course of their struggle to do away with impoverishment in their county can be useful to the underdeveloped countries and regions. To be specific, the experience acquired by the Lankao people in their fight against impoverishment consists of the following:

(1) upholding and widening the influence of Jiao Yulu's morality;

(2) enforcing the rule that it is obligatory for all the government functionaries involved in the mission of curbing impoverishment in a rural area to live in the village he is assigned to carry out the mission for the period his mission is being carried on;

(3) formulating a detailed poverty-alleviation program which should be under-pinned by the principle that it is obligatory for the government to play the leading role in the poverty-alleviation campaign;

(4) indexing various rates that are useful for prescribing diverse allowances or subsidies for the poor villagers;

(5) drawing up a long-term and comprehensive poverty-alleviation project for the county;

(6) encouraging entrepreneurs and luminaries to rally support for the cause of poverty alleviation;

(7) implementing such a policy of poverty alleviation as must be coupled with educating the poor in morality and in common knowledge.

One of the axioms which Chinese for several millennia firmly uphold is this: "Let the world be united, so that the bliss of one of its constituent parts may be freely shared by another." In the course when China is remolding herself into a well-off society, so as to rejuvenate herself by making "Chinese Dream" come true, she has never for once forgotten to avail herself of her own strength for enhancing global prosperity. Never has she for once forgotten about her sincere aspiration that she should exert strenuously to make the world better for humanity to live in. The true happiness ought to be shared by the human race, rather than monopolized by a single nation. Therefore, China

府主导的理念，制定减贫战略规划；提供改善贫困人口教育、医疗、电力、饮水、住房等多维度减贫政策参照；构建大扶贫格局，引导企业家等社会人士参与；实现扶贫与扶志、扶智相结合；等等。

　　世界大同，美美与共，这是中华民族几千年来一直秉持的理念。中国在全面建成小康社会、实现中华民族伟大复兴中国梦的历史进程中，始终把以自身发展促进世界共同繁荣、为人类做出新的更大的贡献作为自己的初心、责任和使命。幸福不应该是一个独立单元的感受，而应该是全人类共同的感受。中国愿同世界各国人民一道，努力构建人类命运共同体，以焦裕禄精神为动力，为更多国家消灭贫困、为世界实现开放包容、互利共赢贡献兰考智慧，提供中国方案，凝聚中国力量。

is bent on creating the community with a shared future for mankind. Being activated by Jiao Yulu's morality, China is determined to help more and more underdeveloped countries and regions with impoverishment alleviation. She would promote the realization of an international win-win situation in the world — a situation in the world where mutual tolerance and goodwill reign supreme.

附录

焦裕禄经典语录

Appendix

Quotations from Jiao Yulu

焦裕禄出身农民家庭，先后当过民兵、企业领导、公职人员、县主要领导等。工作中，他熟悉基层、热爱群众，善于做群众工作，与同事相处融洽，经常帮助他人，被群众称为"热心队长"。生活中，他是一个乐观开朗、积极向上的人，善于总结，幽默风趣，经常使用顺口溜、口头禅来发动群众。焦裕禄的经典语录摘选如下：

一、公仆情怀

1. 没有抗灾的干部，就没有抗灾的群众。

2. 干部不领，水牛掉井。

3. 这些人绝大多数都是我们的阶级兄弟，是灾荒逼迫他们背井离乡的，这不怪他们，责任在我们身上，党把三十六万群众交给我们，我们没能领导他们战胜灾荒，过安居乐业的生活，应该感到羞耻和痛心。

4. 在这大雪封门的日子里，我们不能坐在办公室里烤火，应该到群众中间去。共产党员应该在群众最困难的时候，出现在群众面前，在群众需要帮助的时候，去关心群众，帮助群众。

5. 我们不是人民的上司，我们都是人民的勤务员，必须和群众同甘共苦、共患难。

6. 一个落后地区的转变，首先是领导思想的转变。如果领导思想还没有转变过来，广大群众的积极性就不能得到充分发挥。

二、求实作风

1. 吃别人嚼过的馍没味道。

2. 先顾吃饭，再顾好看。

3. 跟群众打交道，圈要跑圆，理要讲全，心平气和，抓紧时间。

4. 人是最宝贵的。不了解人，不首先做好人的工作，其他工作就会走进死胡同。

5. 要提倡少开会，多做工作，少讲空话，多办实事。

6. 我要把兰考县1094平方公里土地的自然情况摸透，掂一掂兰考的"三害"到底有多大分量。

7. 白天要搞调查研究，晚上要"过电影"。

8. 不读报纸不知道天下大事，不看文件不能领会政策。

9. 当工作感到没办法的时候，你就到群众中去，问问群众，你就有办法了。

三、奋斗精神

1. 革命者要在困难面前逞英雄。

2. 拼上老命大干一场，决心改变兰考面貌！

3. 干革命就得敢闯！成功了，有经验；失败了，有教训。只要敢闯，就能从困难中杀出一条路来。

4. 兰考是个大有作为的地方，问题是要干，要革命。兰考是灾区，穷，困难多，但灾区有个好处，它能锻炼人的意志，培养人的革命品格。

5. 病，是个欺软怕硬的东西，你压住它，它就不欺负你了。

6. 干革命工作嘛，总会有困难的。越是有困难，越要有雄心斗志，越有困难，越要学习毛主席著作。

四、道德情操

1. 要勤俭办事业，不贪玩，不浪费，和人民同甘共苦，吃苦在前，享受在后。

2. 要小小气气地过日子，细细致致地做工作。贯彻自力更生为主的方针，把钱用到最需要的地方去。

3. 灾区面貌没有改变,还大量吃着国家的统销粮,群众生活很困难,富丽堂皇的事,不但不能做,就是连想也很危险。

4. 我死后只有一个要求,要求党组织把我运回兰考,埋在沙丘上。活着我没有治好沙丘,死了也要看着你们把沙丘治好!

5. 不搞特殊,特别是在灾区工作的同志,要注意生活问题,不然就会脱离群众。

五、十条工作经验

1. 要依靠群众;
2. 要发扬民主;
3. 要经常总结工作;
4. 要学习政治;
5. 要利用积极分子做工作;
6. 要了解群众思想,关心群众生活;
7. 要依靠党的领导;
8. 要搞好团结;
9. 要学习党的政策;
10. 要主动向上级汇报工作。

六、干部十不准

1. 不准用国家的或集体的粮款或其他物资大吃大喝,请客送礼;
2. 不准参加或带头搞封建迷信活动;
3. 不准赌博;
4. 不准用粮食做酒做糖,挥霍浪费;
5. 不准拿生产队现有粮款或向社员派粮派款,唱戏、演电影,谁看戏谁拿钱，谁吃喝谁拿粮，一律不准向社员摊派；

6. 业余剧团只能在本乡本队演出，不准到外地营业演出，更不准借春节演出为名大买服装道具，大肆铺张浪费；

7. 各机关、学校、企事业单位和党员干部都要以身作则，勤俭过年，一律不得请客送礼，一律不准拿国家物资，到生产队提取国家统购统派物资，一律不准用公款组织晚会，一律不准送戏票，十排以前戏票不能光卖给机关或几个机关经常包完，一律不准到商业部门、合作社部门要特殊照顾；

8. 坚决反对利用职权贪污盗窃国家的或生产队的物资，坚决禁止利用封建迷信欺骗和剥削社员的破坏活动；

9. 积极搞好集体的副业生产，增加收入，改善生活，反对弃农经商，反对投机倒把；

10. 不准借春节之机，大办喜事（不是不准结婚），做寿吃喜，大放鞭炮，挥霍浪费。

Jiao Yulu was born to a peasant's family. Once he was a militiaman. Later he was appointed to manage an enterprise before he became a government functionary. Still later he was appointed as administrator of a county. He used to endear himself to and familiarize himself with the grass roots and was very skillful in convincing his colleagues, because he was very popular and always earnest to offer help to the people in his surroundings. His nickname was "warmhearted guy". He was optimistic, jocular, insightful, and enterprising. His language was humorous and full of rhymed catchphrases. Below are some quotations from him:

I. Quotations describing his reflection on the role played by a government official

1. If an official who is in charge of campaigning against a natural calamity is undutiful, none of the common people will come to rally support for him.

2. If an official is not dutiful, the common people in his surroundings will do all kinds of folly.

3. Most of them come from the same social origin as you and me. It is the natural disaster that turns them out of their homeland. It isn't their fault at all that they are plunged into such a miserable plight. It is functionaries like you and me who ought to be held responsible for their wretchedness. Our Party has entrusted us with the duty of improving the lot of the 360,000 people. But we funked it. It is us who ought to feel ashamed and deeply remorseful!

4. Snow has blocked access to almost all houses and buildings in the county. We can't so fondly indulge ourselves by staying snug by the stove in our offices and call it a day, can we? No. It is obligatory for us to be together with our people. A communist ought to be in the midst of his multitude whenever adversity looms, and would exert to the utmost in favor of his people whenever they are in need of his exertion. He ought to be deeply concerned about them and give them comfort.

5. All of us are without exception servants of the people. It is incumbent on us to share our people's tribulations and mirth.

6. The remolding of a backward area presupposes the remolding of the outlook of the lead functionary who governs the area. In case his outlook on the prospect of the area remains unaltered, the people living in the area would remain virtually inert.

II. Quotations that mirror Jiao Yulu's down-to-earthness

1. Secondhand knowledge tends to sound stale.

2. Making the starved fed must precede making him feel comforted.

3. The prerequisites for convincing the common people are dispensing with shortcut, perfect reasoning, patience, tolerance, and no procrastination.

4. Nothing in the world is more valuable than a human being. So it is obligatory for us to have a full knowledge of those who are in your surroundings. If you fail to know them well, you are bound to drive yourself into an impasse.

5. We advocate for dispensing with unnecessary meetings, so that we can devote more time to doing our jobs. Don't talk nonsense. Just do things that do pay off.

6. I desire to learn everything that is useful about Lankao which measures 1094 square kilometers, so that I can have a full knowledge of the "three banes" that play havoc here.

7. My daytime should be dedicated to conducting investigation and examination, whereas my evening ought to be spent in reviewing what I did in daytime.

8. Don't miss reading the newspaper, or else you'd be blind to what's going on in the world. Don't miss poring over the documents you ought to read, or else you'd remain ignorant of what policies have dictated.

9. Whenever you're left at the end of your tether in carrying on your job, just go to the grass roots for some inspiration and enlightenment. And then you will know how to get out of the impasse.

III. Quotations that mirror Jiao's indomitability of will and valor

1. A revolutionist should behave the way a true hero does in the face of adversity.

2. I'd stick at nothing and fight to accomplish it even at the cost of my life, since I'm determined to thoroughly reshape Lankao's physiognomy!

3. Being a revolutionist means being irreversibly valorous in the face of adversity. In case you capture what you want to seize, you reap a wealth of experience. In case you miss, you gain a wealth of lesson. When your valor is organically coupled with insight, no success will miss you.

4. Lankao is a climate where auspicious opportunities mushroom. But the crux of the matter consists in whether you want to stir up a revolution there. Being a disaster area, Lankao is pretty hand to mouth and almost choked with impossible problems. But even a calamitous place has its merit: It can strengthen your willpower and refine your revolutionist timber.

5. Illness is a chicken-hearted bully, indeed. When you've the courage to bully him, he gets tamed.

6. A revolutionist career is never all plain sailing. But adversity inevitably thaws in the face of tough will underpinned by a revolutionary ideal. Whenever you're in a blue funk, just go to peruse Chairman Mao's works.

IV. Quotations serving to outline Jiao's morality

1. Be frugal in doing your job and diligent. Don't presume you're privileged to live in better comforts than the ordinary people. Rather you should strive to precede the ordinary people in taking the brunt of any harsh situation and voluntarily let yourself be the last one in your surroundings to take advantage of the benefits bestowed on your surroundings.

2. Be never extravagant, undutiful, or negligent in fulfilling your duty. Never dream of any unexpected godsend, or windfall, or help from the outside world. The official fund should go to where its proper use is guaranteed.

3. Since the inconceivable harsh realities in our disaster area remain unaltered, since the starved multitude here still depend on the emergency rations granted by the state for their survival, and since the Lankao population as a whole are leading a hand-to-mouth way of life, a profligate government expenditure budget is not just a taboo but actually criminal!

4. The last and only craving I cherish prior to my demise is this: The Party organization with which I have been duly affiliated will see to it that my remains, after having been conveyed back to Lankao County, be interred somewhere in a dune there. As I did not succeed in protecting all the dunes there from the encroachment of the gale-force winds in my life, I yearn to see in my afterlife how the local people continue to battle the winds until they are irrevocably subdued.

5. Don't seek to wangle privileges. This is particularly important for those

functionaries who work in a disaster area. I hope they attach great importance to the way they lead their everyday life, or else they would get themselves isolated from the ordinary people.

V. Quotations that summarize the experience Jiao had learned from his official career

1. To perform my duty well, I've to rely on assistance rendered me by the grass roots.

2. I need to have a democratic way with the grass roots and have to push ahead with my task in a way that is compatible with the concept of democracy.

3. I need to regularly review and assess the work I've done in order to enhance my work experience.

4. I need to incessantly enrich my stock of political knowledge.

5. I need to avail myself of the help given to me by the active elements in fulfilling my duty.

6. I need to adequately know about what are on the minds of the grass roots. Moreover, I need to be very solicitous about the welfare and living conditions of the grass roots.

7. I should cling to the directions given me by the Party organization to which I'm affiliated.

8. It is obligatory for me to try my best to be on good terms with everybody in my surroundings.

9. I need to learn and keep myself fully acquainted with policies of our Party.

10. I should always take the initiative in reporting my work to my superiors.

VI. Quotations from Jiao that illustrate the ten taboos for government officials in Lankao

1. No relief funds, relief food, or other relief materials which are allotted to Lankao by the state or owned by a collective may be misappropriated, prodigally consumed, or illegally sent to somebody as private gift.

2. No official is allowed to take part in and/or take the lead in promoting feudal

and/or superstitious activities.

3. No official is allowed to take part in gambling.

4. No grains are allowed to be used for producing alcoholic drink or sugar or for any extravagant consumption.

5. Nobody is allowed to requisition food or fund from a rural collective or individual on any pretext or on the pretext that the food or fund "requisitioned' is to be used as a payment for a dramatic show or a movie. Whoever wants to see a dramatic show or a movie pays out of his own purse. Whoever wants to eat a meal, prepares for it by using his own grain. Nobody is allowed to requisition anything from the rural populace.

6. An amateur ensemble is allowed to perform only within the boundary of the locality where it is native and is allowed neither to stage a commercial itinerant show nor to purchase luxurious costumes or props on the pretext that they are needed for the performances the ensemble is to put on in the Spring Festival.

7. All government organizations, schools, enterprises, and institutions and all party members and government functionaries should act exemplarily in making very thrifty arrangements for the forthcoming Spring Festival. No banquet or presentation of gift is allowed. Nobody is allowed to misappropriate anything that belongs to the state, or to extract from a rural collective materials which only the state is entitled to buy or to allot. No government fund or public fund may be used to pay for the expenses called for by the organizing of the new year's eve entertainment. No theaters in the county are allowed to give off free theater ticket. The tickets of the seats in the ten front rows in a theater are not allowed to be sold to government organizations or to be monopolized by a few government organizations. Nobody is allowed to acquire a preferential treatment from a commercial institution or from a cooperative institution.

8. Severe measure will be taken to crack down on embezzlement or stealth of state property or property of a collective and on feudal or superstitious activities intended for befooling or exploiting the rural population.

9. Nobody is allowed to engage in business activities by giving up his farming activity or engage in speculation or profiteering. Effective measures must be taken to develop sideline production in a rural collective so that income and living conditions in rural area can be improved.

10. Any attempt to arrange for a very luxurious matrimonial ceremony or lush birthday celebration — but that does not mean wedding is forbidden — in the duration of the Spring Festival is strongly objected to. No firecracker may be used. This is for curbing extravagance.

后 记

　　50多年来，人民群众对焦裕禄精神的学习热情不减反增，对焦裕禄精神的时代内涵越挖越深，这充分说明了焦裕禄精神经得起历史、人民和实践的检验。焦裕禄精神是一盏明灯，践行这种精神是时代的选择、人民的选择。这种精神应该是每个公职人员的行为准则，这种精神是任何一个民族都需要的宝贵财富。

　　焦裕禄的事迹被报道后，在全国各地第一次学习焦裕禄的热潮中，1968年2月，年仅17岁的新疆维吾尔自治区哈密县的阿布列林·阿不列孜和5位同学一起，坐火车千里迢迢来到兰考，拜谒了正在修建中的焦裕禄烈士陵园，并拜访了焦裕禄同志的亲属。回到家乡哈密县以后，阿布列林同志不仅长期致力于宣传焦裕禄的事迹，还把焦裕禄精神作为自己的人生准则。在几十年的检察、法院系统工作生涯中，他把公平公正办案当成自己的天职，承办的1000多个案件无一出错，坚定初心，激扬正气，与邪恶势力进行斗争。他在平凡的工作岗位上做出了不平凡的业绩，被誉为"哈密的焦裕禄"。

　　在学习焦裕禄的热潮中，越南、老挝、美国、加拿大等多个国家的留学生、公务员和民众到兰考参观学习。在20世纪60年代，世界和平理事会的一位美国人被焦裕禄精神深深折服，她不仅学习焦裕禄精神，还重新走访了一遍焦裕禄曾经调研过的地方。她每到一处，放下身段，端起简陋的茶具，喝与老百姓一样的水，与当地农民深深地拥抱。

　　焦裕禄是中国的，也是世界的。焦裕禄是个优秀的人，是个无私的人，他的生活充满着真善美，他的身上闪耀着人性的光辉。他的奋斗目标很明确，就是让人民吃饱穿暖，有更好的生活条件。现在还有很多国家没有解决贫困问题，这些国家的政府也希望他们的人民过上好日子。焦裕禄无疑是一个很好的榜样，他的工作方法有很多值得学习和借鉴的地方，他的精神超越时空、超越地域，有广泛的价值，应该成为国际主义精神。这种精神具有恒久的价值，能够激励各国守望相助，促进全球减贫事业，让世界每个角落的贫困人民都能摆脱贫困，过上幸福生活。就像习近平总书记说的那样，世界大同，美美与共。让我们携起手来，为创建一个没有贫困、共同发展的人类命运共同体而不懈奋斗！

  本书的编写工作得到了河南省人民政府外事办公室，开封市委、市政府、市人民政府外事办公室，焦裕禄干部学院，焦裕禄纪念园等有关单位的高度重视和大力支持，由郑州大学外国语与国际关系学院组建团队（钱建成、黄为葳、李洁、张琳琳、贺爱平、李艳芳、杨春丽、杨宏、李文竟）负责翻译方面的相关工作。在此一并表示感谢。

  因焦裕禄事迹年代久远，加上时间仓促，内容难免有纰漏之处，敬请广大读者谅解。

Postscript

The moral fervor and verve displayed by the Chinese people in the nationwide movement of "learning about and following Jiao Yulu" has been incessantly swelling — rather than dwindling — for over half a century. As the movement keeps surging forward, more and more systematic efforts have been made to fathom out the ethical leverage Jiao's morality and his life career can exercise over the contemporary world. This is sufficient to vindicate that universal approval has been irrevocably bestowed on his morality and specific rules of behavior. It has been universally acknowledged that his ethics are an enlightenment called for by our age — ethics which ought to be embraced by every government functionary in the world and are an indispensable asset to all nations across the world.

A nationwide movement — the first of its kind unfurling in China — that motivated the Chinese people to learn about and follow Jiao Yulu was set in motion after the mass media carried for the first time extensive coverage by journalists focusing on Jiao's life and career. In February 1968, Abelelin Abelezi, a 17-year-old youth from Hami County, Xinjiang Uygur Autonomous Region, traveled by train together with his five classmates all the way to Lankao, Henan to respectfully pay homage to Martyr Jiao Yulu's Grave which was at that time still in construction. Later they visited Jiao's relatives. After they returned to their hometown, Hami County, Abelelin Abelezi dedicated himself for a very long time to extensively publicizing Jiao Yulu's splendid and immensely philanthropic deeds and made a point of adhering to Jiao's ethics. He worked for Xinjiang Regional Judiciary and Procuratorate for decades and had been unswervingly adhering to the principle of "upholding justice and equity" in handling cases. And he had never for once erred in his handling of over one thousand cases, because he always and firmly upheld justice and law and combatted social evil undauntedly. He was acclaimed as "a Jiao Yulu in Xinjiang". Although he was an ordinary government functionary, his life was honorable and splendid.

The inconceivable uplift exercised by the learning-about-and-following-Jiao Yulu movement in China swelled globally, students, government officials, citizens from countries such as Vietnam, Laos, America, Canada traveled to China for visiting Lankao. In the 1960s, having been deeply moved by Jiao Yulu's life and career, an American woman who was at that time working for the World Peace Council not just made an in-depth study of Jiao Yulu but also traveled to China exclusively for cruising places, each of which Jiao had gone to for either conducting an inspection or doing an investigation. At each of such places she would drink the plain water from a crude bowl as the villagers in those places habitually did and affectionately hugged those villagers when she had to say farewell to them.

It is true that Jiao Yulu originated with the Chinese nation. But he belongs in the world. He was an outstanding human devoid of selfishness. His life was brimming over with honesty, kindness, and nice sentiments. Humanity is his halo. The goals he set for his life were very definite: He would strive to make the common people not only well fed and comfortably clothed but also enjoy a happy life. In the present-day world there are underdeveloped countries and regions where poverty is still the lethal scourge. Since rulers of these countries, or regions, do hope that their peoples can be lifted out of poverty, it is evident that the life and career of Jiao Yulu may be of appreciable ethical value to them. The way Jiao fought poverty until the latter turned tail is something which may be useful to the rulers just specified above. The ethical bequest Jiao left behind him is an eternal moral asset, which transcends time and space, has a universal value, and should be counted as a specific manifestation of internationalism. The life and career of Jiao Yulu can work as a stimulant helping to lock nations into a cooperative entity aimed at curbing and eliminating impoverishment in these nations and to speed up the global exertion to curb and eliminate poverty in every part of the world.

In winding up this postscript, we would like to quote the following words from President Xi Jinping, "Let the world be united, so that the bliss of one of its constituent parts may be freely shared by another. " Now let us join hands and proceed to unfailingly create the community with a shared future for mankind — community which will be devoid of impoverishment and concentrating on achieving a universal progress and development across the world.

The Chinese version of this book was written with tremendous support from the Foreign Affairs Office of the People's Government of Henan Province, CPC Kaifeng Municipal Committee, Kaifeng Municipal Government, Foreign Affairs Office of Kaifeng Municipal People's Government, Jiao Yulu Executive Leadership Academy, and Jiao Yulu Memorial Park. Its English version was finished by a translation team organized by the School of International Studies at Zhengzhou University (Qian Jiancheng, Huang Weiwei, Li Jie, Zhang Linlin, He Aiping, Li Yanfang, Yang Chunli, Yang Hong and Li Wenjing). We are deeply grateful to all whose contribution has made this book possible.

We sincerely apologize for any potential flaws in this book due to the time limit and the stories of Jiao Yulu being decades old.